THE STRANGER

A STUDY IN SOCIAL RELATIONSHIPS

BY

MARGARET MARY WOOD

AMS PRESS
NEW YORK

COLUMBIA UNIVERSITY
STUDIES IN THE
SOCIAL SCIENCES

399

This Series was formerly known as
Studies in History, Economics and Public Law.

Reprinted with the permission of Columbia University Press
From the edition of 1934, New York
First AMS EDITION published 1969
Manufactured in the United States of America

Library of Congress Catalogue Card Number: 71-82235

AMS PRESS, INC.
NEW YORK, N. Y. 10003

To

ALICE MORROW
SYMPATHETIC FRIEND OF THE STRANGER

PREFACE

This volume embodies an attempt to answer certain questions which have been suggested in part by the writer's own experiences as a stranger in many lands and in part by the controversy concerning the rightful subject-matter of sociology and the methods best adapted for the study of social phenomena. It endeavors to relate these two types of questions, to translate, as it were, social experience into terms of social theory. It seeks to discover an order amid a seeming confusion of diversities, to show, in other words, that the new relationships which are formed when strangers meet are not governed wholly by fortuitous circumstances, but that they are closely correlated with social relationships that are already present in the group which the stranger has entered. It essays therefore to incorporate the new with the old; and, hence, to explain the behavior toward the stranger —the manner of new relationship which is established, whether hostile or friendly, indifferent or curious—from the standpoint of preexisting relationships as these may be affected by the special circumstances of the meeting and by the personalities of the interacting individuals. In following this method whatever knowledge is gained, should any be acquired, becomes of sociological import. It augments the body of knowledge which we already possess concerning the nature of social integration and the relationships which this involves, a problem which is of major import for the sociologist.

In view of this aim the method has necessarily been analytical and interpretative. The field surveyed has been an extensive one since the validity of the argument has rested on determining whether or not it was applicable throughout the widest possible range of social groupings and in varied situations. Variety rather than repetition has been desired. Detail has been sacrificed in the interest of synthesis and no effort has been made to amass a large number of cases in order to verify the existence of a particular kind of behavior in any given community. The citation of specific instances of certain behavior responses has been primarily to clarify the explanation or to add interest. Care has been taken in the selection of this illustrative material that the sources from which it is drawn should be authoritative and that, as far as this is possible, it should be representative and should not tend to give a misleading impression with regard to the prevalence of certain kinds of behavior towards the stranger in a community.

The present study is based upon certain assumptions concerning the nature of social relationships and social structures. A relationship is thought of as existing between two or more persons who are in some way interactive so that the behavior of each is affected by that of the other, or others. Social groupings consist of individuals who are linked together in this way by relationships. Such relationships may be ephemeral or they may be deep and lasting, bulwarked by strong sentiments of affection and loyalty. The character of the group is determined by the nature of the relationships which unite its members. The solidarity of the group is strong if the sense of mutual obligation among its members is strong, and it is weak if these share no feeling of responsibility or affection for one another. The interests, sentiments and emotions which are associated with social relationships are the source of their strength as cohesive bonds.

A stranger who has entered a group for the first time is outside the system of relationships which unite the group, and, if he is to be included, these relationships must be extended to him. The ease or the difficulty with which this is done will depend upon the flexibility of the system of relationships, the personal qualities of the interacting individuals, and the presence or absence of extraneous factors which might tend to hasten or retard the process. If the system is complex, and most systems of social relationships are complicated, certain features of it may be extended while others are withheld. The position assigned to the stranger may include some, but not all, of the privileges and obligations of the original members. Business relations, for instance, may be established with strangers to whom social recognition is denied. The process of assigning a tentative position to the stranger either outside the group as an enemy or within at least the outer circle of group relationships is usually a rapid one. A longer period is required, however, for the stranger to become fully assimilated and the present study does not attempt to trace this entire process. It is interested primarily in the initial stages of the formation of new relationships.

The treatment of the subject has been in no way exhaustive. It is general in nature and suggestive, and has been made from the standpoint of the reaction of the group to the stranger. No effort has been made to delve into the soul of the stranger, to uncover " the well of loneliness " which may be hidden there created by the absence of the personal intimate relationships which exist among friends and relatives who have shared experiences together and who understand and feel affection for one another. Such a sociopsychological study might well be made, and this, in fact, was the writer's original plan when the investigation of the relationship of the stranger was first contemplated. The materials which presented themselves for analysis, however, made it seem imperative that the present volume should be written first to prepare a way for further more specialized work in this field.

It is felt that problems which pertain to the nature of the relationships which form the bonds of social integration and the manner in which these affect behavior toward persons who were not originally a part of the group are of significance and merit the attention of the sociologist. These problems are given emphasis by the increasing mobility which characterizes the growth of modern civilization with its great cities and its marvelous facilities for transportation and communication. No longer for even the least of us need the wish to go to Carcassonne remain unfulfilled throughout our lives. We travel about freely, daily coming into contact with new groups and as frequently those who are strangers to us enter our own groups. This mobility implies the putting aside of old relationships and the establishing of new ones; and if the process is attended with undue difficulties, it may involve an interval of maladjustment the consequences of which may be unfortunate for both the individual and the community. The stranger loses the sense of security with which the familiar is associated. In his new environment he has no recognized and respected status to maintain; he is outside the social group and, hence, under no obligations toward it. This situation is not infrequent among immigrants for whom the processes of assimilation have been slow or imperfect, but it is by no means confined to the immigrant stranger. Other strangers may manifest this same lack of loyalty to the community they have entered because they do not feel themselves to be a part of it and responsible for its well-being. Nor is this attitude that of the stranger only—many times the group absolves itself from responsibility for the welfare of those whom it does not consider as belonging to its fold. The presence of the stranger thus creates problems which are of moment for the student of human relationships.

I wish to take this occasion to express my sincere gratitude to all those who have contributed to the realization of this study. I owe a deep debt of obligation to the many writers from whose works I have drawn so freely for both illustrative and interpretative materials and to my professors of the Department of Social Science at Columbia University who have aided and encouraged me throughout all of my work for the doctorate and to whose inspiration this book is due. I wish particularly to thank Professor R. M. MacIver under whose sympathetic and able guidance the manuscript has assumed its present form; he has given generously of his time and of his talent for this purpose. My thanks are also due to Professors A. A. Tenney, R. S. Lynd and Theodore Abel for reading the manuscript and for advising me on various aspects of the problem. Their suggestions have been fruitful; their criticism, discerning; their interest, heartening. I am also much indebted to Professor A. R. Radcliffe-Brown for his assistance in the interpretation of the anthropological data pertaining to some of the simpler peoples.

M. M. W.

New York City,
March, 1934.

TABLE OF CONTENTS

PART ONE

SOCIAL RELATIONSHIPS

CHAPTER I

SOCIAL RELATIONSHIPS AND STRUCTURE

I. SOCIAL RELATIONSHIPS AS UNITS OF STRUCTURE

THE coming of the stranger creates a dynamic situation that has attracted attention in both modern and ancient times and among highly civilized as well as simpler peoples. Interest in the stranger is a universal trait, and, fortunately for the purposes of the present study, a great abundance of material which portrays, more or less faithfully, the behavior of many different kinds of people when meeting strangers has accumulated. The treatment that has been accorded to the stranger has varied throughout the whole gamut of social relationships from that of an enemy whose fate is to be killed forthwith to that of a god to whom none of the most sacred privileges of group membership are to be denied. Yet, interesting and varied as this material is, very little of it has been brought together and analyzed from the standpoint of the social scientist who would seek to discover an order among these diverse forms of behavior and to relate, if possible, the treatment of the newcomer to certain of the more general social processes and social relationships concerning which a body of information already exists. If such correlations are present, they will prove of value in the interpretation of the reactions called forth by the appearance of the stranger and in the formulation of a basis for the organization and further study of this material. The problem of determining whether or not interrelations of this type do exist is not a simple one, however, since it is difficult to ascertain the precise nature of the phenomena which might be connected in this manner. And unless these particular phenomena are carefully analyzed and the units of which they are composed clearly defined, the conclusions which are drawn will inevitably be confused. Many of the difficulties and ambiguities which arise in dealing with sociological data come from this source; the social scientist has not always been clear about the exact nature of the units which he has attempted to enumerate, to measure, or to trace relationships between, and, hence, the results of his investigations have failed at times to be convincing.

The importance of a clear-cut concept of the units which are being dealt with becomes the more readily apparent when we consider in how large a measure the excellent repute now enjoyed by both the biological and the physical sciences may be attributed to the knowledge possessed today concerning their respective structural units, the cell and the atom. The series of discoveries which led to the formulation of the present well-authenticated theory of the cellular structure of all living organisms marked an epoch in the history of the biological sciences, answering many hitherto puzzling questions, removing impeding fallacies, and giving fresh impetus and direction to the study of innumerable problems in which the biologist is interested. In the physical sciences a like invaluable service has been rendered by the atomic and electron theories which afford a basis for the interpretation of the behavior of the chemical elements as correlated with their structure. These theories have become so generally accepted and so large a fund of knowledge has grown up about them that the recency of the salient discoveries upon which they are based is often overlooked; yet, with few exceptions these discoveries have all been made within the last hundred years, and those of the electron theory within the present generation. This fact lends encouragement to those students of social phenomena who still experience difficulty in satisfactorily defining the units with which they are working. The growth of scientific knowledge is necessarily slow at first, unfolding bit by bit, but gathering momentum as each new discovery or invention reveals further vistas of the truth and suggests new problems and greater possibilities. Scientific progress is accelerated as the fund of accurate information from which to generalize is increased.

A comparison at this point of the kinds of phenomena studied by the different sciences discloses the divergent nature of the social phenomena. Relatively speaking, the phenomena of chemistry and biology have a greater degree of stability, and, moreover, they are capable of being resolved into their component parts in the laboratory for observation and experimentation. The social phenomena cannot be analyzed so easily, for to isolate the human individual is to destroy the very thing which is being studied—the social life itself. The cases of feral men, for instance, which have attracted attention from time to time, have been of interest to the sociologist primarily only as evidence of the importance of social contacts in the development of a normal personality; they have not afforded suitable material for the study of society. It is not the individual as an individual *per se* that is of interest to the sociologist; but, rather, as Professor Giddings has pointed out, the individual who is a companion, the *socius*.[1] It is this fact of companionship, of individuals being associated together, which is significant. The structural framework of society, the living together of men in groups, consists of the forms in which they have become associated, as the family and the community and the various associations which arise within the community as the political, the economic, the religious, and so on. Each of these forms, however, is interrelated with every other, thus

[1] Giddings, F. H., *Elements of Sociology* (New York, 1898), pp. 5-11.

creating an involved complex whole which is baffling in the extreme to the student whose aim is to reduce it to simpler, and more easily understood, elemental terms.

Since a different situation exists when the individual is a companion from that which is present in the case of the isolated individual something must therefore be created by the process of being associated together. It is this spiritual something which we are seeking to understand. It is the inner bond which, uniting man with his fellow man, forms thereby the units out of which the great structure of human society has been evolved. Society is a structure of units, but, unlike an organism, it is not a material but a spiritual structure. Two or more human beings between whom a relationship of some kind exists form a part of the social structure; and thus, in studying the nature of the relationships among people we are also studying the nature of social integration and the social structure of society itself.[2]

2. THE NATURE OF SOCIAL RELATIONSHIPS

In the study of social phenomena attention has been focussed more largely upon the great social structures which

[2] This identification of social relationships with social structure is not new. Among sociologists for whom social relationships, or certain aspects of these, have formed the basis of their theories of the nature of social phenomena may be mentioned Gumplowicz, Simmel, Giddings, MacIver, v. Wiese, Max Weber, Vierkandt, Znaniecki and Abel. Even such writers as E. A. Ross, Ellwood and Hayes, who have stressed the significance of social processes rather than social relationships as the units of sociological investigation, have not decried the importance of the latter. The two viewpoints are not contradictory, but each supplements the other. The question is one of emphasis. Social relationships are created, maintained, modified or destroyed by social processes. The two are so intimately associated that a discussion of the one tends to involve that of the other. The present thesis is concerned with both. It is interested not only in the relationships which are established with the newcomer but also in the processes by which these are brought about.

have arisen through the processes of association than it has upon the nature of the building units, the social relations, themselves. Of what do these consist? This is at once an easy and a difficult question to answer. Its simplicity lies in the fact that the general nature of social relationships as phenomena involving the reciprocal activities of two or more individuals is readily recognized. On the other hand, the analysis, classification and interpretation of the innumerable specific behavior patterns which these activities may assume is a task of far greater magnitude, and one which requires deeper insight and higher powers of discernment. The situation is not unlike that of the botanist who is confronted by an unknown specimen. It may be comparatively easy to determine that it belongs to the *Compositae,* let us say, but it is a much more difficult matter to discover to which genus and species it belongs. If some part of the plant is missing, as is often the case since the blossom and the ripened fruit are separated by an interval of time, it may be impossible to complete the classification. We, too, need a fuller knowledge of the nature of the social phenomena with which we are working before these can be satisfactorily classified. Nor can we hope to achieve quite the same degree of precision that is found in the biological and physical sciences. Man, as Professor Giddings has observed, " wants to change his mind *when he wants to* and to go back for his umbrella ".[3] No matter how carefully regulated our household may otherwise be, this perturbing factor will recur now and again to upset its order. We must anticipate such irregularities, however, and not be disconcerted by them. If they add to the difficulties of the problem, they also add to its interest.

[3] Giddings, F. H., *Studies in the Theory of Human Society* (New York, 1922), pp. 142-43.

An idea of the general nature of social relationships is brought out in the following paragraphs in which Professor MacIver discusses this subject.

Society is the web of social relationships, but what do we mean by social relationship? We may approach the answer by contrasting the social with the physical. There is a relationship between a typewriter and a desk, between the earth and the sun, between fire and smoke, between two chemical constituents. Each is affected by the existence of the other, but the relationship is not a social one. The psychical condition is lacking. The typewriter and the desk are in no intelligible sense aware of the presence of one another. Their relationship is not in any way determined by mutual awareness. Without this recognition there is no society. It exists only where social beings conduct themselves or " behave " towards one another in ways determined by their recognition of one another.

But we have not yet attained our definition. To be mutually aware and to act in that awareness is hardly enough to create a social situation. The hunter and the wolf are aware of the presence of each other and act accordingly, but it would be and undue stretching of language to speak of society as existing between the hunter and the wolf. Society implies some sort of " belonging together ", some sense of what we shall presently describe as community. It involves the recognition of something that is common to its members. Any relationship that is based on the recognition, in any degree, of a common life may properly be termed a social relationship.[4]

This concept of the nature of social relationships given by Professor MacIver is the broadest possible and any less general use of the term will require further definition and explanation. The relationships, for instance, of husband and wife, of parent and child, of brother and sister, of king

[4] MacIver, R. M., *Society: Its Structure and Changes* (New York, 1931), pp. 6-7.

and subject, of employer and employee, of pupil and teacher, of friends and of enemies, all imply that recognition has passed over into more or less well defined ways of feeling and behaving. Each of these relationships signifies that the persons concerned have certain duties, obligations, privileges and restrictions with respect to one another. The more precise nature of these depends upon the customs of the social groups to which the persons belong. They are not haphazard matters despite the wide variations between groups and within the group itself. Loyalty is an obligation of friendship at all times. The duty of parents to provide for their children when small is generally recognized. The privilege of sexual intercourse is everywhere associated with the marriage relation. Restrictions are normally imposed upon persons regarded as enemies. Social relationships of these types have been designated as *social relations* by Professor Abel.[5] They represent more or less permanent behavior sequences which have become established through processes of adjustment and are based on either consent or tradition. Defined in this way the term social relations is more limited in its application than the term social relationships with which it is frequently used interchangeably. It is, in fact, difficult always to keep the two terms separate since the distinction is sometimes largely one of degree, and no special effort has been made to do so in the present study.

Although the behavior of individuals toward one another is the criterion by which we ascertain the nature of the relationships existing between them such behavior is not the relationship itself, but merely an outward expression of it. The relationship between a mother and her child, for instance, is not the activities of feeding and caring for the child, but rather the feeling of affection and of obligation which impels

---

[5] Abel, Theodore, "The Significance of the Concept of Consciousness of Kind", *Social Forces*, vol. ix, no. 1, October, 1930.

this behavior on the mother's part. The action of men in risking their lives in battle is not a relationship; it is, however, the expression of certain relationships, of loyalty to the group whose cause is defended and of antagonism toward the enemy. The initiation ceremonies among native peoples do not constitute relationships, rather they are the means of forming new relationships through creating certain sentiments which uphold these. Behavior thus appears as a process and social relations or relationships as more or less definite psychical adjustments between individuals which have their source and their expression in behavior activities. To return to the relationship in which we are primarily interested, that which is established with the stranger, this, too, represents an adjustment reached by behavior processes. The nature of these processes is again dependent, in its turn, upon relationships which are already in existence, as those between the members of the group with which the stranger is in contact and also between this group and that to which the stranger belongs. This interdependence between behavior processes which are objective activities and social relationships which are psychical adjustments between individuals is brought out more clearly in the chapters which follow, in which concrete instances of the formation of new relationships are dealt with.

3. THE FUNCTION OF SOCIAL RELATIONSHIPS

The significance of social relationships as units of social structure has already been pointed out, but it remains to indicate somewhat more specifically the manner in which such units function in forming social structures. The family relationships perhaps afford the best material for this purpose since they have been the most carefully studied from this point of view. Professor Rivers' studies of the social organization of some of the simpler peoples are particularly enlightening in this respect and a brief consideration of his observations of the function of the bonds of kinship in building social structures may well form a basis for the investigation of the functions of other types of social relationships. Concerning the marriage relation, Professor Rivers says:

I shall lay especial stress on the far more important function of marriage as the means by which every individual born into a society is assigned a definite place in that society, by which his or her social relations to the rest of the society are determined. Each child by virtue of being born as a child of a marriage takes its place in the social structure. Certain members of the group are its relatives; others are not necessarily relatives, but they belong to the same clan or moiety; certain members of the community of the opposite sex are possible mates, while others are forbidden: all these and other such relationships are determined by the act of birth into a family group. Looked at from this point of view, marriage may be an institution of the most definite and highly organized kind although its role as a regulator of sexual relations may be of a very lax and imperfect order.[6]

One has only to reflect for a moment on the unfortunate position of the illegitimate child in most societies to appreciate the significance of Professor Rivers' conclusions concerning the function of the marriage relationship in determining the place of the child in the community. The relations of the child born outside wedlock differ from those of children who are born within it both toward his own kin and toward the group as a whole. His obligations, duties, privileges and restrictions toward others and theirs toward him are not the same as they would have been if his parents had been married. In most instances he is an unwelcome member of the group because of this fact. Through no fault of his own there is no place in the group to which he is legitimately

[6] Rivers, W. H. R., *Social Organization* (New York, 1924), pp. 37-8.

entitled. The organization of any group depends upon its members' each having a recognized position, whether high or low, within it. Otherwise there would be confusion and disorder. In the case of the illegitimate child certain of the criteria which normally determine a child's position in the community are lacking, conventions for maintaining the social order have been disregarded, and resentment is felt because of this.

Social relationships, thus, not only unite individuals into social structures of many kinds, but also determine the positions which the individuals occupy within such structures. That is, if we know what a person's relations are to a group, we also know what his position is, or the other way around; if we know what a person's position is, we also know what his relations will be since certain relations are implicit in certain positions. Position itself is without meaning except as this is given to it by the relationships which it implies. To say that the stranger has been assigned to such and such a position by the group means that relationships of a certain type have been established with him; he is regarded in a more or less specific way and behavior of a particular kind is observed toward him.

In this connection the classificatory system found among simpler peoples in many parts of the world is of especial interest. According to Professor Rivers its primary function would seem to have been to denote relationships rather than relatives, since, in its most complete form, no single term could be used as a means of distinguishing an individual. The same term of address was applied to large groups of persons. The term " brother ", for instance, is used not only for the sons of the same father and mother but also for the sons of the father's brothers and of the mother's sisters. " Sister " is used in a similar wide sense. This system of terminology need not, however, obliterate the facts of actual kinship to others traced genealogically through pedigrees based upon consanguinity or upon those social conventions which serve the same purpose.[7] Its function in regulating behavior is brought out more specifically by Professor Rivers in the paragraphs given below.

It was once supposed, especially by those who had no first hand acquaintance with the subject, that it [the classificatory system] was a mere collection of terms of address. It is now thoroughly established, however, that these terms connote definite social functions, specific duties, privileges, and restrictions on conduct, and that these social functions apply to relatives in the classificatory sense as well as to relatives in the much narrower sense which the terms would bear among ourselves. . . .

Thus there are many peoples among whom there is a special relation between a man and his mother's brother. The nephew has certain definite duties in relation to his uncle, and has certain privileges, including the use of his property, amounting in some cases to a state of affairs in which all property is common to the two. These social relations do not apply merely to the actual brother of the own mother, but to all those whom the mother calls brother, though in most cases the nearer relationship of the actual mother's brother is recognized, and the various social functions are the more strictly observed. . . .

The social duties, privileges, and restrictions which are imposed upon classificatory relatives by traditional custom are of the most varied kinds. They include the duty of mutual helpfulness, either in general, or on special occasions such as funeral and other rites; privileges, especially in connection with property; and restrictions of many kinds. A most important

7 The classificatory system was first noted by Lewis Morgan and was named by him. We are indebted, however, to Rivers, Radcliffe-Brown and Malinowski for the interpretation of its function.

group of the last kind may be classed together as customs of avoidance.[8]

The discovery of the function of the classificatory system as a basis for social organization through the extension of family relationships to include everyone within the group, or within intermarrying groups, is a significant one for the study of the development of social structure. The system is a simple one, relatively speaking, with a limited number of categories for each of which the rights, obligations, privileges and prohibitions are carefully defined. It is an exceedingly rigid system, however, which could function effectively only in comparatively small and isolated societies. It would be inadequate for the needs of groups who were so situated that they were subjected to frequent contacts with varied outside groups. Family relationships could not be extended to all of these and the system would break down through attenuation. As it exists, however, it is an excellent example of the function of social relationships in building social structures and in regulating the behavior of the members of the group toward one another.

4. A THEORY OF THE ORIGIN OF SOCIAL RELATIONSHIPS

In the evolution of such a system as the classificatory system, man has necessarily, though unconsciously, builded with the materials which he had, experimenting with them and changing them to meet the exigencies of his life. Just what these materials may have been in the beginning we cannot say with certainty; but it seems safe to assume that from a very early period in the history of the race some form of the family must have existed, a woman and her child, or a group of women and their children, with the man or men

---

[8] Rivers, *op. cit.*, pp. 63 *et seq.* See also Professor Rivers' article, "Kin and Kinship", *The Encyclopaedia of Religion and Ethics*, vol. vii (ed. James Hastings, New York, 1915).

who were interested in them and who assisted in providing
for them and in protecting them. In so simple a group as
this some forms of behavior would already have become
accepted and established; the mothers would care for the
children while they were small and the men would share the
food which they had obtained with the women and children.
And, as acts are repeated, certain attitudes and sentiments
tend to be developed with respect to them, both in the individuals who perform the acts and in the other persons who
are concerned. An individual who has performed an act a
number of times comes to regard this, if pleasurable, as his
right or privilege and he is prepared, if need be, to defend
this. On the other hand, if the act has been one by which
others have benefited, it will not be long before they will
regard it as their right to receive and the duty of the other
to provide. And they will be ready to enforce this.

Although in both the simpler and the more highly complex
societies of today the conceptions of rights and duties in
most of the important matters of life are handed down as a
part of the social heritage, it is still possible to observe the
manner of their inception in many acts of minor and unprecedented behavior. Such conceptions are formed with great
readiness, if but little permanency, among children. I recall
that as small children my sister and I both had very decided
ideas with regard to our privilege of doing alone, if we so
wished, whatever either of us might chance to be the first to
think of doing. I might, for instance, express the wish to
die and go to heaven, a favorite wish at one time, suggested
by the account of the death of little Eva in *Uncle Tom's
Cabin,* which had impressed me deeply. My sister, who is
younger, would probably repeat the wish, whereupon I would
retort, " I envy your echoing me ", a statement which con-
veyed the same meaning for us that the well-known epithet
" copy cat " does in most groups of children. My sister

would then feel impelled to withdraw her wish and express contentment with life and earthly things. Heaven was closed to her if I got there first unless I should choose to be magnanimous and consent to her coming also. Happily, although claiming rights, we were willing in most cases to waive these and to share our privileges with one another.

Acts and emotional attitudes concerning them come to be associated together, certain things come to be expected of us and we expect certain things of others in return. Social relationships are evolved in this way. We *feel* that we have certain obligations, that there are certain things that we ought or ought not to do; we *feel* that there are certain things which we have a right to do with respect to others. We also *feel* that others should behave in certain ways. As this manner of feeling becomes more definite and organized it develops into a psychological state which may be referred to as an attitude; but which, under some circumstances, is perhaps better expressed by the term sentiment because of the nature of the emotional content which is present. Professor Radcliffe-Brown defines a sentiment as " an organized system of emotional tendencies centered about some object ".[9] Those social relationships which form the cohesive bonds that knit men together into an integrated society involve sentiment in his opinion.

Society depends for its existence on the presence in the minds of its members of a certain system of sentiments by which the conduct of the individual is regulated in conformity with the needs of society. Every feature of the social system itself and every event or object that in any way affects the well-being or the cohesion of the society becomes an object of this system of sentiments. In human society the sentiments are not innate but are developed in the individual by the action of society upon him. The ceremonial customs of a society are a means by

9 *The Andaman Islanders* (Cambridge, 1922), p. 234 n.

which the sentiments in question are given collective expression on appropriate occasions. The ceremonial (i. e. collective) expression of any sentiment serves both to maintain it at the requisite degree of intensity in the mind of the individual and to transmit it from one generation to another. Without such expression the sentiments involved could not exist.[10]

This function of ceremonial or collective behavior in awakening the same sentiments in the participants has been developed by Durkheim in his *Elementary Forms of the Religious Life*. Those sentiments which are shared in common by all the members of a group tend to form strong unifying bonds. The awareness that others feel in the same way toward the same things as ourselves creates a relationship of belonging together. The rhythmic movements of the primitive dance serve not only to engender emotions within the individual but also to communicate these to others, heightening the effect through interstimulation.[11]

Although all unifying relationships are based upon the mutual recognition of something in common they do not all involve sentiment. Professor Abel recognizes two general types of social relations which he has distinguished as *sentiment relations* and *interest relations*.[12] The latter type are

[10] *Ibid.*, pp. 233-34.

[11] An Igorot *canao* dance that I once witnessed in the Philippines, quite by chance and unobserved, impressed me unforgetably with its qualities of emotional appeal. Bare brown bodies swaying in rhythmic unison to the drumming of the *gansas*, the mystery of the shadows beyond the firelit circle, the eery sense of height and of depth—of the mountains behind the village and of the canyon below shrouded in darkness—the distant sound of falling waters, the aroma of roasting meat, all this moved me profoundly although a stranger for whom the ritual itself had no meaning.

That I had lost the trail and had been tramping all day without food, that I was alone, and that it was Christmas Eve may have enhanced my own emotional response to the scene, it is true.

[12] Abel, *op. cit.*

" essentially rational-purposive in their structure; i. e. selection of contacts is made from the point of view of the service they may render towards the realization of the dominant interest." [13]   They are characterized by calculation and the other person is defined as a means for the realization of an end.   Business relations, as a rule, are of this type.   The sentiment relations, on the other hand, comprise " the great number of contacts in which satisfaction of the *desire for response* is the main purpose.   They are based upon intimacy, mutual attachment, and sympathy ".[14]   Relations of sociability, friendship and love, or between members of face-to-face groups are of this type.

Both the interest and the sentiment relations combine in the evolution of social structures, but the fundamental sense of unity, the " feeling of oneness " that holds thousands of men together and enables them to build up a civilization by their united efforts is emotional in its nature as Denison has shown,[15] and, hence, the sentiment relations have played the leading role.   Such unifying relationships have been created by those activities involving others which tend to arouse or to perpetuate pleasurable emotions and a sense of mutual obligation.   In the primitive family group or small horde a comparatively simple system of social relationships, largely of the sentiment type, would suffice to integrate the group and to regulate the activities of the members toward one another; but as the horde increased in size or in the number of its contacts with other groups the need for establishing new social relationships would arise.   The problem of the formation of new social relationships thus becomes the crux of the problem of social development as Professor Radcliffe-Brown points out.

[13] *Ibid.*   [14] *Ibid.*

[15] Denison, J. H., *Emotion as the Basis of Civilization* (New York and London, 1928), *passim.*

The development of society depends upon the organization of personal relations. The task of man in primitive society is therefore similar to the task of a child. The needs of his life compel him above everything else to devote himself to organizing that part of his experience that relates the actions of persons upon one another; all else is subordinated to this supreme need.[16]

Contacts with strangers call for the formation of new relationships, and, hence, they form a part of the general problem of the development of society. The behavior toward the stranger will, in a large measure, be dependent upon the system of social integration which is already present in the group since this forms the foundation upon which the new relationship must be erected. A study of new relationships and the processes by which these have been formed must of necessity take into consideration the materials men have to do with, the social relationships with which they are familiar and which form the unifying bonds of the group. Can these be extended to include the newcomer or are they too inflexible for this? Is it desirable to extend them or is it not? And for what reasons? These are significant questions for the interpretation of the manner in which the stranger is received and the next step in our analysis of the problem is therefore to discover something of the nature of the processes by which relationships may be extended.

[16] *The Andaman Islanders*, p. 380.

CHAPTER II

The Extension of Social Relationships

I. RITES OF PASSAGE

WE have already noted that as the family or small horde increased in size or in the number of its contacts with other peoples a certain strain would be placed upon the organization of the group and some form of readjustment would become necessary in order to relieve this tension. Not only must a more or less definite system of relationships be established with the new arrivals, but the fact of their presence within the group will also react upon it, producing changes in the system of relationships which had previously existed among its members. In the family, for instance, the birth of each child calls for a certain realignment of the relations among all the members; the situation is not the same for the second child that it was for the first now that there are four persons to be considered instead of three. The advent of each additional individual within intimate face-to-face groups involves some changes in the social organization. Similar situations also arise within larger groups, but in this case it is not so much the presence of the stranger as an individual but as the representative of a class which makes reorganization necessary. The agitation in California against the Japanese and Filipinos is not directed toward them personally as individuals, but rather as members of alien groups whose presence for one reason or another has caused dissension and with whom satisfactory relationships have not yet been established.

34

As the group endeavors to accommodate itself to the changed social situation brought about by the intrusion of persons from without the tendency has been to follow lines suggested by the nature of the relationships which comprise the existing social order. The types of relationships that are involved will differ, however, as one feature, or combination of features, it stressed more definitely than another. Such lines of development are not simple and they change as conditions within the group itself are changed; at one period in the history of a people one form of relationship may be the dominant motif, and, at another stage, a different one. If the group is one that has had frequent and varied contacts with outsiders, its social organization will have become adjusted to such intercourse and the arrival of the stranger will not create a new problem. On the other hand, if the contacts have been infrequent and also varied, the question of the behavior toward the stranger will still be more or less unsolved. Where the former contacts, though few, have all been of a certain kind, a definite attitude toward strangers as a class may have been formed and the reaction toward the newcomer may be an organized but undiscriminating one. He may be heralded as one who brings glad tidings or he may be summarily killed according to the nature of the former contacts of the group. In any case the manner in which the stranger is received will depend upon the organization and background of the group—subject, however, as will appear later, to the modifying influence of the particular circumstances of the meeting and of traits of personality.

The correlation which exists between new relationships and the nature of the social relationships which constitute the unifying bonds already present in the group is a vital one. Any event which affects these relationships also affects the social structure of the group and is a matter of moment. It is necessary, therefore, that the appropriate emotions upon which these relationships depend should be maintained when changes occur; and hence, some form of ritual is usually employed to arouse or to strengthen them. In modern civilized societies the significance of such ritual ceremonies has been largely lost sight of; and their performance, if still retained, is often carried out in a prefunctory manner and little thought is given to their original purpose. Among simpler peoples, however, *les rites de passage,* as Van Gennep has termed them, are an integral part of the social system. A change in the life of the individual which also results in a change in his position in the group and in his relations to others is an occasion to be celebrated by such rites. Birth, initiation, marriage and death are events in the life of the individual which also affect the group; relations within the group are changed by them, and this must be done in the accepted way. The individual is passing from one position to another, or, as it were, from one world to another, from the world of the profane into that of the sacred; and, inasmuch as these two worlds are incompatible, there must be an intermediate stage in passing from one to the other. Thus, Van Gennep points out, *les rites de passage* tend to assume a three-fold nature; first, rites separating the person from his former associations such as rites of separation; second, rites of preparation, during the marginal period; and third, rites of aggregation incorporating him in his new existence. The sharing of food is such a rite.[1]

Time is required for any change in social structure. In Australia the rites of separation during initiation represent taking the boy from his mother when he is old enough for initiation. These rites are symbolic, showing that social

[1] Van Gennep, Arnold, *Les Rites de Passage* (Paris, 1909), p. 27. "Je propose en consequénce de nommer *rites préliminaires* les rites de séparation du monde antérieur, *rites liminaires* les rites exécutés pendant de stade de marge, et *rites postliminaires* les rites d'agrégation au monde nouveau."

bonds are being broken.   Then follows the marginal period
in which the boys are outside of their own camp for perhaps
a year.   In the Andaman Islands the name is dropped and
the boy wears a special costume.   He may also be shut up in
a special hut.   This is the marginal period and during it the
boy is a ritual object, he is *tapu,* that is sacred in a certain
sense, he is dangerous even to himself.   The marginal period
is followed by rites symbolizing death and rebirth.   The bull-
roarers used in the initiation ceremonies in Australia are
supposed to be the voice of the god Baiame who kills the boy
and he is then reborn into his new status as a man.   Throughout these ceremonies a great deal of emotionalism is involved,
mystery and awe are evoked, and pain is inflicted which the
initiate must bear with self-control.   All this is to bring about
a change in the individual in conformity with his change in
position within the group.   It is primarily the social order
and not the individual which is sacred and it is the change in
this that is the real object of the ritual attitude.   The individual himself becomes sacred only because of the position
which he occupies in the social structure.

The initiation ceremonies among the Bagesu, of which
Roscoe has given an interesting account,[2] afford another instance of *rites de passage* in which the three stages noted by
Van Gennep are readily distinguished.   The time set for the
ceremony was two or three days after the appearance of the
new moon during the harvest season.   The priest and the
chief of the village went to the mountain shrine of the
creator, *Weri,* taking a fowl, usually white, and two eggs.
The fowl was killed and left at the foot of the sacred tree,
and the eggs were broken in the path for a snake which was
supposed to be in the tree.   The boys were then brought by
the chief and the priest to the forest.   An animal was offered

[2] Roscoe, John, *The Bagesu and Other Tribes of the Uganda Protectorate* (Cambridge, 1924), pp. 27 *et seq.*

to the god, after which it was killed and the contents of the stomach, mixed with water, were smeared over the bodies of the boys. A sacred meal was then prepared and eaten and the priest pronounced the god's blessing on each boy. When this was over they went back to the village at a rapid trot and the boys joined in the dancing, brandishing heavy sticks or clubs. There was a good deal of beer drinking, excitement ran high, and the boys were supposed to be under the influence of some spirit. This went on until early in the afternoon when the boys were summoned by the priest to the mountain shrine, blessed, and smeared with white clay, after which they returned at a run to their own villages to be operated upon. An elderly man described to the boys their duty to the clan, admonishing them to be faithful. Vows were sealed by a further ceremony, and the operation of circumcision was then performed by a medicine man and his assistant in a painful manner. These were rites of separation after which a marginal period followed during which the boys lived in a special house until they healed. From one to two months were allowed and then the boys were washed, smeared with white clay, and given men's dress. An offering was made to the god and a feast was celebrated, concluding the rites of aggregation. The boys were now allowed to join the men's councils, to drink beer, and to find wives at the next harvest festivities.

The elaborate initiation ceremonies of boys among many of the simpler peoples have an interesting parallel in our own civilization in the formal coming-out ball and other social functions by which the daughters of wealthy families are introduced to society and their eligibility for marriage tacitly announced. Dancing, dress and food have an important role in these ceremonies as in the rites of the more primitive groups. The expenses of the society girl's debut are borne by her own family, however, and are not a group affair as among the Bagesu, for instance, where presents of food were contributed for the initiation feasting. That the debutante should meet "the right people" is a matter of serious consideration, particularly for those families whose social position is an insecure one; and not infrequently the coming-out ball is an occasion of impressive outward display [3] and of inward trepidation on the part of the debutante's family. The lot of the debutante who is unpopular socially is not an enviable one, although the variety of interests to which young women may now turn has alleviated the sting somewhat and the status of an unmarried woman has become a less ignominious one than was formerly the case.

Death ceremonies are also rites of passage originating in the efforts of the group to adjust itself to a change brought about by the loss of one of its members, a loss which may be greater or less according to the position of the person who has died. The passing of the dead person from the world of the living into the spirit world is thought of as a change in his relationship to the group, but not as complete annihilation. To the primitive mind the ancestors are still a part of the community; the clan includes the ancestors; they are still in connection with it; but death has brought about a change in their relations to it. A change in the social structure has thus taken place for which an interval of time and appropriate rites are required. In the Andaman Islands the dead person is not thought of as dead until he has been put outside of the group by the rites of separation, the burial of the body or the placing of it in a tree with accompanying ceremonies. A marginal period of perhaps a year follows during which the name is not used, after which rites of aggregation incor-

---

[3] An article, "The $3,000,000 Machine" in *Fortune*, December, 1930 estimates the cost of the coming-out ball at $11,500 and of the debutante's clothes for the social season at $10,500, and adds, somewhat sardonically, that the same result could be achieved by announcing the fact that the young lady was ready to enter society in the newspapers.

porating him into his new position among the ancestors are performed. At Ontong Java [4] in the Solomon Islands the body is buried after appropriate mourning ceremonies lasting throughout the night. The mourners then move to the cemetery to live for the period of mourning, perhaps a year or longer; they are *tapu*, work is avoided, and they conceal their identity by wearing old hats and wrapping their bodies in old mats or strips of calico. The chief mourner sleeps on the grave for a portion of each night. At the end of the period of mourning two baskets of *taro* are presented at the temple, a night is spent in ritual mourning and then the hat is removed from the mourner by a woman relative and the name of the dead person is pronounced. The proper adjustment to the change in the social order created by the death of a member of the group is now completed.

The purification rites to which strangers entering many primitive groups are subjected are adaptations of separation rites.[5] The object is to remove from the stranger anything adhering to him from his former associations which might be detrimental to the community. Some form of ritual employing fire or water is often used for this purpose; for instance, when the ambassadors sent by Justin II, Emperor of the East, to conclude peace with the Turks had reached their destination they were subjected to a ceremonial purification by fire. Having deposited the goods brought by the ambassadors in an open place, the shamens carried burning branches of incense around them while they rang a bell and beat a tambourine, snorting and falling into a state of frenzy in their efforts to dispel the powers of evil. Afterwards they

[4] Hogbin, H. Ian, " Transition Rites at Ontong Java (Solomon Islands)", *Journal of the Polynesian Society*, vol. 39, September, 1930, pp. 201-20.

[5] See Frazer, J. G., *The Golden Bough* (3rd ed. in 12 vols., London, 1915), vol. iii (London, 1911), pp. 101-16 for examples of such rites.

purified the ambassadors by leading them through the flames. Such ceremonies supposedly disarm the stranger of the magical power which he has possessed as a member of another group. He is thus separated from his own group before he becomes eligible for entrance into the new community where his presence involves establishing certain new relationships to include him as an additional member.

On returning to his home from a journey in a foreign country a man may be required to undergo purification rites before he can reenter the society of his tribe. His absence and his return are events which have a bearing on the organized group life and the changes produced by these must therefore be marked by some form of ritual ceremony. Ceremonies of a ritual nature may also be performed by a group on entering a strange country. These are essentially separation rites, the group is passing from under the aegis of the spirits of their own territory, which involves a change in their social life that must be adjusted. Moreover, they are entering the jurisdiction of the spirits of a new region, as it were, and these, if offended by the intrusion, are capable of doing harm. Ritual ceremonies must be performed to ward off such impending dangers or to evoke the protection of the god, or gods, of the country. The observance of these rites indicates that although the social order is an adjustment of the system of relationships among living individuals, it is nevertheless intimately linked through tradition with the spirits of the ancestors and with objects of the physical environment with which these are associated.

A change of environment also involves changes in the social relations of the group which become the object of the ritual attitude. Even in our own highly evolved social life a change of environment as from the country to the city brings about changes in the system of relationships of the family or other group that are the result of different physical as well as social conditions. We may experience homesickness not only when we are separated from the loved members of our own group but also when we are afar from familiar scenes that have become dear to us through association. Among primitive men homesickness on being removed to a new territory is even more poignant than it is for more highly civilized peoples because of the greater intimacy that exists between the primitive group and its surroundings through the medium of its ancestors. The difficulties of making the readjustments necessary to taking up its life in a new abode may lead to the disintegration of the group. It is not strange then that leaving one's own country, even though temporarily, should be regarded as a ritual occasion; a change is foreseen and a readjustment of relations with reference to this must follow. It is the function of the rites of passage to create an emotional state that will facilitate this, bridging the gap between the old order and the new. Rites of this nature still exist with varying degrees of intensity in highly civilized groups; birth and marriage and death are still ritual matters. Ceremonies of confirmation, dedication, convocation, and so on, all symbolize certain changes in the relations of the persons concerned with respect to the group, and, hence, a change in the social structure itself. All of these rites tend to call forth an emotional response and to become an object of sentiments regulating the behavior of the individual in conformity with the needs of the group.

When the function of rites of passage is understood in this way, one of the fundamental problems of group life is brought into relief, that of establishing new relationships with members whose status within the group has changed or with strangers who have come into contact with the group. This latter situation is the one about which the interest of the present study revolves. The growth of modern civilization with its marvelous facilities for transportation and com-

munication has tended to bring all the peoples of the world
into more or less close touch with one another, thus necessi-
tating rapid changes within the social structures of the different groups in order to keep pace with ever widening, and
deepening, circles of contacts.

2. THE CONCEPT OF THE STRANGER

Before continuing further with an analysis of the processes
involved in the formation of relationships with the stranger,
it is perhaps well to follow the procedure that is generally
adopted by those who set out to explore an unknown region
in quest of treasure, whether they be pirates or sociologists,
and to pause a moment to locate certain landmarks.   In the
romantic tales of the search for the lost treasures of a
Morgan or a Kidd on the faded chart, which has in some
mysterious way fallen into the hero's hands, there are always
such landmarks, the blazed tree, the scarred rock and so on,
which must be located before the exact position of the buried
chests of gold can be discovered.   The difficulties of the
hero's task are invariably accentuated, however, by the ambiguities of the old freebooter's chart or by the obliteration
of the landmarks themselves with the passage of time.   We
are also confronted by similar obstacles, for the terms which
we are using as guide posts to point the direction of our
further search have been worn by long exposure to the
weathering of daily usage and their precise meaning is difficult to decipher.   The stranger is such a term which forms
one of the landmarks of the present problem.   Although the
essential core of its meaning remains unchanged, it may be
subjected to somewhat varying interpretations; and unless it
is specifically defined we may become confused and lose sight
of the trail.

We shall describe the stranger as one who has come into
face-to-face contact with the group for the first time.   This

concept is broader than that of Simmel, who defines the stranger as " the man who comes today and stays tomorrow, the potential wanderer, who although he has gone no further, has not quite got over the freedom of coming and going ".[6] For us the stranger may be, as with Simmel, a potential wanderer, but he may also be a wanderer who comes today and goes tomorrow, or he may come today and remain with us permanently. The condition of being a stranger is not, for the present study, dependent upon the future duration of the contact, but it is determined by the fact that it is the first face-to-face meeting of individuals who have not known one another before. The question of whether or not the contact is to be a temporary or a lasting one is, however, as we shall see later, of importance in determining the character of the initial relationship.

The stipulation just given that the contact shall be a first one between the people concerned separates our concept of the stranger for another current one, that of the person who is socially isolated from the members of his group even though he is in daily contact with them. The unhappy plight of these little understood, or misunderstood, individuals has been a frequent theme in literature. The prophet, the genius, and those who occupy high executive positions may in this sense be isolated from their groups because they stand beyond them and are not understood by them. The psychopathic case and the unfortunate person who, through physical deformities or disease, is prevented from participating in the normal activities of the group or is avoided by others may also suffer from the loneliness of isolation. So, too, may the individual whose race or whose customs and mores are different from those with whom he is associated. In all these instances, however, these persons are thought of as strangers to their groups because in certain respects their

[6] Simmel, Georg, *Soziologie* (Leipzig, 1908), pp. 685 *et seq.*

situation is comparable to that of the individual who has entered the group for the first time; they are in the group but not of it.   The intimate relationships which unite the others of the group have not been established with them; the feeling of strangeness and of social isolation which comes from the absence of such relationships still persists.   The others share sentiments and associations and experiences in which the outsider has had no part and he can come to feel that he belongs to the group only as relationships are established with him through his sharing some part of the common life of the group.   Although such relationships normally require a considerable period of time for their complete development, a beginning will be made in the first meeting; and, if there are no marked barriers to their growth, the feeling of strangeness will wear off more or less quickly in subsequent meetings as an increasing appreciation of common interests gives a basis for the further extension of group intimacies to include the stranger.

In those cases, however, in which obstacles such as differences of race, nationality, class or temperament prevent the ready extension of the group relationships, the stranger may remain indefinitely outside the group.   The situation of such a person differs nevertheless from that of the individual who is outside the group because he has only just arrived.   It is, for instance, quite a different matter if one is not invited to join in the social activities of the group because he has just entered it and is a stranger in this meaning of the term, or if, after long association with the group, the invitation is still withheld because he continues to be a stranger through the inability to establish relationships of intimacy and understanding.   In the first case the question, perhaps the doubt, which naturally exists as to whether or not the stranger will prove a congenial addition to the group is yet an open one; in the second case this question has already been answered in the

negative, and the stranger is not included. The first of the
situations just described is the more dynamic, an adjustment
of relationships has not yet been made and further contacts
will affect this. The later situation is more static, the relationship with the outsider has become stabilized and it will
change but slowly unless some new element is introduced
into the situation. The distinction is a significant one and
it seems justifiable to place these two concepts of the stranger
in different categories, and to devote our attention to the
situation of the newly arrived stranger as a distinct problem.

3. THE CONCEPT OF THE GROUP

The concept of the group as we shall use the term is another
landmark which needs careful definition. In defining the
stranger the group has been spoken of somewhat as though
the two terms were antithetical concepts. It must not be
overlooked, however, that the members of the group are just
as much strangers to the unknown individual who comes
into their midst as he is a stranger to them. The contact is
one between strangers; but, for purposes of analysis, the
person entering the group from without is distinguished as
the stranger. Thus we give to the stranger something of
the attribute of mobility It is he who comes among us,
perhaps from the far ends of the earth, perhaps, if we are
city-dwellers, from the apartment across the hall. In any
event it is the stranger who comes and the group who receives.
The group is, as it were, at home. To it we have attributed
something of stability, both in its location and in the relationships of the members of the group to one another. The
behavior of each has been adjusted toward every other.
Each feels himself to be a part of a larger whole and his
reaction toward the newcomer is influenced by this. The
consciousness of belonging to the group is fundamental to
the existence of the group. The presence of this feeling

creates a different situation from that in which none of the persons who are meeting for the first time can be said to have entered the group of another but each is equally remote from former associates and surroundings. The contrast between the two situations appears in instances frequently met with in traveling. The passengers on board of a ship may all be strangers to one another at the beginning of the voyage, no groups of relatives, friends or acquaintances may be present; but this situation does not remain for long. Group-forming factors are present and the "poor sailor" who does not appear in the dining room or on deck for the first few days will probably find that when he does most of his fellow passengers will already have formed fairly definite little cliques. Relationships will have sprung up among them based on a cogeniality of interest in the life on board the ship, and, though of a temporary nature, such relationships will carry with them a certain measure of obligation toward the original members of the little band as opposed to outsiders. The newcomer must remain more or less alone or be accepted into one of the cliques that already exist, a process which is unlike that which was involved in the first formation of the group, temporary and unorganized as it is. He comes into the group, and if it is a small one, he must be approved by all the members within it or friction will arise because of his presence. He is not a charter member, the others have certain privileges which are not immediately his. They may, for instance, have their deck chairs on the port side of the ship and he would have preferred the starboard side, and, had he been one of the group when it was first forming, he could have urged this. Now, if he is tactful and there is room, he has his deck chair placed with theirs and says nothing about his preference. If there are too many for bridge or the deck games, it is he who must offer to drop out and look on unless some arrangement is made for taking turns

or enough people can be found for another set. The con·
sciousness of belonging together as opposed to others grows
quickly under favorable circumstances.

A student who enters a class after it has met for the first
few times does not stand in quite the same relationship to
the others that he would have done had he been present at
first. Certain adjustments will have been made among the
members of the class and he may encounter these. If seats
are unassigned and he sits where another did at a previous
meeting, his neighbors make a comparison. They may be
glad that he has done so or they feel resentful if the former
occupant has been more congenial to them. He may even
be asked to move—a request that would hardly have been
made at the initial meeting of the class. His relationship to
the instructor may also be affected. If the class is already
over-crowded, he is less welcome than if he had been one of
the original group, while, on the other hand, if additional
students are desired, he may be greeted more warmly than
those who were present at first.

In a theater audience and in similar gatherings of people
who are unacquainted with one another the factor of the
consciousness of being a part of a group may seem at first to
be negligible. There appears to be complete indifference on
the part of each to all of the others, yet this very indifference
is a form of relationship, a pattern of behavior, unformu-
lated, unexpressed, but nevertheless agreed upon by those
present. It represents an adjustment of people to one
another under the exigencies of the conditions imposed by
the nature of the circumstances. An individual who failed
to conform to the accepted standard of conduct and in so
doing offended another would discover that in spite of the
apparent oblivion an actual unity of feeling is present, and
that the injured one's protests are more vehement than they
would be if he did not realize that he had the sympathy of

those about him to whose presence he had paid no heed before the incident.

It would be an ill-assorted aggregation indeed in which no relationships whatsoever existed among the members and in which no group-forming factors were present as quiescent, if not active, common interests, capable, if called forth by an appropriate stimulus, of producing a degree of unity. At first thought the crowds traveling on the New York City subways during the morning and evening rush hours may appear to be such aggregations, devoid of all human unifying relationships, ever changing, lacking all cohesion; but a closer examination reveals the opposite. There is relationship, mutual understanding, forbearance, and agreement of a very definite character which makes what would otherwise be an unendurable situation at least tolerable. Pressure, physical and circumstantial, crushes the finer courtesies which are ever sensitive to over-crowding; each considers himself alone, but if he grants no quarter, he asks none. If he mercilessly shoves those in front of him, he is as mercilessly shoved in his turn by those behind him, and he accepts the buffeting. These are the rules of the game, unwritten but understood, and to be angry because of them gains one nothing. The subway crowds are singularly good-natured under one of the most trying of conditions, the restriction of the freedom of bodily movements through the hindrance of others; neither is the crowd altogether ruthless in its self-interest. The need of the elderly and the weak may be over-looked, and generally it is; but if it is actually observed, a seat or other assistance will be offered. A polite request for information will elicit a kindly answer, a real desire to be of service on some one's part.

Although the feeling of belonging together which is the distinguishing characteristic of the group is ordinarily in abeyance in such gatherings as the subway throng or the theater audience which have been brought together by like interests rather than a common purpose,[7] this is not altogether lacking as was noted. Certain fundamental bases of unity are present which may be aroused by an appropriate stimulus. The persons who comprise such miscellaneous aggregations will probably belong for the most part to the same nationality and community groupings and on occasion these relationships may spring into the foreground, creating an awareness of unity among those present as compared to outsiders. During the World War raising the flag or singing the national anthem in miscellaneous gatherings created a group spirit through an aroused patriotic sentiment and drew those of the same nation together as opposed to the enemy nation. The coming of the stranger often proves to be such an incentive for quickening quiescent group relationships; those who belong to the same group become aware of their relations to one another in contrast to the outsider who does not share these.

In the present thesis the stranger has been defined from the standpoint of the group—he is one who has entered the group who did not formerly belong to it—inasmuch as the problem we are primarily interested in studying relates to the manner in which existing group relationships affect the formation of new relationships. The problem of forming new relationships when all group support is lacking on both sides is a somewhat different one as we noted in the case of the passengers on shipboard. Such relationships are more largely a matter of individual initiative, of personality, of consciousness of kind and of difference, or of the expediency of the

[7] See MacIver, *Society: Its Structure and Changes*, p. 8 for a discussion of the distinction between the use of the terms *like* and *common.* " The like is what we have distributively, privately, each to himself; the common is what we have collectively, what we share. . . . Observe that while the like is not the common it is often the source of the common."

moment than is true when the stranger has entered into contact with another who is aware of himself as a part of a group and whose actions are influenced by this. New relationships tend to reflect the nature of the group relationships. If the stranger is incorporated into the group, the relationships which unite the group must be extended to him also through the process of developing in him the sentiments upon which these relationships are based. The relative ease or difficulty of this process will in a large measure depend upon the character of the sentiments which form the basis of the unifying bonds of group organization and which serve as a means for distinguishing certain broad categories of group relationships.

4. FUNDAMENTAL TYPES OF UNIFICATION

The multiplicity of groups is so great and there is so much overlapping among them that the problem of discovering the nature of the relationships upon which they are based is not an easy one. If we attempt to utilize the distinction between communal and associational groups,[8] which is clearly a fundamental one in certain respects, we find that the associational groups have their roots so thoroughly embedded within the larger life of the community that it is often impractical or even impossible to disentangle them. To illustrate, although church congregations may be regarded primarily as associational groups organized to further certain specific interests, the manner in which the stranger is received by a church group will be complicated by other factors derived from the basic communal life. To be welcome he must fit into a social scheme that extends beyond the fact of conformity to the standards of conduct and belief required for membership in the church. The request of a Brooklyn pastor that the colored members of his congregation withdraw from it and

[8] For a discussion of this distinction see MacIver's *Community* (New York, 1928), pp. 28 *et seq.*

attend a church for their own race is an instance of this. Again even in those professional groups whose interests are most highly specialized and in which the influence of extraneous factors has been reduced to a minimum, such factors have not been entirely eliminated; latent, they may still be aroused by some crisis. This was the case during the World War when cultured Germans in this country who had formerly been welcomed to professional groups suddenly found themselves ostracised because of their nationality. Participation in the specific activities of associational groups is thus seen to be dependent upon other relationships which are communal in their nature.

Racial and national differences which, theoretically, would not in themselves debar their possessors from belonging to certain associational groups may do so at times. A pride in one's own race and a prejudice against that of another are seen to transcend the tenets of brotherly love preached by the church. An awakened patriotism, a loyalty to one's own national group, is seen to be dominant over the claims of smaller associations existing within the nation. The special abilities and qualifications which would normally be required for admission to professional groups are subservient in a crisis to the major criterion of nationality. Associations thus are revealed as partial in their nature and dependent in a greater or a less degree upon an underlying community which is integral.[9] We can never wholly remove an associational group from its context; it must be considered in relation to its background. The problem of classifying groups from the standpoint of the present analysis thus becomes one of differentiating among communal groups. The essential differences between the two great types of groups, the communal and the associational, are not lost sight of, but these groups are not dissociated.

[9] *Ibid.*, p. 24.

The communal group or community has been defined by Professor MacIver as "any circle of people who live together, who belong together, so that they share, not this or that particular interest, but a whole set of interests wide enough and complete enough to include their lives".[10] A community is always a group occupying a territorial area. The tribe, the pioneer settlement, the village, the city, and the nation are examples of communal groups. Such groups vary greatly in the complexity of their social structures, but the basic feelings of unity which underlie these are less diverse in nature. In general two main types of group relationships or structures may be distinguished from the standpoint of the sentiments in which they are grounded. In the one type feelings associated with the primitive "Father idea" predominate, and in the other the feeling of brotherhood has been extended. These types Denison has designated as the "patriarchal" and the "fratriarchal".[11] They are different in principle and in application and the groups which develop from them are also structurally different.

In the patriarchal type individuals are bound together by their relation to the father. Even if they have no sense of unity with one another, they remain together because each feels his unity with a common ancestor. They hang upon him as many separate weights may hang from one hook or as bits of iron adhere to a magnet. In the fratriarchal type the authority of the father is disregarded and the members hang together because of a sense of union with one another, as bits of iron once magnetized hold together without any compelling force. In large groups of the patriarchal type where men are held together by the feeling which each has for the official above him, while nothing holds him to the masses at his side, we may term the cohesive force "vertical".

[10] MacIver, *Society: Its Structure and Changes*, pp. 9-10.
[11] Denison, *op. cit.*, pp. 8-10.

In a democracy or brotherhood where each man is bound to his fellow the unifying emotion is " horizontal " in action.

Each of these two major types of unifying social relationships from which the social structures of complex societies have been evolved has developed through the extension of sentiments based upon the blood ties, real or fictitious, which unite the primitive family group, horde or clan. In relationships of the patriarchal type the sentiments of loyalty and of obedience to the superior authority of the father, whether prompted by affection, reverence or fear, have served as a nucleus for the principle of authority which Hobhouse distinguishes as the bond of union belonging to " epochs of expansion in culture and improvement in the arts of life "[12] It is one method by which large communities can be formed with greater facilities for self-preservation and for the maintenance of internal order than the primitive clan or village commune can enjoy. Ancestor worship as a system of social organization is an extension of the patriarchal type of unification. The idea of a common father gives cohesion and social continuity to the group. Social systems based on a class distinction between men are also an adaptation of the patriarchal relationship; the authority of the father becomes merged in that of the ruling class to which others are subordinated. In relationships of the fratriarchal type, on the other hand, although descent from a common father is implied by the fact of common brotherhood, the authority of the father is not emphasized. The stock or kinship group who share the same blood is the social unit rather than the family as such.[18] Hence, a certain equality of rights exists since all are blood brothers and are bound by the same ties. No one has authority over another, but all share common

[12] Hobhouse, L. T., *Morals in Evolution* (New York, 1906), pp. 58-9.

[18] Smith, W. Robertson, *Kinship and Marriage in Early Arabia* (London, 1903), pp. 69 *et seq.*

duties and responsibilities from which no member of the group can withdraw. The unifying principle is that of mutual obligations which give rise to social structures differing in form and spirit from those based on authority. Citizenship as it was first evolved in the Greek city-states and later among the Romans was based on the theory of a common blood brotherhood which shared rights and responsibilities. During the Medieval Period the feudal contract between vassal and suzerain always involved duties for both, and, hence, the sentiments on which it was based were fundamentally unlike those of the patriarchal relationship in which the subject had no legal rights. The Christian Church of this period also advocated the brotherhood of man, but combined this with the fatherhood of God, thus uniting both principles in one system. The bonds of nationality which unite the great national states of the present time are a further extension of the principle of a common brotherhood with mutual obligations to include all those who share a certain measure of common living.

The nature of the bonds which unite men into communal groups thus offers a key for the classification and study of such groups from the point of view of their relations to outsiders. To include the newcomer it is necessary, as we have seen, to extend to him the relationships which unite the group through a process of inculcating in him the appropriate sentiments which sustain these relationships. An interpretation of the reaction of the group to the stranger must therefore begin with an analysis of the social structure of the particular group with which the stranger is in contact. This is the method adopted for the study of the material which we wish to consider. The major systems of social integration are subject, however, to various modifying influences that may not be overlooked. Smaller communities are formed within the larger units and these tend to develop other relationships peculiar to themselves which supplement the larger system of social integration. The social organization of the small town differs from that of the city although the inhabitants of both may belong to the same nationality groups. The rural neighborhood differs in its turn from the small town, and the retarded isolated community from the frontier settlement. Nationality groups which have been transplanted in a new environment and are subjected to the pressure of an alien population about them undergo changes which are reflected in their systems of social relationships.

The unique patterns of social integration which have evolved in local groups such as these we have mentioned give a distinctive character to the manner in which the stranger is received. In many instances, particularly if the newcomer is of the same race and nationality as the members of the group, the problem of his reception is mainly one of establishing these more special relationships since he is already included within the larger circle of relationships. The effort to seek out that which is common in the treatment of the stranger can hardly neglect the influence of that which is special. Each contact between strangers is after all a unique situation some features of which are general and others of which are special. To interpret the behavior which is manifested the influence of both types of factors must be evaluated. A careful discrimination between the role of factors which are common to many situations and that of factors which belong to the special circumstances of any specific meeting should therefore prove enlightening. It is the aim of the chapters which follow to differentiate such factors and to consider their relative importance for various kinds of situations. The material relating to the treatment of the stranger has been oriented from this point of view and falls into three major categories: first, situations in which the relationship is determined primarily by the nature of the fundamental system of social integration; second, situations in which the relationship is determined not so much by the fundamental system of the whole society as by the characteristics peculiar to the local pattern of the particular community which the stranger enters; and, third, situations in which the particular circumstances of the meeting and the unique personalities of the individuals involved are the significant factors in deciding the character of the initial relationship.

PART TWO

THE STRANGER AND THE SOCIAL ORDER

CHAPTER III

THE OBLIGATIONS OF KINSHIP

I. THE ANDAMANESE SYSTEM OF HORDE RELATIONSHIPS

EVERY individual belongs to a cultural group and more intimately to a greater or a less number of smaller groups within this larger community. He may also belong to other groups whose membership, either directly or indirectly, cuts across the unity of different cultural groups and binds together individuals of like or complementary interests throughout a far greater area. The form that the social organization of a group assumes is an adjustment to the varied and sometimes conflicting demands which are made upon individuals as members of these interrelated groups. The degree of complexity of the social structure of a people is a function of the number of interdependent groups which lie wholly or partially within its domain, and the manner in which communities differ in this respect has been taken as a basis for distinguishing between simpler and more highly civilized peoples. The cultures of such peoples as the Andaman Islanders, the Australian aborigines, the Trobriand Islanders, the American Indians, the Eskimos, and the Negro tribes of Africa are all spoken of as simple or primitive. Although differing from one another in many ways, each of these peoples has a simple social organization in comparison with the highly involved, interrelated social structures of the so-called civilized nations of Europe, Asia and the Americas. In the Andaman Islands, for instance, an individual belongs to his horde of perhaps fifty persons which is the territorial and war-making unit. Within the horde he is a member of a family and of his own age and

61

sex groups.   His membership within these few groups regulates his behavior toward all other persons in the horde.
Toward each he has certain duties, obligations, privileges and
restrictions which are determined by his position in the
groups to which he belongs.   Outside of his own horde he
has contacts with a number of other hordes within the district
who speak the same language and share the same general
customs.   Toward some of these the relationships are
friendly, visits and gifts are exchanged, and intermarriage
occurs; toward others the attitudes are unfriendly, sometimes
to the point of bloodshed.   Before the intervention of the
white man, the circle of contacts of a native of the Andaman
Islands did not, with few exceptions, exceed five hundred
persons at the most.   These contacts were all direct and
personal and the relations which were formed all involved an
element of sentiment.   The contacts of a member of a
modern civilized community, on the other hand, are practically unlimited, reaching out in one form or another to
embrace millions of people throughout the world.   The
great majority of these contacts, however, are indirect and
impersonal in their nature and are entirely lacking in
emotional content.

Among the Andaman Islanders a simple social organization sufficed to meet the need for regulating behavior within
the group because of the small size of the horde and the comparative freedom from outside contacts of a varied or unfriendly nature.   The various relationship patterns, although
fairly definite in character, were not intensified.   A man
might take up his residence with another horde if they were
willing.   Children might be adopted or, what happened more
frequently, be exchanged for a period of time.[1]   This novel

[1] Man, E. N., "On the Original Inhabitants of the Andaman Islands",
The Journal of the Anthropological Institute, vol. xii (London, 1882-
1883), pp. 124-26.

custom would seem to indicate the greater importance of the relationship of the child to the group as a whole than to his own immediate family. Children were kindly treated at all times. The Andamanese did not trace relationships beyond the third generation.[2] Family relationships, although recognized, were not accentuated and thus the Andamanese social system possessed a certain measure of flexibility. The main features of the relationship system are summed up by Professor Radcliffe-Brown as follows:

The duties that one person owes to another are determined much less by consanguinity and marriage, than by their respective ages and social status. Even within the family, which is nevertheless of importance, the duty of a child to a parent is very little different from his duty to any other person of the same age. There is very little of any special customs relating to conduct towards different kinds of relatives. Corresponding to this we find very few terms to denote relationships and a considerable development of the terms which denote age and social status. Thus a man's duties to his elder brother are much the same as those toward other men of the same age, and we find that there is no word for " elder brother ".[3]

The fact that age and social status rather than consanguinity and marriage determine the duties of one person to another makes it possible to assign a place within the group to the stranger if his status is made known through common friends. Strangers who are thus properly introduced are always warmly welcomed by the whole community and the parting guest is graciously speeded among the Andamanese.[4] Other strangers are repelled since there is no recognized place for them in the community. Early accounts have pictured

[2] *Ibid.*, p. 127.
[3] *The Andaman Islanders*, pp. 81-82.
[4] Man, *op. cit.*, p. 148.

the natives of the Andaman Islands as ferocious and canni-
balistic. Sailors avoided the islands for fear of being ship-
wrecked on their inhospitable shores. That this attitude
toward foreigners should have been taken by a people who
are not quarrelsome or blood-thirsty among themselves Professor Radcliffe-Brown attributes to the unhappy nature of
their first contacts with outsiders. In former times raiding
parties from the mainland had killed or carried off some of
their number, thus conditioning the reaction of the natives
toward all other foreigners. Strangers were thought to
come from the spirit world; they were unfriendly, and if they
were killed their bodies did not receive burial rites. Instead
they were thrown into the sea or cut up into small pieces and
burned, but not eaten. This custom of burning the bodies
probably gave rise to the mistaken impression that the
Andamanese were cannibals.[5]

2. THE AUSTRALIAN CLASSIFICATORY SYSTEM

The Australian aborigines are another of the simpler
peoples for whom the horde was formerly the land-owning
and war-making unit; but their social organization was more
highly integrated than that of the Andaman Islanders. The
relationships of every individual toward the others of his
own horde and to the members of related hordes had assumed
definite behavior patterns which were based upon kinship.
The implications of such a system based on kinship are
brought out by Professor Radcliffe-Brown.

In Australia we have an example of a society in which the
very widest possible recognition is given to genealogical relationships. In a tribe that has not been affected by white
intrusion, it is easy to collect field pedigrees for the whole tribe.
Further, these genealogical relationships are made in Australia,
the basis of an extensive and highly organized system of re-

[5] *The Andaman Islanders*, pp. 7-8.

ciprocal obligations. While among ourselves the question of genealogical relationships only affects our relations to a few individuals, our nearest relatives, in native Australian society it regulates more or less definitely the behavior of an individual to every person with whom he has any special dealings whatsoever. . . .[6]

So far as Australian tribes are concerned it can be laid down as definitely proved that the kinship terminology of a tribe is an integral and essential part of the social organization. At every moment of the life of a member of an Australian tribe his dealings with other individuals are regulated by the relationship in which he stands to them. His relatives, near and distant, are classified into certain large groups, and this classification is carried out by means of the terminology, and could apparently not be achieved in any other way. Thus in any part of the continent when a stranger comes to camp the first thing to be done, before he can be admitted within the camp, is to determine his relationship to every man and woman in it; i.e., to determine what is the proper term of relationship for him to apply to each of them. As soon as he knows his relation to a given individual he knows how to behave towards him, what his duties and what his rights are.[7]

Such a social system based exclusively on relationships of kinship is extremely rigid and inflexible. In the Australian system there was " no provision by which a man could leave his own horde and be 'adopted' or 'naturalized' in another ", nor could social relations of any type be established with strangers unless these could demonstrate that they were connected by kinship ties with someone within the horde.[8] A stranger from an unknown tribe, unless he came accredited as a sacred messenger, would most probably be promptly

[6] Radcliffe-Brown, A. R., "The Social Organization of Australian Tribes", *The "Oceania" Monographs*, no. 1 (Melbourne, 1931), p. 12.

[7] *Ibid.*, p. 95.

[8] *Ibid.*, p. 4.

speared, according to Spencer and Gillen.[9]   There was no
place for him in the group, no basis for bringing him into
relationship with its members. The peculiar dread that the
native has of evil magic from a distance attaches to the
stranger. He is feared and therefore to be killed. Just why
the natives should have attributed evil magic to the strangers
must be purely conjectural in the absence of a more complete
history of the previous contacts of the group. It seems
probable, however, that the presence of a stranger in a group
all of whose social relations were strictly ordered on the basis
of kinship would be a disturbing element. His presence
there would create an uncomfortable tension for which some
outlet would be sought. If the stranger is killed, this tension
is removed and the anticipated evil averted. Indeed, this
would be the most direct solution for the problem in a group
whose social organization provided no means for assigning
a definite position to the stranger and in this way removing
the condition of uncertainty and of apprehension brought
about by his intrusion.

When the element of fear has been removed the natives of
Australia are not inhospitable. Although no members of
any one local group could enter the camp belonging to another
local group until they had been formally invited to do so,
Spencer and Gillen observed visitors in most camps of any
size.[10]   They also speak of the friendly manner in which they
were received by one strange tribe due to the fact that, unknown to them, the tribe among whom they had last been
working had sent messengers in advance to say that they
were friends and that they were to be told things without
fear.[11]   These same authors give an interesting account of

[9] Spencer, B. and Gillen, F. J., *The Northern Tribes of Central Australia* (London and New York, 1904), p. 31.

[10] *Ibid.*, p. 31.

[11] *Ibid.*, p. xi.

the behavior manifested toward messengers whose relationship toward the group they are entering is a special one.

When important ceremonies are about to take place messengers are always sent out, often to distant tribes, and the etiquette observed illustrates well one aspect of aboriginal character. Each messenger is provided by some important member or recognized leader of the group that sends him out with an object, the possession of which at once indicates to all whom he meets that he is a messenger. In the southern parts of the Territory this will take the form of a sacred stick called a churinga, or popularly, a bull-roarer. The bearer of this is absolutely safe anywhere. On approaching a camp he sits down waiting until the local men choose to take notice of him, which may not be until after an hour or so. They all go on meanwhile, quite unconcernedly, as if he did not exist, and then one or two of the older men will go over to him; he will show them his credentials and deliver his message, after which he is brought into camp, made free of the special men's camp and provided with food. This same thing goes on at every camp that he visits and exactly the same etiquette is observed when the visitors arrive at the camp from which the messenger was sent. In the northern parts, as, for example, in the Alligator River district, when boys are to be initiated, they are sent out on a journey to distant camps amongst strange tribes that often lasts for months. Each of them carries a small wand and under the protection of this they travel in perfect safety. When they come to a strange camp they stand close together, leaning on their wands and singing a special corrobboree song, which must be replied to by women in camp.

It is interesting to find that the natives have also, as it were, extended this feeling of sacredness of the persons of their own messengers to those of aboriginals who are carrying messages for white men. A letter is always spoken of as a " paper yabber " and is carried in a cleft stick so that it can be seen easily. The cleft stick acts as a safe passport.[12]

[12] Spencer, B., *Native Tribes of Northern Territory of Australia* (London, 1914), pp. 34 *et seq.*

Although the Australian system of social organization made provision for certain formal contacts outside the horde, such as those which have been described in the paragraphs above, it was essentially a closed system. Limitations were imposed by the method of classification which could not be exceeded. There was no way of extending the system of genealogical relationships to include outsiders who did not fall within its narrow circle, and under the pressure of the rapidly changing conditions brought about by the intrusion of the white man the system has disintegrated.

3. PARTNERSHIP SYSTEMS OF GIFT EXCHANGE

Not all of the simpler peoples are as restricted in their contacts and relationships with outsiders as the natives of the Andaman Islands and of Australia. In these groups the unifying relationships within the horde were strong while those of the tribe as a whole were relatively weak or almost non-existent. Among many native peoples, however, this order is somewhat reversed and the tribal relationships are strengthened while those of the horde become more restricted. The tribe, for instance, becomes the land-owning and war-making unit. The extension of group relationships to include the tribe increases the complexity of the social order. The number of persons with whom an individual has contacts is increased and there is a correspondingly greater differentiation among the various kinds of relationships; some relationships are nearer and more personal and others are more remote and impersonal; some are reserved for the individual's more immediate circle of relatives and friends and others are extended to the tribe. The larger number within the tribe and the greater area occupied also increases the opportunities for contacts with other tribes. Such contacts are frequently, though not always, of a war-like character. Malinowski has given a delightful account of a system of ceremonial exchange of gifts known as the *Kula* which binds together members of tribes among the Melanesians which differ in language and culture and probably even in race.[18] These tribes occupy a wide ring of islands which form a closed circuit to the north and east of the east end of New Guinea.

Along this route articles of two kinds, and these two kinds only, are constantly travelling in opposite directions. In the direction of the hands of the clock, moves constantly one of these kinds—long necklaces of red shell called *soulava*. In the opposite direction moves the other kind — bracelets of white shell called *mwali*. Each of these articles, as it travels in its own direction on the closed circuit, meets on its way articles of the other class, and is constantly being exchanged for them. Every movement of the Kula articles, every detail of the transactions is fixed and regulated by a set of traditional rules and conventions and some acts of the Kula are accompanied by an elaborate magical ritual and public ceremonies.

On every island and in every village, a more or less limited number of men take part in the Kula—that is to say, receive the goods, hold them for a short time, and then pass them on. Therefore every man who is in the Kula, periodically though not regularly, receives one or several *mwali* (arm-shells), or a *soulava* (necklace of red shell discs), and then has to hand it on to one of his partners, from whom he receives the opposite commodity in exchange. Thus no one man ever keeps any of the articles for any length of time in his possession. One transaction does not finish the Kulu relationship, the rule being "once in the Kula, always in the Kula", and a partnership between two men is a permanent and lifelong affair. Again any given *mwali* or *soulava* may always be found travelling and changing hands, and there is no question of its ever settling down, so that the principle "once in the Kula, always in the Kula" applies also to the valuables themselves.

[18] Malinowski, Bronislaw, *Argonauts of the Western Pacific* (London and New York, 1922).

The ceremonial exchange of the two articles is the main, the fundamental aspect of the Kula. But associated with it, and done under its cover, we find a great number of secondary activities and features. Thus side by side with the ritual exchange of arm-shells and necklaces, the natives carry on ordinary trade, bartering from one island to another a great number of utilities, often improcurable in the district to which they are imported, and indispensable there. Further, there are other activities, preliminary to the Kula, or associated with it, such as the building of canoes for the expeditions, certain big forms of mortuary ceremonies, and preparatory taboos.

The Kula is thus an extremely big and complex institution, both in its geographical extent, and in the manifoldness of its component pursuits. It welds together a considerable number of tribes, and it embraces a vast complex of activities, interconnected and playing into one other, so as to form one organic whole.[14]

In the discussion of this unique system Malinowski has made it clear that the objects which are exchanged have little or no actual value in themselves, but that the reasons why so much satisfaction is derived from their temporary possession are purely sentimental ones. To give or to receive a gift lends prestige in the Trobriands; it creates a bond between the two individuals concerned. The one who receives is under an obligation to the giver which it is his duty at a future time to repay with an equivalent gift, or, if possible, he will give a better one since to do so would enhance his own prestige. The natives compete with one another in generosity rather than in war. The function of the Kula is therefore to create a new type of social structure through the formation of friendships with individuals belonging to different local units. It is a method for giving a recognized status with respect to the local group to certain persons who do not

14 *Ibid.*, pp. 81-3.

belong to it otherwise. Although the Kula objects are exchanged between individuals and the relationship is personal and direct, it is a group affair in that it affects the social order of the community as a whole. It is this aspect of the Kula that has made it a matter of ceremonial ritual; through it a change in social structure has been brought about and it is this which is of ritual significance. The exchange of such commodities as yams for pots which goes on in connection with the Kula is of secondary importance. Barter is an interest relation, and in spite of its utility it does not form so strong a link between the persons or groups concerned as does the giving of a gift, which is a sentiment relation and one which augments the prestige of both the giver and the receiver.

The tribes among whom the Kula is carried on are matrilineal in descent and women are well treated in all of them. They differ, however, in their moral standards and this difference is reflected in their attitudes toward strangers. Among the Amphletts, where strict chastity is the rule, the women hide from strangers, while among the Trobriand natives, where sexual relations are very lax, the women mingle freely and are genial. " As soon as an interesting stranger arrives, half the village assembles around him, talking loudly and making remarks about him, frequently uncomplimentary, and altogether assuming a tone of jocular familiarity." [15]

The village rather than the horde is the unit and then comes the district. The totemic clans cut across the political and local divisions, and among the Trobriands social differentiation into rank has made its appearance with a definite chief and commoners. The ghosts of ancestors are not feared, but black magic is, and unless he is under the protection of his Kula partner no native would feel safe and comfortable in a strange district for fear of foreign sorcery.[16]

[15] *Ibid.*, p. 52. [16] *Ibid.*, p. 92.

From the standpoint of complexity the social organization of the Trobriands is a higher type than that of either
the Andaman Islanders or the Australian aborigines both in
the greater number of sub-groups into which the local unit is
differentiated and in its specialized relations with a much
wider and more varied circle of outsiders. The creation of
social ties through the exchange of gifts, as distinct from
barter, has afforded a method for expanding the social structure within certain limits by giving to it a degree of flexibility.

Although the details of the Kula system could hardly have
originated more than once the underlying principle upon
which it is based, that of a gift followed by a counter gift,
has been widely applied as a means for establishing social
bonds. The Potlatch ceremony of the West Coast Indians
of Vancouver Island and British Columbia had a similar
function.[17] The chief of a tribe as its representative, gave
the Potlatch to a neighboring tribe and the greater the amount
of property that was given away on the occasion, the greater
was the prestige of the givers. It was expected, however,
that after the lapse of a proper interval of time the Potlatch
would be returned and that they would receive in their turn
blankets, coppers, and other property equivalent in value to
what they had themselves given. The whole matter of giving and receiving was nevertheless a social affair and not a
business transaction. The obligation to make an adequate
return for a Potlatch was felt as something quite different
from the obligations involved in trade, somewhat as gambling
debts are regarded as "debts of honor". The relations were
based upon sentiment rather than utility.

A formal organized system of gift exchange such as the
Kula or the Potlatch could hardly flourish as a means of

17 A good description of the Potlatch may be found in Boas, *The
Social Organization and Secret Societies of the Kwakiutl Indians*
(Washington, 1897), pp. 353-58.

maintaining social relations except among neighboring tribes of the same general culture area. Though widening the horizons of the local community it makes no provision for giving a position within the group to a stranger from a distance. The question of the manner in which a stranger is treated will depend upon whether or not friendly relations exist with the group from which he comes. This distinction is seen in the treatment of castaways among the Melanesians.

A stranger as such was generally throughout the Islands an enemy to be killed. Thus at Florida a stranger who had escaped from a wreck onto an islet was killed when seen, and spoken of as a cocoanut that had floated ashore. There was a common belief that a stranger would bring with him disease or some other mischief. But it was often a question whether a castaway was a stranger. If he were recognized as belonging to an hostile district, there was no doubt of his fate; but if he fell into the hands of those to whose division, *kema* or *veve,* he belonged, he would probably be saved. It is not an uncommon thing that canoes should be blown from Santa Cruz and the Reef Islands to Malauta and Ulawa; the men on board them were not wholly strangers, though personally unknown, they were men from known lands, not strange beings like white men from without the world. They were therefore received as guests, sometimes establishing themselves after a while by marriage, sometimes awaiting an opportunity to return. . . .

A refugee or a castaway is not a slave but a guest; his life is naturally less valued than that of a man of the place, and useful services are expected from him, while he mixes freely and on equal terms with the common people.[18]

Although organized systems for establishing social relationships with other groups by means of a formal exchange of gifts which are associated with sentiment and which con-

[18] Codrington, R. H., *The Melanesians* (Oxford, 1891), pp. 345-46.

vey prestige are rare, the principle of establishing or strengthening bonds by means of gifts is a universal one.[19] The
giving of a gift, even when a gift of equivalent value is
expected, is a sentiment relation and its implications are
unlike those of barter. The gift is personal; it enhances the
prestige of both the giver and the receiver. The spirit in
which the gift is given is important, but no more so than the
manner in which it is received. Although all giving is not
altruistic in its purpose, the sentiment, " Not what we give,
but what we share", is in a measure implied. Bonds are
created between persons through sharing and gifts create or
maintain ties of a very definite nature. The obligation of
the person who has received the gift is a specific one: gratitude is expected even if a return gift is not. Gifts may be
embarrassing at times because of the obligations which they
impose, and they may offend as well as give pleasure. The
psychology which is involved in the giving of gifts and the
function which these perform in establishing relationships
are social phenomena worthy of further study.

4. ADOPTION

Adoption is a device which has been widely used by both
primitive and civilized peoples for the purpose of including
an outsider within the social organization of the group. By
means of adoption the newcomer is given a definite status in
the group and his relations to the other members are determined by this. Although the outsider is adopted by a particular family the sanction of the gens is necessary among
primitive peoples since the ties that unite the group as a whole

---

[19] The importance of gifts in establishing friendly relationships also
appears in early Anglo-Saxon poetry. In *Beowulf* and in *Widsith, the
Far-traveler*, particular emphasis is placed on the gifts which are made
to the stranger as reflecting honor on both the giver and the receiver.
The gifts have a sentimental value and are not regarded as ordinary
remuneration for services.

are so closely knit that the addition of a new member is a matter of moment to all and an occasion for ritual ceremonies. Among the Iroquois, according to Morgan, a distinctive right of the gens was that of admitting new members by adoption.

Captives taken in war were either put to death, or adopted into some gens. Women and children taken prisoners usually experienced clemency in this form. Adoption not only conferred gentile rights, but also the nationality of the tribe. . . . A declining gens might replenish its members through adoption, although such instances were rare. . . . Among the Iroquois the ceremony of adoption was performed at the public council of the tribe, who turned it practically into a religious rite.[20]

Morgan was himself adopted into the Hawk gens of the Senecas, doubtless as an honorary member without active duties and obligations.[21] Adoption provides a method for extending group relationships and thus it gives a modicum of flexibility to the social order. Ceremonial adoption of this nature must not be confused, however, with the informal type observed in the Andaman Islands which did not involve including the stranger but was carried on among the members of the group by the temporary exchange of their own children. Formal adoption is a ritual matter in which an adjustment is made to the change in group life that is brought about by the introduction of a stranger. Even in civilized societies unless a child has been legally adopted he has no recognized claim to certain rights in the inheritance of property from his foster parents. His position is dependent upon the per-

[20] Morgan, Lewis H., *Ancient Society* (New York, 1878), p. 80.

[21] Although white men have occasionally been honored by such initiation into primitive tribes as in the instances of Morgan and of Spencer and Gillen in Australia their position in the tribe is a purely nominal one in Prof. Radcliffe-Brown's opinion. It involves certain rights and privileges, but enforces no duties and obligations, and, hence, the individual is not fully a member of the tribe.

formance of a ceremonial function which, although it has lost its picturesque attributes, has still retained its essential meaning.

Among the American Indians some tribes had the custom of adoption while others did not. No ceremony, for instance, existed by which a stranger could be adopted into a gens of the Omahas; [22] but among the Osage, a tribe cognate to the Omahas, a captive taken in war might be adopted by anyone who had lost a child, or was without children. After the ceremony the person became in all respects as one born in the tribe and was subject to the duties and requirements of the family into which he entered by a kind of new birth. In an account given of the ceremonies of adoption among the Osage the characteristics essential to rites of passage are revealed.[23] The person wishing to adopt the captive sent an invitation to the leading men who were the peace makers and also to those who had charge of the war rites. Food was prepared and set before these leaders, and the host in a solemn speech expressed his desire to adopt the captive. These leaders then sent for men who were versed in the rituals of the ceremony and when all were assembled, the captive was brought and placed in the back part of the lodge opposite the entrance, the seat of the stranger. Then the ritual used in the initiation and naming of a child born in the tribe was given. This ritual recounts the creation and history of the tribe and the four stages of man's life. At the close the captive was passed from the chief of those who made peace to those who made war, thus symbolically traversing the tribal circle, an act indicating that he was to share in all that

[22] Dorsey, J. Owen, " Omaha Sociology ", *Third Annual Report of the Bureau of Ethnology*, 1881-1882 (Washington, 1884), p. 225.

[23] Fletcher, A. C. and La Flesche, F., " The Omaha Tribe ", *Twenty-seventh Annual Report of the Bureau of Ethnology*, 1905-1906 (Washington, 1911), pp. 61-62.

concerned the tribe. He was then given a sharp cut on the nose and the blood which flowed was washed away. This was a rite of separation, symbolizing that the blood of his former tribe was washed away. He was then given food, the new blood of the Osage, and this was sanctified by smoking the peace pipe. He was now anointed with buffalo fat to bring him within the tribal rites and his face was painted with black stripes in recognition of the war god. These were acts of aggregation. The name Ni'wathe (made to live) was given to him and he became the child of his adopted parents. Later the name Ni'wathe was dropped and he was given another name belonging to the tribe without further rites.

The method of adoption provided a means for giving the stranger a definite place in the group, but it was inherently limited in its scope. A small native community could not adopt any considerable number of outsiders, and, unless they chanced to be captives, adult persons would hardly consent to being adopted. The method was best suited for children and young persons who had been deprived of the usual ties of relationship through warfare or other misfortune and who did not need to relinquish former ties in order to establish new ones. The bonds of adoption were personal and permanent and the adopted individual became a member of the tribe for always. Where the contact with the stranger was of a more general nature some other basis for establishing relationships of a temporary form was needed and the guest relationship was evolved to meet this requirement among peoples of many kinds.

5. GUESTS AND GODS

Hospitality within the primitive group itself is the accepted custom and friendly visiting between groups which are on good terms with one another is common. The relationship of guest and host is not a new one. What is new is the ex-

tension of this relationship to include the stranger who comes
as a guest under the aegis of his host, or under the protection of some god or of some taboo.[24]   In any case his rights
within the group do not attach to him as a person, but he is
dependent for his protection upon hospitality which in some
instances is restricted by custom to a definite length of time.
For the time, however, that he remains a guest his position is
an honored one which among certain peoples includes even
the privileges of sexual hospitality.   In explaining the
reasons for this custom Briffault says:

To primitive man all men are either tribal brothers or strangers,
and the latter term is equivalent in primitive society to
"enemy": there is no middle status between those two opposite
relations. If a man, not being by birth a tribal brother, is
admitted into the community, if he is found to be well-disposed,
if he is regarded with good will or affection or admiration—if,
in short, he is not an enemy—he must needs be a tribal brother.
Hence the sacredness of hospitality in all primitive sentiment;
a man who has been admitted into the relation of guest is
necessarily to be regarded and treated as a tribal brother.[25]

In accepting the stranger as a tribal brother a change is
effected in the social structure through the addition of a
new member and this is regarded with the ritual attitude.
The sacredness which characterizes the hospitality shown to
the stranger guest emanates from this source, although it is
not infrequently complicated by other factors, as Westermarck points out.

The custom of hospitality is also associated with superstitious beliefs. The unknown stranger, like everything un-

[24] Hobhouse, L. T., *Morals in Evolution* (New York, 1906), vol. i,
p. 240.
[25] Briffault, Robert, *The Mothers* (New York, 1927), vol. i, pp. 635
et seq.

known and everything strange, arouses a feeling of mysterious awe in simple minds.   The Ainu say, " Do not treat strangers slightingly, for you never know whom you are entertaining " (Batchelor, *Ainu and Their Folk-lore,* p. 259).   According to Homeric notions, the gods, in the likeness of strangers from far countries, put on all manner of shapes, and wander through the cities, beholding the violence and the righteousness of men (*Odyssey* xvii, 585 *et seq.*).   It is significant that in the writings of ancient Greece, Rome, and India guests are mentioned next after gods as due objects of regard.   When properly treated the stranger may bring with him great blessings; for if efficacy is ascribed to the blessings of even an ordinary man, those of the stranger are naturally supposed to be still more powerful.   And there is yet another reason for pleasing him. He is regarded not only as a potential benefactor, but as a powerful source of evil.   He is commonly believed to be versed in magic; and the evil wishes and curses of a stranger are greatly feared, owing partly to his quasi-supernatural character, partly to his close contact with the host and his belongings, which makes it possible to transfer evil to them.[26]

In the theories of both Westermarck and Briffault the concept of the stranger as a possible god in disguise offers an explanation of the rites of sacred prostitution among uncultured peoples and in the ancient world.   In ancient literature the man who is invited to take advantage of them is expressedly described as a stranger.   The belief that when a stranger is honored a god has been entertained unawares seems to have been widely spread among peoples of different culture areas.   The American Indians regarded the first white men with whom they came in contact as gods, but, unfortunately, it was not long before they had reason to think differently and to assume a hostile rather than a respectful manner toward the newcomers.   Codrington gives an

[26] Westermarck, E., *The History of Human Marriage* (5th ed., New York, 1922), vol. i, pp. 226 *et seq.*

interesting account of the impression of the Banks Islanders with regard to white men, which is similar to that of the American Indians.

In the Banks Islands, for example, the natives believed the world to consist of their own group, with the Torres Islands, the three or four northern New Hebrides, and perhaps Tikopia, round which the ocean spread till it was shut in by the foundations of the sky. The first vessels they remembered to have seen were whalers, which they did not believe to have come from any country in the world; they were indeed quite sure that they did not, but must have been made out of the sea, because they knew that no men in the world had such vessels. In the same way they were sure the voyagers were not men; if they were, they would be black. What were they then? They were ghosts, and being ghosts, of necessity those of men who had lived in the world.

When Mr. Patterson first landed at Mota, the mission party having been seen in the previous year at Vauna Lava, there was a division of opinion among the natives; some said that the brothers of Jat had returned, certain supernatural beings of whom stories are told; others maintained that they were ghosts. Mr. Patterson retired from the heat into an empty house, the owner of which had lately died; this settled the question, he was the ghost of the late householder, and knew his home. A very short acquaintance with white visitors shows that they are not ghosts, but certainly does not show that they are men; the conjecture then is that they are beings of another order, spirits or demons, powerful no doubt, but mischievous. A ghost would be received in a peaceful and respectful manner, as European visitors have always in the first instance been received; a being not a living man or a ghost has wonderful things with him to see and to procure, but he probably brings disease and disaster.[27]

[27] Codrington, *op. cit.*, pp. 10 *et seq*. See also Lucian Lévy-Bruhl, *Primitive Mentality* (London and New York, 1923), pp. 352-83, for further instances of the superstitious attitude toward the stranger shown by native peoples.

By primitive people the ancestors and gods were regarded as a more definite part of the social group than is the case in more advanced communities; and at times it was thought to be well to take measures to renew or to strengthen the bonds with these spiritual members of the group. This was the function of sacrifice. The gift of sacrifice created a feeling of unity with the unseen world, and it was expected that the gods or ancestors would in their turn give a counter gift by furthering the well-being of those who offered the sacrifice. Among primitive men the gods were naturally thought of as having the same needs as themselves and so food was offered to them in sacrifice and women in the form of sacred prostitution, which, as Briffault has shown,[28] was a surrender of individual rights that was the equivalent of sacrifice.

Both sexual hospitality and sacred prostitution are customs which have a unifying function; but in the first a new bond is created by granting this privilege to one who is a stranger guest, yet nevertheless a man, while in the second case the ties of a relationship thought of as already existing are being strengthened. That is, the stranger is supposedly a god, and as such he has a recognized place and rights within the group. The relations established by both of these customs are ritual in their nature. Sacred prostitution was associated with the religious observances of various cults and some form of ritual ceremony usually preceded the granting of the privileges of sexual hospitality. Professor Boas gives an interesting description of the ceremonies for admitting the stranger into the group among the Central Eskimo who practice the custom of sexual hospitality.

If a stranger unknown to the inhabitants of a settlement arrives on a visit, he is welcomed by the celebration of a great feast. Among the southwestern tribes the natives arrange

[28] *Op. cit.*, vol. iii, pp. 203-204.

themselves in a row, one man standing in front of it. The stranger approaches slowly, his arms folded and his head inclined to the right side. Then the native strikes him with all his strength on the right cheek and in his turn inclines his head awaiting the stranger's blow. While this is going on the other men are playing ball and singing. Thus they continue until one of the combatants is vanquished. . . . The meaning of the duel, according to the natives themselves, is that the two men in meeting wish to know which of them is the better man.[29]

A great deal of visiting goes on among friendly groups of Eskimo and much hospitality is displayed. This includes wife-lending, a courtesy on the part of the host that it would be an insult to refuse.[30]

The numbers of instances of friendly visiting which have been noted among groups of simpler peoples is in contrast to the somewhat general impression that primitive man is a kind of Ishmael whose hand is against every man and who believes that every man's hand is against him. Many groups have solved the problem of establishing friendly relations with their nearer neighbors and the attitude of hostility to strangers has become special rather than general in its application. It is manifested only toward foreigners whom these groups have some particular reason for fearing, as the unfortunate nature of former contacts with other like strangers or a superstitious dread of magic from a distance. In those groups whose social organization includes the guest relationship a basis exists for forming new relationships. The social system is more flexible than one which includes only the kinship relations. The guest relationship, although a personal one involving definite obligations and the privileges

[29] Boas, Franz, "The Central Eskimo", *Sixth Annual Report of the Bureau of Ethnology*, 1884-1885 (Washington, 1888), p. 609.

[30] *Ibid.*, pp. 574-76 and pp. 779-81. See also J. W. Bilby, *Among Unknown Eskimo* (London, 1923), pp. 62-64.

of kinship, is not necessarily a permanent one. In this connection Grierson's conclusions from his study of the early trade relations of native tribes are of interest.

It is not the entertainment of guests, but the entertainment of strangers as guests, which is unfamiliar to primitive man. In the early stages of this novel relation the stranger is still regarded as an enemy, but is treated as a friend for a limited time, and for a specific purpose. He can count at least upon food and shelter, and protection, as long as he is actually in residence with his host. In some cases he can prolong his stay as long as he likes; in other cases, he must bring it to a close on the expiry of a fixed period. Sometimes his entertainer protects him, even after his departure, by escorting him to the next village, or by protecting him with a token which will ensure his friendly reception. Not infrequently this relation is indicated by an exchange of names, or by some ceremony as that of blood-brotherhood. At first it seems to have been strictly personal to the individuals concerned. We find, however, instances in which it does not cease on the death of the original parties to it. Further, in many cases the stranger is treated by his protector's tribe as its protégé; and in this attitude of a community towards an individual, we see the beginning of that public hospitality which forms a marked feature in the life of classic antiquity. Lastly, it is to be observed, that to refuse hospitality is generally regarded by public opinion as blameworthy, and is, in some cases, punishable by law.[31]

The relationship of the host and his stranger guest is one which involves deep sentiments and which, in most instances, must be confirmed by some form of ritual ceremony. Such rites frequently have taken the form of a covenant or sacred agreement and the relationships thus confirmed became permanent. The common life into which the two were brought by the covenant bound them irrevocably. Among rites of

[31] Grierson, P. J. H., *The Silent Trade* (Edinburgh, 1903), pp. 83-4.

this nature those of the covenant of blood, or of some variation of this, have been widely dispersed and are of particular
interest.

6. THE COVENANT OF BLOOD

Trumbull's studies of the covenant of blood, the covenant
of salt, and the threshold covenant have illuminated the
function of these rites, and his conclusions are of interest.
He says:

As I have come to see it, as a result of my researches, the very
idea of a "covenant" in primitive thought is a union of being,
or of persons, in a common life, with the approval of God, or
of the gods. This was primarily a sharing of blood, which is
life, between two persons, through a rite which had the sanction
of him who is the source of all life. In this sense "blood-
brotherhood" and the "threshold covenant" are but different
forms of one and the same *covenant*. The blood of animals
shared in a common sacrifice is counted as the blood which
makes two one in a sacred covenant. Wine as "the blood of
the grape" stands for the blood which is the life of all flesh;
hence the sharing of wine stands for the sharing of blood or
life. So, again, salt represents blood, or life, and the covenant
of salt is simply another form of the one blood covenant.[32]

In his volume, *The Blood Covenant*, Trumbull quotes a
body of evidence which shows how universal some form of
this covenant has been. The inter-mingling of the blood of
two persons was viewed as "equivalent to the inter-com-
mingling of the lives, of the personalities, of the natures, thus
brought together; so that there is, thereby and thence-
forward, one life in two bodies, a common life between two
friends".[33] In the course of Stanley's travels among the
negro tribes of Africa he became the blood brother of a con-

[32] Trumbull, H. Clay, *The Covenant of Salt* (New York, 1899), p. vi.
[33] *The Blood Covenant* (Philadelphia, 1898), p. 38.

siderable number of the native chiefs so that it was jokingly
said of him that the blood of a fair proportion of all of the
first families of Equatorial Africa coursed in his veins; and
that, if ever there was an American citizen who could appropriate to himself pre-eminently the national motto *E pluribus
unum,* Stanley was the man.[34]   The exchange of blood makes
unity, whereas eating together shows union.   Thus with the
Arabs, as with the Hebrews, the real covenant-union in sacrifice was *represented* by blood-sharing, and was *celebrated*
by the feast-partaking.[35]   Later, salt became the symbol of
blood among certain peoples and the eating of salt formed a
bond of friendship.

Trumbull has shown an interesting relationship between
still another form of covenant, which he has called the threshold covenant, and the beginning of religious rites.

The primitive altar of the family would seem to have been
the threshold, or door-sill, or entrance way, of the home dwell-
ing place.   This is indicated by surviving customs, in the East
and elsewhere among primitive peoples, and by the earliest
historic records of the human race.   It is obvious that houses
preceded temples and that the house father was the earliest
priest.   Sacrifices for the family were, therefore, within or at
the entrance of the family domicile.

In Syria and in Egypt, at the present time, when a guest
who is worthy of special honor is to be welcomed to the home,
the blood of a slaughtered, or a " sacrificed " animal, is shed
on the threshold of that house as a means of adopting the
newcomer into the family, or of making a covenant union with
him.   And every such primitive covenant of blood includes an
appeal to the protecting Deity to ratify it as between the two
parties and himself.   The guest becomes a member of the
family by the threshold covenant. . . .[36]

[34] *L. c.*   [35] *The Blood Covenant,* p. 351.

[36] *The Threshold Covenant* (2nd ed., New York, 1906), p. 3.

Thus it would seem that, from the beginning, on the national threshold, as on the threshold of the temple and of the home, sacrifices were offered, and boundary markers were set up, in recognition of the peculiar sacredness of the border line — which is itself a foundation and a limit. These boundary marks were commonly a pillar or a tree, in apparent symbolism of a fructifying or a fruit-bearing agency, of the transmission or the continuance of life. And the establishment and protection of these boundary marks was deemed well pleasing to God or to the gods, and in the nature of a holy covenant service.[87]

Among the Arabs if a man has but touched the tent-rope of his host's tent, his life must be defended against all enemies, and to tell an Arab that he has neglected his guest is the greatest of all insults.[88] The Arabs have some recourse against entertaining unwelcome guests, however, according to Burckhardt.

If strangers are seen approaching a tent with an apparent intention of alighting there, and if the owner of the tent suspect that they belong to a hostile tribe, induced by untoward circumstances to fly for refuge, which must not be refused, he cries out to them from afar:—" If you belong to a hostile tribe, you shall be stripped." After this warning, they are not entitled to claim *dakheil* (protection) from that person, but they may endeavor to find another tent.[89]

On the other hand if the stranger does not belong to an enemy group, he may be eagerly sought after as a guest. The first person who sees him approaching may claim him for the night by crying out, " There comes my guest ". Even

[87] *Ibid.*, p. 192.

[88] Burckhardt, J. L., *Notes on the Bedouins and Wahábys* (London, 1830), p. 102.

[89] *Ibid.*, p. 189.

children have this right, and women may take an active part in entertaining the guest.[40]

It is interesting to note in this connection that among the Semitic peoples, for whom the bonds of the covenant of blood-brotherhood were particularly strong, the stock or kinship group and not the family was the unit of the system of social organization.[41] The blood-bond of the group itself embraced all who bore a common name, according to Robertson Smith.

Kinship then among the Arabs means a share in the common blood which is taken to flow in the veins of every member of a tribe—in one word it is the tribal bond which knits men of the same group together and gives them common duties and responsibilities from which no member of the group can withdraw.[42]

The extension of tribal membership to include the outsider through some ceremony which symbolized the blood relationship of the group is in keeping with the general process of establishing new relationships which has been traced throughout simpler societies. The principle of social organization within the group determines, with certain limitations, the form of the relationship which is established when the stranger enters the group. The nature of the obligations involved in the guest relationship among the Semites appears in the following discussion by Robertson Smith.

From a very early date the Semitic communities embraced, in addition to the free tribesmen of pure blood (Heb. *ezrāh*, Arab. *sarīh*) with their families and slaves, a class of men who were personally free but had no political rights, viz. the pro-

40 *Ibid.*, p. 198.
41 Smith, W. Robertson, *Kinship and Marriage in Early Arabia* (London, 1903), pp. 69 *et seq.*
42 *Ibid.*, p. 27.

tected strangers (Heb. *gerim,* sing. *gēr;* Arab. *jīrān,* sing. *jār*), of whom mention is made so often both in the Old Testament and in early Arabic literature. The *gēr* was a man of another tribe or district, who coming to sojourn in a place where he was not strengthened by the presence of his own kin, put himself under the protection of a clan or of a powerful chief. From the earliest times of Semitic life the lawlessness of the desert, in which every stranger is an enemy, has been tempered by the principle that the guest is inviolable. A man is safe in the midst of enemies as soon as he enters a tent or even touches the tent rope. To harm a guest, or to refuse him hospitality, is an offense against honor, which dyes the perpetrator with indelible shame.

The bond of hospitality among the Arabs is temporary; the guest is entertained for a night or at most for three days, and the protection which the host owes to him expires after three days more. But more permanent protection is seldom refused to the stranger who asks for it, and when granted by any tribesman it binds the whole tribe. The obligation thus constituted is one of honour, and not enforced by any human sanction except public opinion, for if the stranger is wronged, he has no kinsman to fight for him. And for this very reason it is a sacred obligation, which among the Arabs was often confirmed by oath at a sanctuary, and could not be renounced except by a formal act at the same holy place, so that the god himself became the protector of the stranger's cause. . . . Newcomers sought admission to the sanctuaries of the " god of the land " as clients. The relation was submission on the worshipper's side and bounty on the god's.[43]

Another aspect of the significance of a ceremonial compact of a specific type between groups is brought out by Briffault in a discussion of the difficulties with which the rule of exogamy is sometimes attended among primitive peoples.[44]

[43] Smith, W. Robertson, *Lectures on the Religion of the Semites* (London, 1914), pp. 75 *et seq.*

[44] *The Mothers,* vol. i, pp. 560 *et seq.*

The difficulties in the path of true love are indeed formidable in primitive life owing to the hostilities between the clans, according to Briffault, and hence there arises the necessity for some formal provision for overcoming these.

There is, in fact, but one way in which the otherwise insuperable difficulties of providing for the needs of reproduction, while at the same time observing the prohibition of incest, could be overcome in the conditions of primitive society; and that is by some pact or agreement between two groups, such as that which the son of Hamor proposed to the sons of Jacob: " Then will we give our daughters unto you and we will take your daughters to us " (*Genesis,* xxxiv, 16).

And this is, in fact, what takes place in primitive societies. There is in nearly all the surviving examples of such societies an understanding whereby the members of a given group obtain their sexual partners from some other particular group, or groups, the members of which have intermarried with their own for generations. To marry into a totally strange group, between which and the group of the suitor there exists no established custom of intermarriage and no understanding in this respect, is an unusual and difficult procedure. Those elaborate tribal conferences, negotiations, diplomatic parleys, and concilatory exchanges of presents, which have been noted in Australia, Melanesia, or Polynesia, do not of course, take place on the occasion of every marriage; but they are necessary in case of the marriage of members of two different tribes between whom a regular practice of intermarriage has not already become established. A man cannot marry into a strange group without an agreement being concluded by the two groups which will permit the intermarriage between their members. Those negotiations and that agreement have reference secondarily and incidentally only to the particular individuals concerned; it is not the relation between those individuals, but the relation between the two groups which is considered and discussed. The contract, if concluded, is not an individual contract, but a group contract and will permit of further intermarriage between members of the two groups without the necessity of new negotiation. . . . Marriage is a formal juridic transaction. . . . The original purpose of the institution of marriage was thus quite other than the regulation of sexual relations or the safeguarding of claims of individual possession. It had not reference to individuals, but to collective groups; it was not an individual marriage contract, but a group marriage contract.[45]

Intermarriage between groups represents an exchange of values; the most highly prized of all its possessions, a part of the group itself, one of its own members, is given as a gift for which in due time a reciprocal gift of like value is expected. Thus, theoretically at least, intermarriage should form one of the strongest possible of social bonds between groups. And this in general would seem to be true although instances have been cited of intermarrying clans between whom a state of perpetual warfare existed.[46]

In the customs of primitive peoples with regard to the stranger which have so far been considered the newcomer has either been rejected outright or ceremonial measures have been taken to give him a position within the circle of the group. There has been no intermediate position. Among some primitive groups, however, conditions do exist under which the presence of the stranger is tolerated although he is not received into the membership of the group itself. Some ceremonial precautions are usually taken in such cases in order to free the stranger from his power to do evil. Such rites in themselves do not establish a bond; they are rites of purification or of separation which may, or may not, be followed by further rites of aggregation. Unless these latter rites are performed the stranger is still an outsider who has simply been permitted to enter the territory of the group.

[45] L. c.
[46] Roscoe, op. cit., pp. 176-77.

Its members are under no particular obligation to befriend him because of this. The rites of purification for removing taboos on intercourse with strangers, or on entering or leaving a strange land, are ceremonial in their nature, but they differ from a compact or covenant in their purpose. Their function is to ward off the possible harm of a stranger's magic by providing a form of counter-magic. These rites do not involve sentiment as the rites of a covenant do, and the two types should not be confused. Primitive thinking is so permeated by the belief in magic that ritual ceremonies are indubitably colored by this belief, if they have not actually arisen in magical observances; but, as in the case of many of the ritual ceremonies practiced by civilized peoples, the earlier significance of the ceremonies has often been lost sight of and they have become symbols for perpetuating certain sentiments. Crawley, for instance, in *The Mystic Rose* regards the blood covenant as a form of mutual inoculation against evil magic.[47] This interpretation of the ceremony harmonizes it with certain other primitive beliefs concerning the magical power of one person over another if he possesses something that has been intimately connected with the other, as a lock of his hair or the parings of his finger nails. It does not, however, tell the whole story although it may account for its origin. The covenant ritual as generally performed symbolizes the establishment of a bond of relationship which involves mutual obligations and which is associated with profound sentiments.

The nature of the duties, privileges, obligations and restrictions which exist between persons are the measure of the kind and of the strength of the social bonds by which they are united. The obligations of adoption, of gift exchange, of host and guest, and of blood-brotherhood are all

[47] Crawley, Ernest, *The Mystic Rose* (2nd ed., London, 1927), vol. i, ch. xi.

deeply imbued with sentiment and cannot readily be dissolved. These relationships are intimate and personal, and hence they are restricted to a somewhat limited number of individuals. When groups are subjected to numerous and diverse contacts with outsiders some more impersonal basis for establishing new relationships must be devised if the relations are to be other than those of hostility. The principle of barter, as distinct from that of gift exchange, has been utilized as a nucleus for developing a system of such indirect and impersonal relationships. The individuals concerned regard each other as a means through which certain desired objects are to be secured and not as ends in themselves. In such relationships the element of sentiment is minimized or eliminated and the needs which are gratified belong to a different order from those of the personal relationships. In the Kula system, for instance, the exchange of gifts to which sentiment is attached fulfils a different function from that of the trade which is carried on in connection with it. In the one case prestige is gained by displaying generosity while in the other it is secured by cleverness in making a good bargain or in getting the best of a transaction either fairly or, at times, otherwise.

7. THE SILENT TRADE

One of the ways by which the exclusiveness of a primitive group and their fear of strangers may be overcome to the extent of establishing trade relations with aliens is described by Grierson in *The Silent Trade*. This, in its simplest form, " is a transaction by way of exchange between persons who not only do not address, but do not see, one another." [48]

The principle which underlay these transactions was that of giving on the understanding or, at all events, in the expecta-

[48] Grierson, *op. cit.*, p. 41. For specific examples of the silent trade see Sumner and Keller, *The Science of Society* (New Haven, 1927 and 1928), vol. i, pp. 155-57 and vol. iv, pp. 46-49.

tion of receiving an adequate return; and it was this principle which they applied in their dealings with strangers. They chose some spot on the borderland between their own country and that of the tribe with which they wished to traffic; and there they set out their wares in the hope of disposing of them and obtaining what they wanted in exchange. And all the while they secured their own safety by keeping out of sight. Having once succeeded in opening a trade, they would naturally endeavor to renew it from time to time. And, if those with whom they traded were desirous that the trade should continue, they would refrain from either carrying off the articles offered without leaving a return, or attempting to capture or maltreat those who made the offer. Thus a trade in which self-interest is the guarantee of good faith would become established at a fixed place, and, probably, at fixed times; and, if the articles were such as to command high prices in the markets of the world, and if the spot where they were offered was readily accessible,—if, for example, it was situated on a river-side, at the seashore, or where ways converged, — this trade would attract not only near neighbors but merchants of distant countries.[49]

The silent trade contained within it the germ of the primitive market of which Grierson writes:

Viewed as a factor in the constitution of relations which, if not friendly, are at least not hostile, the primitive market, except in its rudest forms, shows a marked advance upon the previous practice. Those who engaged in the silent trade secured their safety by keeping apart from those with whom they were dealing but those who frequent the market are safe, for the time being at all events, although they associate with one another in the prosecution of their affairs. For the place itself is regarded as neutral, and in some cases as sacred; in other words, the conception of a " peace " has been formed,— a peace attached to a certain spot, and observed while the

[49] Grierson, *op. cit.*, pp. 64-7.

market held there lasts. Sometimes the peace extends beyond the limits of the market-place to the paths which lead to it; and further advance is made when the privilege becomes personal rather than local,—becomes, that is to say, the privilege of the trader rather than of the place of trade.[50]

At the present time there are but few primitive groups who have not had some contacts with more highly civilized peoples, and who have not become acquainted to some extent at least with the principle of establishing relations with strangers through trade. An interesting account of the manner in which such a relationship was opened is given by Dr. Dickey in a description of an encounter with the Guaharibos Indians of the Upper Orinoco River in South America, a timid, little-known tribe whose customs and mode of life are still those of the Age of Stone.

Just as we were about to emerge into the main stream, there came a cry from the forest, and another, and then a yell in chorus, " Guaica, guaica! "

We pulled up to the bank, and presently a group of naked, light yellow savages appeared. They twanged the strings of enormous bows, continuing to cry, " Guaica, guaica! "

I jumped to the bank and the savages retreated a little way. I stood my ground and shouted " Chori, chori," which, in the Guaharibo tongue, means " Friend, friend," and raised my arms to show that I had no weapons.

The Indians returned a few steps, and they too shouted " Chori, chori," and beating their breasts they added, " Ma, ma, ma "—all of this meaning " Friend, friend, yes, yes, yes." I placed some food on a leaf on the ground. The Indians motioned me to back away, approached the food, picked it up, ate it. But not yet convinced of my bona fides, they would occasionally stop eating, snap their bow strings most disconcertingly in my direction and shout " Guaica! "

[50] *Ibid.*, p. 68.

" Guaica," apparently, was something quite unpopular.

We backed and filled for some time. As I advanced, they retreated, and I, acquiring the habit, retreated as they advanced. But the space between us gradually lessened, and we finally, but not without a number of exhausting manifestations of friendship, achieved a community of interest—that of barter.

They wanted knives, machetes. They demonstrated how hard it was to use their bone and finely sharpened bamboo knives, their stone axes. The jazz whistles and other noise-producing toys I had brought as propitiatory gifts were simply disdained. Nothing but steel cutting instruments were desired.

As I wanted their implements and weapons for the museum, and they wanted our knives and machetes, each was made happy by the trade.[51]

After his stock of cutting instruments had been exhausted, Dr. Dickey observed that the Indians became restless and were evidently anxious to be let alone. The relationship of trade which had been established terminated naturally after a brief interval without involving any further obligations on either side. However, by the formation of even such a simple transitory relationship as the one just described, a new element was introduced into the system of relationships which constitutes the social structure of the group. In the future the bahavior of the Guaharibos Indians toward white strangers at least will be affected by it. This initial relationship having been a satisfactory one there will be a desire to renew it as a means of procuring more of the coveted cutting tools, if for nothing else. Fear, hostility and suspicion will have been somewhat allayed by Dr. Dickey's friendly behavior, and unless some untoward factor should enter into the situation, new relations will be more readily established in the future.

[51] Dickey, Herbert Spencer, "Up the Orinoco into the Age of Stone," *The New York Times Magazine*, November 2, 1930.

In the opening of new relationships, even though these are impersonal in their nature, formalities of some kind are generally observed which purport to assure each party of the goodwill of the other and which lend a certain dignity to the occasion. The Punt Reliefs of the Der el-Bahri temple at Thebes which belong to the Eighteenth Dynasty (1580-1350 B. C.) give a graphic impression of the formal procedure whereby the Egyptian expedition sent by Queen Hatshepsut succeeded in establishing trade relations with the more primitive Puntites of the Somali Coast.[52] On the arrival of the Egyptians in Punt, the " king's messenger " is shown advancing at the head of her soldiers while the Punt-ite chief comes forward to meet them. He is followed by his enormous wife, mounted on an ass, and by their three children. The Egyptians have brought necklaces, hatchets, daggers, and other things for trade with the Puntites although giving them ostensibly as an offering to the goddess Hathor. A friendly contact having thus been made, " the king's messenger " then pitches his tent on the myrrh terrace by the sea and receives the Puntites, presenting them with food and " everything found in Egypt ". The Puntites in their turn give in exchange the products of their country and the vessels of the Egyptians are heavily loaded with frag-rant woods, ivory, apes, monkeys, dogs, and the skins of panthers. Natives and their children also accompany the Egyptians on their return.

Among other early records of methods of establishing trade relations is that given by Herodotus, who describes the system of silent trade carried on by the Carthaginians with the natives of Libya. Such relations, although lacking the intensity of feeling which characterizes the sentiment rela-tionships, mark an advance in the social organization of the

[52] Breasted, James Henry, *Ancient Records of Egypt* (Chicago, 1906), vol. ii, pp. 102-22.

community nevertheless. They are more readily extended than the intimate relationships of kinship and they afford a different basis for treating the newcomer from that which unites the members of the group itself. As the relationships which constitute the social organization of a community become more highly differentiated there will be a corresponding increase in the diversity of the reactions toward outsiders. The behavior toward the stranger becomes more varied and more discriminating. Other categories than those of the tribal brother or the enemy are formed and the social system has a greater degree of flexibility. The group is better able to adjust its social order to the demands put upon it by contacts with a large number of foreigners or with widely different alien types. Obligations and privileges of certain kinds may be extended to the stranger while those of other types are reserved exclusively for the group members or for particular strangers whom the group especially chooses to honor. The development of the interest relations through trade thus introduces a new principle of social integration into the community structure, but one which, although augmenting the bonds of kinship, does not supplant these.[53] Sentiment relations growing out of the primary patriarchal or fratriarchal kinship ties form the new fundamental unifying bonds which have gradually evolved to meet the needs of communities as they became more complex in social structure.

[53] It must be borne in mind at this point that economic development has no necessary connection with improvement in the relations between members of a society. This has been made clear by Hobhouse, Wheeler and Ginsberg in their painstaking study, *The Material Culture and Social Institutions of the Simpler Peoples* (London, 1915).

CHAPTER IV

The Principle of Authority

I. ANCESTOR WORSHIP

AMONG the simpler peoples the basis of the social organization was seen to be some form of kinship grouping which, growing out of consanguinity, had evolved into an order of society. Within this order the relationships were largely of the sentiment type and the various duties, privileges, obligations and restrictions associated with these were carefully defined by custom. Such a system was by its very nature relatively inflexible and hence better adapted to smaller more isolated groups. Frequent contacts with outside groups or a considerable increase in the numbers of the group itself would place a strain upon a social order of the kinship type and necessitate changes within it and the development of new forms of relationships if the group was to maintain its integrity and at the same time to expand. This need was met in part through the establishment of trade relations with neighboring peoples. Desired goods were obtained in this way rather than by force. Interest relations, however, if based wholly on utility and devoid of ties of sentiment, do not constitute a strong cohesive bond. Groups may trade with one another without merging their identities or sharing a sufficient measure of common life to overcome their distrust of one another. To bring together or to hold together in a functional unity large numbers of people whose varied material interests are often opposed as well as complementary, utilitarian relationships must be embedded, as it were, in an

underlying matrix of common life. Interest relationships in
themselves will hardly suffice to replace the former bonds of
consanguinity with their rich emotional content in creating a
unified social structure. Some further and more fundamental basis of unity must be engendered to bind together
into a larger community numerous smaller groups whose
immediate interests tend to be separative.

In many communities of the world, in India, China, Japan,
and Africa, this extended feeling of belonging together has
been achieved by the transfer of certain obligations from a
nearer to a more remote kinship grouping through the
medium of ancestor worship, which gives expression to the
sentiment of social continuity. Among the Zulu-Kaffir
tribes of South Africa, for instance, the group is thought of
as consisting of the living and the dead, between whom a close
intimate harmony must be maintained. The ancestors are
the guardians of custom; they must not be offended. The
social order becomes an external thing with a sacred origin,
and a strong bond of cohesion is created among all those who
are able to trace their descent from a common ancestor. All
the clans of a tribe are regarded as coming from the same
original stock and the tribe takes its name from the original
ancestor. The chief's tribe is the senior one and he is the
chief of the whole tribe, the eldest son of the eldest son and
so on back to the beginning of time. The clan sub-divides
into households and the head of each family household is
responsible to the head of the clan, who in turn is responsible
to the chief of the tribe. Absolute loyalty is the rule and
thus a close tribal integration is secured without depriving the
family or clan of their local autonomy. The tribe rather
than the clan is the effective unit for larger enterprises such
as war-making. Although such an organization is at once
strong and yet flexible in so far as the growth in numbers of
the tribe itself is concerned, it does not provide a ready basis

for the inclusion of outsiders of a different ancestry. If the stranger has recommended himself to the group, some such ritual as that of the blood covenant is required to bring him within the circle of group relationships.

The Chinese system of ancestral worship also made use of the patriarchal system of unification; but the ancestors of the different local groups did not develop into definite gods and the groups could not be combined into a nation by the method of amalgamation of gods which was used in consolidating the empires of Egypt and Mesopotamia. The Chinese family and clan or village groups were so self-sufficient and independent of one another that, as Denison shows,[1] it was necessary in order to unite them to break down in part the original system and to superimpose upon it another culture of a different type. This was done through the development of the tradition of a " father " god of the patriarchal type who was identified with heaven and whom all must revere and obey. The emperor was presented as the son of Heaven and it was his peculiar function to worship at the Temple of Heaven from whence he derived his authority. The people had no direct contact with the emperor, but a sense of unity was maintained through officials appointed by the emperor. The system was one of graded authority—the ancestral culture uniting the district, the culture uniting the district to its governor, and that uniting all the governors in the service of the empire. The emotional power of such a complex system was naturally much less effective than that of a system in which each subject felt his unity directly with the king. The bonds of the family and village group were strong while those of the nation as a whole were weak.

The system of ancestral and emperor-worship in China was supplemented by two religions, Taoism and Buddhism. Taoism " created a certain sense of national solidarity by

[1] *Op. cit.*, ch. viii.

giving to all who followed its rites a horror of strangers or
' foreign devils ', together with the sense that all adherents of
the religion shared in a certain favor of the gods or ' good
luck '." [2]   It has been a dominant influence in preserving the
customs of the lower classes.   Buddhism as it was practiced
in China resembled Taoism.   Neither of these religions conflicted with the original system of ancestral worship on which
the social order was based.   "Each recognized the gods
taught by the others and the people participated in the cere-
monials of all three at appropriate crises or seasons.   For
many centuries all strangers were admitted to China and all
religions were permitted." [3]   The difficulties which eventually led to the prohibitions against Christianity were based
on the exclusive nature of the Christian religion.   Christian
religious authorities refused to permit their creed and customs to be combined with those of the Chinese.   The Chinese
emperors, realizing that to renounce the old ancestral culture
would mean the disintegration of Chinese civilization, therefore excluded a religion whose avowed purpose was to destroy
that culture.   The coherence of Chinese civilization rested
on ancestral worship, and influences from without which
tended to weaken the ties within the family group were re-
sisted.   Foreigners failed to behave as the Chinese thought
strangers should behave when entering a foreign country.
"When you enter the frontiers inquire respecting the prohibitions; when you enter into a country inquire into its customs " is an old Chinese saying which Westerners have not
heeded and the Chinese have kept apart in an effort to preserve their culture from deteriorating through contact with
the intruding foreigners.

Ancestor worship as a system of social integration is relatively inflexible and is limited in its application unless some

[2] *Ibid.*, p. 116.

[3] *L. c.*

means can be found for identifying the loyalties of the outsider with those of the group. In Egypt this was done through a union of the gods of local groups into a family of gods; and in Persia under Zoroaster an attempt was made to achieve world unification by replacing many gods with One God of all the earth. The authority which the ruler possesses by virtue of his relation to the ancestral gods tends to pass over, as we shall see, into one which is based on material possessions and which gives rise to a social system of a more autocratic type.

2. SUBORDINATION AND CONTROL

Within a tribal organization such as that evolved by the Kulu-Kaffir peoples can be detected the germ of another type of social structure—that of subordination and control. The chief is not only the head of the tribe in religious and material matters but he is also the tribal capitalist. The wealth of the tribe is amassed in his hands, theoretically for the use of the tribe as a whole. In practice, however, the accumulation of wealth in the hands of a privileged few has been generally fraught with an abuse of the power that is inherent in wealth. Through its possession an original system of tribal democracy based on kinship and ancestor worship tends to be displaced by a class structure comprising a small controlling group and a large subject class whose adherence is secured through sentiments of traditional loyalty or, as in the case of a conquered people, through fear. A social structure of this type, despite the weakness of submission to a common over-lordship as a cohesive bond, possesses certain advantages; it is capable of a far wider expansion than a kinship organization. A measure of unity of action may be attained throughout a large area with a minimum of unity of feeling. In describing a social structure of this type, Professor MacIver says:

A community, so organized, presents a striking contrast to the primitive tribe. We may take as illustration the earliest known stage of the ancient civilization of Egypt. Here we find nothing to correspond to the clan or tribe. The order of society is based not on kinship but on status determined by class and occupation. These distinctions are for the most part hereditary, though fortune and official favour may raise a man to any eminence. The divisions of the double kingdom of Upper and Lower Egypt are territorial, and each territory or province has its local usage and its local gods. But they are all set like mosaics in the framework of the state. Originally they must have been, save for a few merely administrative divisions, autonomous communities. But the conflicts of power have issued in an overruling might, wielded by the conjoint authority of king and priest. A repressive religion, for the most part grotesque, gloomy, and dread-inspiring, has elevated a few of the local gods into deities of universal range and common cult, like Osiris and Horus and Seth. The king too has become a god, and one symbol, the " falcon of Horus ", stands alike for " god " and " king ". Thus palace and temple dominate the land, and all men are subjects. The institution has become lord of life. Its origin is forgotten, and the strong influences of superstition and rank dominate the mind. Men are no more blood-brothers or comrades, free-men of a community whose institutions are their own; they are servants of power. The building of the king's palace or of his tomb or of another temple to one of the many gods they serve, is a duty paramount over the mere well-being of the folk. The state, doubly armed with weapons of military force and religious awe, is over all.

No other community may have exhibited so extreme a diversion of the state from the principle of common service as did ancient Egypt, but in varying degrees all early peoples which attained the conditions of civilization, to wit, a surplus of wealth over immediate necessities and a form of city life, passed through a similar process of satisfaction and subjection. In Sumeria as in Babylon, in India as in China, the way of empire was prepared by subordination, within the at first small city-centered state, of the mass of the people to the class or classes which held the institutions of power. Not always is the "spiritual" dominance so clearly associated as in Egypt with the political—sometimes the priestly order is withdrawn from the political, and sometimes it wins a superior place. But always the two powers are united in this at least, they reinforce one another in stabilizing, along lines of authority and subordination, the order of society. The class system becomes in consequence deeply impressed upon each community. When this has been achieved the time is ripe for a leader who, with the instrument of power now forged for his hand, will carry the principle of dominance from out of his own state and impose it on others. Such was the role of leaders like Sargon of the Akkadians, Tiglath-Pileser I of the Assyrians, and Wu Wang, the founder of the Chow dynasty. These were no mere victors in common warfare; they were men who incarnated the idea of power to which their individual states were already committed, and carried it to its logical conclusion of empire.[4]

Some of the oldest historical documents which have been discovered recount the extension of the principle of subordination and control upon which the earliest civilized states were based to alien peoples with whom they had come in contact. Among the inscriptions on the Palermo Stone, so-called because since 1877 it has been in the Museum of Palermo, mention is made of:

> Hacking up the land of the Negro.
> Bringing up 7,000 living prisoners, and 200,000
>   large and small cattle.
> Bringing of 40 ships (with) cedar wood.[5]

In these events of the reign of King Snefru of the Third Dynasty (2980-2900 B. C.) two types of relationships with

[4] MacIver, R. M., *The Modern State* (London, 1928), pp. 56-58.

[5] Breasted, J. H., *op. cit.*, vol. i, pp. 65-66.

foreigners are disclosed. In retaining captives of war as prisoners whose fate it was to become slaves a relationship of enforced submission was established with the Land of the Negro. With Lebanon, the source of the cedar wood, the relationship at this time seems to have been a commercial one although at a later period this region too came under Egyptian dominance. In inscriptions engraved on the rock walls of the Wadi Maghara in the Peninsula of Sinai, where the Egyptians had carried on copper-mining operations from as early as the First Dynasty, Snefru, who came to be regarded as the patron god of the region, is called " Smiter of barbarians ". The relief which represents his victory over the Bedouin symbolizes in an interesting way the principle of subjection. The crowned king is shown with upraised war-club about to strike a Bedouin whom he has seized by the hair of his head and forced to his knees. Other inscriptions at Wadi Maghara refer to King Khufu (Cheops) of the Fourth Dynasty, the builder of the famous pyramid, as " Smiter of the Troglodytes ", and King Sahure of the Fifth Dynasty as " Smiter of all countries ".[6]

The Code of Hammurabi, King of Babylon about 2250 B. C., also contains evidence of the principle of subordination of outsiders through the institution of slavery. A distinction is made, however, between those slaves who are natives of the country and those who are of foreign birth. The Code reads :

If a man purchase a male or female slave of a man in a foreign country, and if, when he comes back to his own land, the (former) owner of the male or female slave recognize his male or female slave—if the male or female slave be a native of the land, he shall grant them their freedom without money. If they be natives of another land, the purchaser shall declare before god the money he paid (for them), and the owner of

6 *Ibid.*, vol. i, pp. 75-6.

the male or female slave shall give to the merchant the money which he paid out, and he (the owner) shall receive into his care the male or female slave.[7]

The right of freedom is thus secured to native-born slaves under certain conditions while being denied to slaves of foreign birth. A social structure based on class is subject to gradations within it although retaining the same principle throughout of a unity based on submission to control. This distinction between subject classes is also hinted at in an interesting way in the stipulations of the " Tribute of Yu ", an ancient Chinese document which forms a part of the *Shu King or Chinese Historical Classic,* which contains an historical record covering a period of more than sixteen centuries from the reign of Yaou, 2355 B. C. to 719 B. C. Some of the material in the *Shu King* is doubtless of a legendary character, but it is nevertheless of significance in indicating the way of the wind. According to the stipulations, the territory is divided with reference to the distance from the seat of government. The first and nearest region is spoken of as the Tribute Holding; the second region is that of the Nobles; the third region, called the Peaceful Tenures, is alloted to literary workers and for military defense; beyond this, and outside the defended area, lay the Prohibited and Unstrained territories. The Prohibited territories were divided between foreigners and transported convicts, and the Unstrained territories, which were the most remote of all, were the abode of barbarians and felons.[8]

This zonation of the entire territory seems a most ambi-

---

[7] Harper, R. F., *The Code of Hammurabi* (Chicago, 1904), pp. 95 and 97.

[8] Old, W. G., *The Shu King or the Chinese Historical Classic* (New York, 1904), pp. 50-51. See also " The Texts of Confucianism " translated by James Legge in the *Sacred Books of the East* (Oxford, 1879), vol. iii, pp. 75-76.

tious instance of regional planning, though not perhaps an altogether happy one. By its restrictions foreigners were compelled to dwell in the same neighborhood with criminals and their contacts would thus be with the least desirable element in the population rather than with the best. Other passages from the *Shu King* are suggestive of the nature of social integration within the Empire and of the novel manner in which these were impressed upon outsiders. A paragraph from the " Canon of Yaou " reads:

He showed his talent and virtue in binding together the nine degrees of kinship which, being thus in accord, equalized, and enlightened, reflected their virtues in equal degree upon all the people of the Empire. These, his own people, being instructed, rendered the various states of the Empire harmonious, and the black-haired people, ah! even they were impressed by this compact! [9]

The black-haired people were the hill men and border tribes, and probably also the Tartars, who were not included in the Chinese nation proper. They annually paid tribute through their chiefs at the Chinese court. The impression made upon them by the harmony within the Empire does not seem to have been a lasting one, however, for a few generations later in the reign of the Emperor Yu-Shun about 2222 B. C. the hill men resist the decree of the Emperor and harrass the peaceful communities of the plains. In the " Deliberations, the Ta-Yu " an account is given of the solution of this problem. Ta-Yu, the superintendent of works, has sought the Emperor Yu-Shun for advice as to the best method for controlling the hill men, here called Meaovites, and the Emperor says:

Only virtue can compel Heaven and there is no distance to

[9] Old, *op. cit.*, p. 1.

which it cannot reach. Fulness is predisposed to decrease
while humility receives increase. This is Heaven's way. . . .
And if superlative integrity can move the gods, how much
sooner these Meaovites?

Yu acknowledged these excellent words, saying " True ". He
then withdrew his army and quartered his troops.

The Emperor thereupon spread abroad his wisdom and virtue,
displaying the shields and feathers on both sides of the grand
staircase; and in seven decades (seventy days) the Meaovites
surrendered.[10]

Whatever the reasons may have been which prompted the
action of the Meaovites their position is one of subordination
to control after their surrender, whether this is to a superior
military power or to one of superlative virtue. In the
Chinese social system the well-being of the group depended
not only on harmony within the group but also on the relationship of man and heaven. The emperor was the religious
head of the nation, and because the greater spirits were
supposed to be his exclusive ancestors, their worship was
deemed his exclusive privilege. And for any other man to
presume to sacrifice to the spirit associated with heaven was
tantamount to a declaration of rebellion. The source of the
emperor's power was thus a religious one.

In India the earliest Sanscrit literature, the Vedic Hymns,
like the earliest Chinese literature, is lacking in data of a
strictly historical nature. It is suggestive, nevertheless.
There are numerous intimations of conflicts with other
groups. Among the Hymns of the Atharva-Veda there are
those to the battle-drum, the terror of the enemy, prayers for
help in battle, charms for confusing the enemy, a battle-charm
against arrow wounds, and a curse upon the enemy: " Be he
our own, or be he strange, the kinsman, or the foreigner,
who bear enmity towards us, these enemies of mine Rudra

[10] Old, *op. cit.*, p. 26.

shall pierce with a shower of arrows ".[11]   Indeed, life in the
Vedic period seems to have been active and war-disturbed.
The individual clans, Aryan and non-Aryan, or even Aryan
among themselves, oppress and drive each other from the
homes just conquered.[12]   The aboriginal inhabitants who
were displaced by the Aryan invasion are spoken of as *Dasyus*
(foes) and those who did not escape to the hills were made
slaves and later became the fourth caste, the Sudras.   However, despite their imprecations against these *Dasyus*—" May
then Atri, O Agni, overcome the Dasyus who do not give
(to the Brahmans) "—there is evidence that the Aryans
made matrimonial connections with them and that the off-
spring formed a new class which were considered as of more
or less pure blood and social position.[13]

A class system which eventually crystallized into a rigid
caste structure was being formed during the Vedic period.
The unifying principle among the conquering group, and the
one which was ultimately extended to the conquered aborigines, was that of submission to a controlling class which
derived its justification from a religious source.

In the extension of the principle of subordination and control it is necessary to distinguish between those conquests in
which the victors either brought back the conquered as slaves
or settled in the territory of the subdued group, as the Aryans
did in India, and other conquests in which the defeated people
were governed as a subject province.   In situations of the
first type assimilation and amalgamation occur in spite of
the inferior status which is assigned to the subject class.
This was noted in the Ayran invasion of India and it is also

[11] Bloomfield, Maurice, " Hymns of the Atharva-Veda " in the *Sacred
Books of the East*, vol. xlii, p. 120.

[12] Kaegi, Adolf, *The Rigveda: The Oldest Literature of the Indians*
(tr. R. Arrowsmith, Boston, 1886), p. 78.

[13] Frazer, R. W., *A Literary History of India* (New York, 1898), p. 20.

true in the case of the negro slaves brought to the United States. In the process of time the subject classes tend to lose their own identity and to become incorporated into the social system of their conquerors. They form an integral part of the community although their position may remain an inferior one. On the other hand if the conquered people are governed as a subject province, the routine of their daily lives may be changed but little. There are isolated communities in the Near East which have retained their ancient customs relatively unmodified by the dominance of the various great empires which have held successive sway over them during the last two thousand years. Their allegiance has been a superimposed one and social integration in the true sense has not extended beyond the confines of their own local communities. This limitation of the feeling of unity has been noted by Spengler.

Classical man felt as " Home " just what he could see from the Acropolis of his native city. Where the horizon of Athens ended, the alien, the hostile, the " fatherland " of another began. Even the Roman of late Republican times understood by " patria " nothing but Urbs Roma, not even Latium, still less Italy.[14]

The extension of common shared interests and sentiments of a more intimate nature to include the people of an outlying conquered province is at best a slow process and in the earlier empires the nearer and stronger loyalties were to one's own kinship or neighborhood group. The early empires were mosaics of local entities whose common setting was obedience to a ruling authority which derived its sanction from a religious source by identifying the king as the representative of the god, or gods, of the various communities.

[14] Spengler, O., *The Decline of the West* (tr. Atkinson, London, 1926), vol. i, p. 334.

No plan could have been better adapted for building up a vast empire and civilization than the old patriarchal system, accompanied by the ingenious devices of the kingship and the amalgamation of the gods. Each patriarchal group clung about its god as bees around their queen, and could be shifted into new group relations by moving the god into a new family. Each group was controlled in its purpose and action through the office of kingship, which was like a central telephone-office, with wires to every post in the nation. The conqueror had only to slip into the place of the former king and he could bring his will to bear upon every section of the conquered country. To take the king's place he had merely to prove himself the representative of the national god. . . . Every conqueror who was a statesman used these devices to the full, and thus created out of a congeries of antagonistic tribes an empire, held together not by force but by the sense of unity which centered in the throne.[15]

The basis of a system of subordination and control is the feeling of reverence, or of fear, of the common people for the king and a belief on his part that he deserves the worship which they give him. The divinity which " doth hedge a king " is the fundamental groundwork of the system and once this is destroyed the social structure disintegrates. In ancient communities which were organized in accord with the principle of authority the position of the stranger was generally an inferior one. He was regarded as a barbarian and without personal rights. He was subject to the king's will but he could become an integral part of the community only by accepting its gods as his own. He might, however, be regarded at times as a god in disguise and have been granted the utmost hospitality because of this. Both of these relationships which are extended to the stranger are a part of the social order of the group, but in the first case the

[15] Denison, *op. cit.*, p. 193.

status of the stranger is conceived as a subject one and in the second he is accorded the privileges of the ruling class. Which form is extended will depend upon the particular circumstances of the meeting. As the social structure becomes more highly differentiated and the distinctions between classes more marked the attitudes toward the stranger also show more variation. Graduations appear between the extremes of tribal brotherhood or of enmity although the characteristics of the we-group and the others-group relationships continue throughout.

The patriarchal method of securing unity of action through the authority of the king is simpler and more direct in its application than the methods of systems which are based on the extension of the idea of common brotherhood and common responsibilities; and hence the first great civilizations and empires tended to be patriarchal in form. The idea of mutual obligations and of a unity of purpose which is not superimposed, but which is the common will of the group developed more slowly although it seems to have been present in some groups from the first. It was most effective in small groups who could meet face to face in the tribal council or village assembly but it failed to unify widely scattered groups. Leadership was necessary for carrying out the common purpose, but the authority of the leader was derived from the group and not from a religious source. Fratriarchal assemblies did not cultivate an atmosphere of awe and fear, but they sought rather to arouse men by eloquent appeals, and to stimulate and fuse their emotions by music and dancing.[16]

The growth of cities among groups which had the brotherhood idea facilitated the formation of assemblies for discussion and for awakening a feeling of unity among those belonging to the city in opposition to the outlanders who were

[16] *Ibid.*, p. 195.

attracted to the city by trade. Cities afforded opportunities for two types of contacts, those between the original inhabitants themselves and those with foreigners. These two kinds of contacts occurring simultaneously tended to bring into relief both likenesses and differences. The city-dweller became more conscious of the resemblances which existed between himself and the members of his own group as opposed to the differences which separated him from the stranger. The idea of a common brotherhood based upon the possession of common characteristics, customs and interests was strengthened. Those having the same racial and cultural attributes came to regard themselves as belonging together in contrast to others who differed in these respects, and a new basis of social integration, that of citizenship, was recognized.

CHAPTER V

The Principle of Mutual Obligations

I. CITIZENSHIP

THE bonds which originate in the awareness of sharing certain things in common with others of a group are more flexible as a rule than the ties of kinship and less so than those of subordination and control. They possess an important advantage over the latter, however, in their greater degree of cohesiveness. The principle of authority although establishing a strong direct link between ruler and subject does not unite one subject with another except indirectly by virtue of the fact that all are bound by like ties to the same authority. Destroy this single source of cohesion and the social structure falls apart. The bonds of a common life on the other hand are direct, linking each member of the group at once with every other. Their strength, however, varies with the value that is placed upon those things which are shared. These may mean much or little. The status of citizenship, for instance, confers certain rights and privileges which may be more or less highly coveted and it imposes certain obligations which may be regarded either as a sacred duty that it is an honor to fulfil or as a burden to be evaded if possible. The meaning or content which is given to the relationships that are involved in citizenship determines the relative strength or weakness of a social structure which is based on this principle. If citizenship is an expression of a like participation in a common life, its bonds have strength because of the firmness of their foundation. If, however, citizenship has been conferred upon outsiders who do not value the same things nor share in this underlying feeling of unity, its mere possession may prove ineffectual as a basis of union. In the United States, for example, the fact that citizenship has been granted to an alien through the processes of naturalization cannot be regarded as a reliable index of his cultural assimilation. The status of citizenship may have been sought solely for its economic advantages and the individual who has attained it may have no feeling of loyalty to the institutions of the new community and no desire to establish other relationships than those of an economic nature. On the other hand many foreigners in the United States who have not sought to become naturalized citizens or who, for one reason or another, have been denied citizenship may have established intimate relationships in the community in which they reside and may share in all the various aspects of its life except those which are specifically denied to non-citizens. It is true nevertheless that immigrants who wish to feel at home in their new environment tend to seek citizenship as a means to this end. To such persons the conferment of citizenship is prized, not for its economic advantages alone, but because it enables them to participate more fully in the activities of the new community. It signifies the establishment of a new and nearer set of loyalties replacing certain former ties of adherence.

These instances of the different meanings which may be associated with the status of citizenship are an indication of its nature. Citizenship is membership in an association belonging to the community—the state.[1] As an association the state possesses such powers as have been delegated to it, among which is the right of determining its own membership. The qualifications demanded for this membership may be few or many, according to the manner in which the pur-

[1] See MacIver, *The Modern State*, pp. 3-8 for a discussion of this distinction of the state as an association of community.

poses of the state are defined. If these are so far-reaching that they control many of the activities of the citizen and regulate his relations with other individuals, it will be difficult for an outsider to gain citizenship since this would mean extending to him not one set of relationships but many. The more involved the relationships are which a given status implies the more difficult this status is to attain. This does not overlook the fact that a given status is sometimes granted without the establishment of the accompanying relationships. Such a position is, however, something other than it purports to be. The granting of tribal membership by primitive groups to distinguished white visitors is an instance of this. The obligations of such membership are not imposed and the position is honorary rather than actual and active. This is true of the honorary membership in most organizations: a different set of relationships is involved from that belonging to regular membership. In cases in which status has been conceded without the establishment of the relationships which it implies, the outsider is not actually brought within the circle of group relationships. His position is an anomalous one. He is outside the circle of group relationships although assigned a position within it. To a certain extent this is the situation of Greeks and Armenians who were born in Turkey and are living there at the present time. They are classified as citizens of the Turkish Republic and are required to identify themselves in this manner although they have not yet come to regard themselves as Turks and a sympathetic, unified feeling is still to be created.

In the evolution of the principle of citizenship the individual emerged as a person apart from his family group. His status as a citizen depended upon qualities which he himself possessed. That many of these qualities were kin-determined is true, but a different interpretation was placed upon them which made them the criteria of a new status in the community and a new set of relationships. This new status, as we noted before, was city-born, but eligibility was dependent upon personality and not upon domicile. It was inclusive of those who possessed certain characteristics and exclusive of those who did not. Rarely, if ever, were all the members of a community brought within the circle of relationships. In democratic Athens the slaves and the resident aliens, the outlanders, outnumbered the citizens themselves. The relations of the citizens were so intensive and the privileges so highly regarded that the numbers who could enjoy them were necessarily limited. Aristotle felt that " the citizens should be not too many to hear the orders of a single general or the announcements of a single herald ".[2] He criticizes Plato's ideal state of 5,040 free households as an impossibility since " the number of 5,000 citizens just now mentioned will require a territory as big as Babylonia or some other vast country, if so many persons are to be supported in idleness together with their women and children and attendants, who will be a multitude many times as great." [3]

Although the relationships involved in Athenian citizenship were too all-embracing and too personal to be freely extended, the attitude toward foreigners was not an illiberal one, as Hadow points out.[4] Foreigners were invited to immigrate, especially if they were skilled craftsmen, and they were given free trade and intermarriage and even a place in the military service. Political rights, however, were reserved for citizens of pure descent on both sides. In this regard the foreigner was always an outlander even if imbued with the spirit of the Athenian community. Nicias com-

[2] Aristotle, *Politics*, bk. vii, ch. iv. 11.

[3] *Ibid.*, bk. ii, ch. vi. 6.

[4] Hadow, W. H., *Citizenship* (Oxford, 1923), p. 7. See also A. E. Zimmern's *Greek Commonwealth* (Oxford, 1922), pt. ii, ch. vi.

mended the outlanders in his army against Syracuse, telling them that they have won the admiration of Greece by their knowledge of the language and their assimilation of Greek ways. They are all but Athenians. The strength of other bonds than those of hereditary citizenship is recognized in this speech. Nicias' appeal is to a broader community spirit which transcends the narrower limits of civic bonds which are confined to those who enjoy membership in the association of the state.

For so long as Greek citizenship was determined solely by birth it formed the basis of a social system which was relatively closed. Reforms were necessary to accomplish its extension and these were generally made under social pressure. The ten new tribes which Cleisthenes created to replace the four ancient and exclusive tribes to which citizenship had formerly been limited enrolled as citizens many poor people, immigrants, freed slaves and their descendants who had not been members of a tribe before, and hence had been without political rights. The number of citizens was thus materially increased, but facilities were not provided for the admission of new citizens in the future. The system had not lost its rigidity; the reforms which were to bring this about were an achievement of the Romans. In contrasting Greek and Roman citizenship, Hadow says:

At Rome the conception of citizenship was more complex than at Athens, and its history more turbulent. It comprised the public right to vote and of eligibility to office, the legal right of appeal and of action, and the private right of free trade and lawful marriage: it was stratified in varying degrees from full citizenship, which included all six privileges, to the grade of the *civitates sine suffragio,* who had the private rights alone: it was often supplemented or traversed by special treaties concluded between Rome and her most powerful allies. To the Romans it was perhaps less of a sentiment and more of an established order than it was to the Greeks.[15]

5 Hadow, *op. cit.,* p. 11.

Although the Greeks like the Romans had distinguished between classes of citizens with respect to wealth and had granted privileges and rights accordingly, they had not made wealth the criterion of eligibility for citizenship. The citizen and the non-citizen were separated by the insuperable barrier of birth. The Romans on the other hand grasped more clearly than the Greeks had done the relation of the state to those who occupy the territory which is governed by it, and thus a more flexible system of social integration was made possible. Citizenship was based on the sharing of common interests rather than on the possession of like hereditary attributes. The plebeians and patricians were alike Roman citizens; but the patricians possessed an undue share of the privileges and the good things of life and they held on to these tenaciously, yielding to the plebeians their portion only under the pressure of civil disturbance or warfare.

These two features of Roman citizenship, the distinction between civil and political rights and the recognition of common interest as the basis for the extension of these either wholly or in part, gave a wide latitude to the system. Gibbon notes that " a nation of Romans was gradually formed in the provinces by the double expedient of introducing colonies, and of admitting the most faithful and deserving of the provincials to the freedom of Rome ".[6] Both measures facilitated social integration, but failed in the end to achieve an enduring unity. Cultural assimilation is a slow process and in the outlying provinces it was incomplete, particularly in the eastern provinces which already possessed old, well-developed cultures of their own that were not easily displaced. There was little of common interest between these peoples and the citizens of Rome except the privileges of citizenship and these were emptied of their meaning by the failure to

[6] Gibbon, Edward, *Decline and Fall of the Roman Empire* (London, 1897 ed.), vol. i, p. 35.

provide a method for participating in them.   Theory became divorced from practice and a republican form of government gave way to a military despotism.   A system of subordination and control destroyed the cohesive bonds of pride and loyalty engendered by the principle of citizenship, and it was many centuries after the disintegration of the Roman Empire before this sense of belonging together recovered its due place as a unifying force.

Under Roman law freemen who were citizens of independent states or of dependent communities which did not have the rights of Roman citizenship in whole or in part were termed *peregrini*.   " Such a freeman, when at Rome, secured protection either through a treaty made by his state with Rome, through the offices of the *praetor peregrinus,* who administered the *ius gentium,* or by an *hospitium privatum* arranged with a Roman citizen, who was thus put under moral obligation to protect him to the extent of his power." [7] Hospitality of this nature to guests and to strangers was a pleasant feature of both Greek and Roman life.   In the Homeric Age to refuse hospitality or to injure a guest was to offend the gods.   The gods, taking the disguise of strangers from other lands, walk up and down cities in all sorts of forms.   Indeed, the Trojan War, so Homer tells us, was fought to avenge an outrageous violation of hospitality. Paris, a foreign prince who had been royally entertained, took his host's wife with him when he departed.

In the disordered centuries which followed the collapse of the western half of the great Roman Empire under the impact of the Germanic invasions, citizenship as a system of social integration was submerged and two new principles of organization appeared, fealty, or the loyalty of the vassal to his lord, and faith, or the obligations of fidelity to the Christian church.

[7] Abbott, F. F., *A History and Description of Roman Political Institutions* (Boston, 1901), p. 249.

2. FEALTY AND RELIGIOUS FAITH

Fealty like subordination and control gave rise to a class structure, but with a difference in principle. If the vassals owed obedience to their lord, he in turn was bound to render justice to them to the best of his ability. The feudal contract involved duties for both. Precedents for such contracts already existed in the old Roman relationship of patron and client (the Roman "patronage") and in the German custom (called "comitatus") of young braves' attaching themselves as loyal personal followers to some elder warrior of famed prowess.[8] The nature of the loyalties involved in the contract removed even the lowest class of vassals, the serfs, from the status of the slaves, although they were not freemen in that they were "attached to the soil" and could not leave the manor without the lord's consent. Unequal, however, as the social classes of the feudal period were, and marked as the cleavage was between them, they were nevertheless held together by sacred contracts and by cooperative interests. The importance of the cooperative spirit and also its limitations have been ably pointed out by Professors Hayes and Moon.

Coöperation was the outstanding characteristic of social life in the Middle Age, but it was coöperation on a comparatively small scale. The smallest and most basic agency of coöperation was the family—father, mother, and children—who conducted a joint household. Father worked on the farm or in the shop; mother did the housework and made the clothing; the boys helped father, and the girls helped mother. Work of all sorts, in town as well as country centered in the home and proceeded from the household. A young man could not become a full-fledged master, or freeman, or villein, until he was a householder; and to be a householder he had to marry and have a

[8] Hayes, C. J. H., and Moon, P. T., *Ancient and Medieval History* (New York, 1929), p. 524.

home. The family was a contractual relationship; it was an economic unit; and it was a moral force of great strength.

The manor, as a larger unit of agricultural life and labor, was also coöperative. It represented joint ownership and joint action on the part of a group of families living close together in a village and working close together in the same way on common arable lands, common meadows, and common woodlands. Corresponding to the manor in the country, were the merchant gild and craft gilds in the town. They too represented joint action on the part of a group of families living close together and working in the same way at the same jobs under common rules and regulations of their own making.

The very intensity of the spirit of coöperation in family, manor, gild, and town, was hostile to the development of wider loyalties, particularly to any such thing as national patriotism. The serf in Germany might be very loyal to his family, to his manor, and even to his lord. The craftsman in Italy might be intensely loyal to his family, his gild, and his city. But neither the serf nor the craftsman had much feeling about Germany as a whole or about Italy as a whole. So long as his intimate and local loyalties were not interfered with, he troubled himself very little about king or emperor or about his own nationality.[9]

The extremely personal and local character of the loyalties which held any particular feudal community together tended to repel all others who did not belong to it. Jealousies and dissensions were frequent and petty private wars were one of the worst features of feudalism. Commerce was seriously hampered, travel was hazardous, and the status of the stranger was a precarious one. His safety depended upon securing the protection of some feudal lord of importance, perhaps by an appeal to his sense of chivalry. The defense of the weak, especially of women and orphans, was inculcated in the teachings of chivalry. However, despite the lack of

[9] *Ibid.*, pp. 551-52.

safe and easy means of transportation, trade became increasingly important throughout the Middle Age and merchants traveled greater distances in search of desired commodities. Trade gave rise to the merchant gild, an association of the medieval town which regulated trade and protected its own members from the commercial competition of outsiders. In England, for instance, alien merchants were not allowed to trade directly with one another, thus insuring the middle man's profits to merchants of the local gild. Foreign merchants were also obliged to reside in the houses of citizens, and to leave after forty days.[10]

Strangers generally were regarded with suspicion although the wandering minstrel and troupes of entertainers found a welcome. Beggars, too, seem to have been regarded with a measure of tolerance, and to have formed a more or less recognized class which got a living by begging from monastery to monastery and from house to house. The different craft gilds which flourished during the medieval period also protected their members from competition with non-members; but the more specialized each of the crafts became in its own line, the more dependent it likewise became upon trade to supply its needs in other lines and to furnish a market for its wares. Wider trade relations thus tended to undermine the insular character of the loyalties which dominated the feudal community. Another powerful influence, the church, was also working toward this same end.

Among primitive peoples and in the earlier civilizations, religious interests had coincided with other interests of the community and had been interlocked with them in the system of social integration; but during the Middle Ages all three of the great religions, Christian, Buddhist and Moslem, gradually became sufficiently distinct in their own right and sep-

---

[10] Lipson, E., *An Introduction to the Economic History of England* (4th ed., London, 1926), pp. 444 *et seq.*

arate from the system as a whole to be extended independently. New converts were sought over wide areas; even as early as the thirteenth century Christian missionaries were to be found in the far-off court of Kublai Khan in Peking. Unfortunately, however, although a degree of separateness which made possible the rapid extension of religious interests and their accompanying ties was a relatively early achievement, confusion as to the real relation of these obligations to other obligations of the community still existed; religious and secular loyalties conflicted and a long struggle ensued before the issue was clarified and the respective functions of the associations of the church and the state within the community were defined.

During the feudal period the church fulfilled other functions in addition to providing for the religious life of the people. The monasteries took the place of hotels for strangers and travelers, and they were charitable institutions providing for the aged, the sick, and the poor. There were no public schools and education was conducted by the church. Moreover, the church exercised important functions of government which it sought to extend. The church, however, was often a house divided against itself. Its temporal power and its spiritual principle were not in harmony. Though zealous for converts and ready to receive newcomers within its fold, the church was intolerant of those who held religious doctrines contrary to its own. Such persons were known as " heretics ", and were regarded as dangerous persons to be bitterly persecuted. The influence of a common religion and the united effort called forth by the Crusades served nevertheless to break down other prejudices and to extend the narrow horizons of the feudal communities. These religious bonds did not, however, possess the cohesive strength that was needed to weld together the small, self-centered feudal communities into a larger unity. The fusions and the cleavages which eventually occurred between the various feudal states were not determined by the relationships of religion or of trade—though influenced by both. The unifying principle which drew certain groups together in opposition to other groups in the latter part of the Middle Age was *nationality,* a new sense of community which being common to all within a certain area " demanded that its community should be protected, ordered, and furthered by the state ".[11]

3. NATIONALITY

The sense of nationality differs from the conceptions of social unity which preceded it, and in considering these differences, which are summarized in the following quotation from *The Modern State,* we come nearer to its own meaning.

The sense of nationality has a content more pervasive and more real than the conceptions of social unity which had preceded it. It belongs to a stage where social consciousness is diffused through the various classes of a society. It belongs to an era which advances to democracy and parliaments, where monarchy disappears or becomes a symbol of a unity that it does not create. It contains a claim of equality, for nationality has no degree within its range. It applies to all men, rich or poor, high or low. It is not external, like the fact of a common subjection to dynasty. It is not transferable, except by a long process of assimilation. It cannot be merely accepted or rejected, like a creed of the days of Julian or of that prince of Adiabene who turned his whole state to Judaism. No easy formula, like the famous *cuius regio eius religio,* can solve its problems of jurisdiction. It is no mere boast or subjective expression of collective pride, like the claim of distinctive race. And, although communal in character, it unites far greater areas of society than ever in the past felt themselves to be one community.

[11] MacIver, *The Modern State,* pp. 135-36.

A spirit so pervasive, so complex, so subtle, and yet so strong, seeks embodiment in an association, inevitably in the state. No other association could serve its end, as the church serves the religious spirit or the family the primary needs of sex. The state becomes, or seeks to become, the embodiment of nationality.[12]

The development of a new type of community spirit which sought determinate ends in the organization of a governing association which should maintain the universal external conditions of social order within a given territory evolved in response to the needs created by the difficulties and dissensions of the feudal period. Wearied of incessant quarreling and of the confusion of conflicting loyalties men gradually came to a realization that their personal ends were identified with common ends which could best be served through union. This vision of a unified community, though far broader than the cooperative activities of the feudal manors and cities had been, was still limited in scope. It did not include all men, or even all civilized men, or yet all men of one race, or of one religion, or of one language, or of one continent. It did, however, include all men within certain lesser areas who shared a common environment and a common social life in contrast to other surrounding groups who either did not share these so intimately or whose interests were opposed. For, as Professor MacIver notes, " it is the very essence of nationality that it rests on the consciousness of difference no less than on that of likeness. Each nationality is determined by contrast with others, and a nationality regards itself not only as distinct from others, but nearly always as possessing some exclusive common qualities, being thereby separated from others as well as united within itself." [13]

[12] *Ibid.*, pp. 132-33.

[13] MacIver, R. M., "The Foundations of Nationality", *Sociological Review*, July, 1915.

Differences are more readily discerned than likeness and the feudal period had been dominated by narrow loyalties which accentuated the differences. Nationality emerged with the recognition of likenesses throughout an enlarged community. Those things which were regarded as common and of significance in one community were not necessarily the same as those for another community, nor were they necessarily the same at all times within a given community. Any quality or interest whatever if it is regarded as common by those who possess it can become a basis for nationality, and no quality or interest, however common, can become a basis of nationality unless it is regarded as common by those who possess it.[14]

It is not necessary for nationality that there should be any "pure determinant" whatever. The essentials are a common environment and a common social life. The qualities which are recognized as common and which form a basis for the sentiment of nationality need not be alike in any two communities. There are, however, certain chief qualities which are important although no one of them can be called imperative since a strong sentiment of nationality can exist in its absence. These qualities, Professor MacIver has listed as: race, language, territory, i. e., as occupied effectively, not as politically owned, economic interests, culture, i. e., characteristic standards and modes of life, religion, political tradition, political subjection or political domination.[15] In no one of the instances of nationality examined by Professor MacIver were all of these qualities found to be present and no two instances exhibited the same combination of qualities. Nationality, then, cannot be defined in terms of any one particular quality or combination of qualities, but rather it must be defined in terms of the sentiment which the possession of common qualities, whatever these may be, gives rise to.

[14] *Ibid.*

[15] *Ibid.*

Professor Muir defines a nation provisionally as " a body of people who feel themselves to be naturally linked together by certain affinities which are so strong and real for them that they can live happily together, are dissatisfied when disunited, and cannot tolerate subjection to peoples who do not share these ties." [16]   At another point, he says:

We can only say that a nation is a nation because its members passionately and unanimously believe it to be so.   But they can only believe it to be so if there exist among them real and strong affinities; if they are not divided by any artificially maintained separation between races from which they spring; if they share a common basis of fundamental moral ideas, such as are most easily implanted by common religious beliefs; if they can glory in a common inheritance of tradition; and their nationality will be all the stronger if to these sources of unity they add a common language and literature, and a common body of law.   If these ties, or the majority of them, are lacking, the assertion of nationality cannot be made good.   For, even if it be for the moment shared by the whole people, as soon as they begin to enjoy the freedom and unity which they claim in the name of nationality, they will fall asunder, and their freedom will be their ruin.

Nationality, since it is not based solely or even mainly upon racial homogeneity, can be nursed into existence, even where most of the elements of unity are to begin with lacking.[17]

Of the significance of the unity of race as an element in nationhood, Professor Muir writes further:

There is no nation in the world that is not of mixed race; and there has never been a race (Teutonic, Celtic, or the like) which has succeeded in including all its members within a single national entity.   Some degree of racial unity is, indeed, almost

[16] Muir, Ramsay, *Nationalism and Internationalism* (London, 1916), p. 38.

[17] *Ibid.*, pp. 51-52.

indispensable for nationhood: but it is enough that the various elements in the nation should have forgotten their divergent origins, and that there should be no sharply drawn cleavage between them. In other words, racial mixture is not hostile to the growth of a national spirit so long as the races are merged, and there is free intercourse, by marriage and otherwise, between them. What is fatal to the upgrowth of a sense of nationality is that one of the constituent races should cherish a conviction of its own superiority, and that this conviction should be embodied in law or custom. The mixed races of Hungary might have developed into a nation if the Magyars had not from the beginning held themselves aloof from their Slavonic and Roumanian subjects, and treated them as inferiors. And the greatest obstacle to the growth of real nationhood in India is the rigid caste system, whereby the Aryan conquerors have succeeded through many centuries in preventing themselves from being merged with the mass of their subjects.[18]

It would seem, then, that racial similarity after it has become dissociated from its more primitive connotation of the bloodbond in kinship groupings does not in itself create a system of social integration; yet, on the other hand, the presence of racial differences may prove a powerful obstacle in preventing the development of social unity.

Another type of difference which always threatens solidarity is that which is expressed in race-consciousness. For racial antagonisms are bitterly subjective. They are easily inflamed and most apt to blind men to a reasoning consideration of their common interest. Even in long established communities they not infrequently remain half-submerged, ready to intensify other disturbances, as in the situation of the Swedes and the Finns in Finland or of the Flemish and the Walloons in Belgium. Differences of speech, as in the instances just mentioned, tend to perpetuate racial distinctions. So do marked external signs of race—what Park calls "racial visibility".

[18] *Ibid.*, pp. 39-40.

The most conspicuous of these signs is color, and the "color line" is thus the most formidable barrier to solidarity where groups of different color meet.[19]

The two ideas of race and nationality should therefore be distinguished in attempting to analyze the reactions of strangers toward one another. Either may be present as a potent factor without the other, or both may be present together. The prejudice towards the Negro which exists in the United States is racial in its nature, whereas the antagonisms which arise at times in contacts between English and American nationals are accentuated by an exaggerated sense of nationalism. Both kinds of factors, those of race and those of nationality, complicate the relations of the Americans and the Filipinos, and of the English and the Indians. Not only are the racial differences sufficiently marked to constitute a color-line barrier socially, but the Filipinos and the Indians also have national aspirations which are thwarted by their present political status. The Americans and the English on the other hand as the dominant groups politically are under the necessity of maintaining their national prestige and a conflict situation ensues which tends to emphasize unduly the distinctions of nationality. Specific examples of the manner in which the relationship of the stranger is affected by such situations will be considered in the following chapter, which is devoted to a more detailed discussion of the formation of new relationships under circumstances in which the factors of nationality play an important part. For the present we are more directly interested in ascertaining the nature of nationality itself as a means of social integration.

In an analysis of the social psychology of international conduct, Professor Stratton has made certain observations

[19] MacIver, *Society: Its Structure and Changes*, pp. 73-74.

which throw further light on this problem. He points out that " both the higher animals and men *have to learn at what to be angry* ".[20] " Friendliness is as truly rooted in the nature of men as is antipathy. For either of these attitudes comes forth instinctively according to circumstances, according to the total situation past and present ". [21] Racial prejudice is not inborn, but it has arisen as a reaction to losses threatened or experienced and it is continued by tradition and by fresh impressions of harm received. The sentiment of nationality, of belonging together as distinct from other groups, has likewise been acquired, but it has for its basis the recognition of shared interests and of common benefits. This has come about through training, for, as Professor Stratton shows, " while the impulse behind social solidarity is natural, yet the actual groups of men which have been welded into the two opposing States which modern war requires have attained their particular sense of union only by an intensive social cultivation ".[22] " There could be no nation," he concludes at another point, " without solidarity, without psychic fusion, without a sense of community of desire or interest, acquired by training." [23]

The circumstances which have afforded this training have varied. In Western Europe the reaction against the difficulties and evils of the feudal system led to an appreciation of a wider conception of community. The awakening of the sentiment of nationality among Asiatic peoples has been a later development growing out of their contacts with western civilization. Various of these peoples have become nation-conscious through a desire to maintain their own independence and dignity on terms of equality with the nations

[20] Stratton, George Malcolm, *Social Psychology of International Conduct* (New York, 1929), p. 272.

[21] *Ibid.*, p. 204.   [22] *Ibid.*, p. 255.

[23] *Ibid.*, p. 287.

of the western world. The Japanese, for instance, are animated by an intense nationalistic fervor, while the Chinese on the other hand have not yet fully merged their ancient familial and community loyalties in the larger sentiment of national unity. In India the national spirit is being fostered by the political subordination of the people to an alien governing power. It is cut across, however, by the religious differences of the Hindus and the Moslems and by the rigidity of the caste system. In Turkey the humiliating conditions imposed by the Treaty of Sèvres fanned a smoldering sentiment of nationality into a consuming white heat that destroyed opposition and transformed the Turks through suffering and achievement into an acutely nation-conscious people, sensitive and proud.

The experiences which have served to inculcate the spirit of nationality throughout a people have also served to limit its expansion. A double service has been fulfilled. Through the consciousness of nationality a ground has been provided for the union of localities and for the reconciliation of divergent class interests while at the same time an " important protest against *false* universal claims, the claim, for instance, of political Rome over the world, or, again, the claim of ecclesiastical Rome over the world " has been signified.[24]

The fact of common nationality is definitive and determinative, not to be denied or renounced, a real basis of unity and condition of common action. . . . All the laws of life conspire to give a common and distinctive character to every area of community, and especially to those areas bounded by the frontiers of States. The great currents of culture that sweep over continents and even over the world along increasing channels of communication will never obliterate but rather enrich that character of national individuality.[25]

[24] MacIver, *Community*, p. 278.
[25] *Ibid.*, p. 279.

With the exception of the more conspicuous external signs of race, as color, the traits which distinguish the different nationality groups are, as a rule, the ones most readily apparent when strangers confront each other. It is seldom difficult to determine whether or not the other person belongs to our own nationality group, even though we may not be familiar with the traits peculiar to the nation to which he does belong and he may simply be " some kind of a foreigner " so far as we are concerned. The classification of the stranger as a member of our own group in regard to nationality or as an alien at once establishes certain relationships; certain assumptions can be made which afford at least a tentative basis for determining the nature of our behavior toward him. If the nationality of the stranger is the same as our own, we can feel reasonably well assured that he possesses certain loyalties, customs, and ideals in common with ourselves, whereas, if his nationality is different, these also will be different. The initial relationships are largely given direction by this fact. If the problem of nationality differences does not enter in, the situation is simplified and other factors such as those of class and personality receive more immediate attention in establishing the stranger's position with reference to the group. If, however, the stranger is a foreigner, these other factors are often obscured and the character of the relationships which are formed at first tends to be decided almost wholly from the standpoint of nationality.

When the stranger enters a foreign group he encounters certain preexisting attitudes which have been determined in part by the relations between the two nations represented as a whole and in part by the previous experiences which the group may have had with other foreigners, possibly with those of his own nationality. If the relations between the two nations are friendly, and if the former contacts have been pleasant, the reaction toward the newcomer will probably be a friendly one unless some untoward factor intervenes. But if the international relations are strained, or if former contacts with foreigners like the stranger have been unfortunate, the situation will be a less favorable one. Where nations are at war with each other these antagonisms affect the personal relations between individuals of the two opposing groups, as, for instance, when friendship was changed to hate between many Germans and Americans at the time of the World War. If loyalty to one's nation is, or appears to be, incompatible with other loyalties, the loyalty of nationality takes precedence. It is essential for the integration of the national community that this should be the case for otherwise the effective unity of the nation would be destroyed by a confusion of loyalties. It is not, however, essential that national loyalty should degenerate into chauvinism. In an interrelated world the needs and rights of one's own nationality can best be served by also recognizing the equal needs and rights of other nationalities. Another attitude which, although outwardly the opposite of chauvinism, is none the less akin to it in the lack of an appreciation of the actual values involved is manifested by those persons who continually deprecate their own local or national group in favor of the foreigner, irrespective of the merits of the case. The foreigner is assumed to be in the right simply because he is a foreigner; foreign goods and foreign ways are assumed to be superior simply on this ground alone. This type of disloyalty is usually, however, more seeming than real and in times of actual crisis when the larger interests of the country are threatened persons with this attitude can generally be counted on to stand by their own group.

The spirit of nationality which seeks to express itself through an organized state also seeks to regulate the relations with other nations through this channel. The state determines which foreigners may or may not enter its territory, not, however, as a rule, without some diplomatic consideration of the attitude of other nations in this matter. Nations are sensitive with regard to the privileges which are granted or refused to their subjects by foreign states. The system of passports and visas is a protective device which serves a double function, affording safety to both the traveler and the nation visited. Without these credentials the foreigner is debarred while with them he has a recognized status which permits him "safely and freely to pass". The surveillance to which the stranger is subjected after he has entered a foreign country varies greatly, not only in different countries but also at different times within the same country. Strangers may be watched with suspicion during a crisis who would be unnoticed in normal times. Some states more than others maintain a guarded attitude at all times, as, for instance, Japan and Turkey. The traveler in Turkey is irked by the necessity of obtaining official permission in advance to go from one point to another within the country and by having to check in and out with the police at each stopping place. I have spent hours in calling on the Turkish police for this purpose, albeit not unpleasantly. I found them courteous and obliging. They always called me "Margaret", naively unconscious of any familiarity since the use of the surname has not been customary in Turkey. And over my unmarried status they invariably shook their heads sadly as though the reasons for this were quite incomprehensible, which was gratifying.

The questions of the stranger's purpose and the probable duration of his stay are important. The distinguished foreign visitor is fêted, his wishes are anticipated, and his approval is eagerly sought. The tourist in general is tolerated, perhaps even welcomed as a source of income, and, to a greater or a less extent, his wishes are also catered to. The immigrant, however, finds a different situation. He has come to stay and the burden of accommodation and adjustment falls largely upon his shoulders. He is not a guest, and there is no one to give particular heed to his likes and dislikes. Even if he is fortunate enough to enter a community which is not prejudiced against him and his reception is a friendly one, he is nevertheless a probationer. With all the good will in the world nationality cannot be transferred. It can only be acquired by a long process of assimilation. Allegiance, however, can be transferred; the stranger can loyally serve the interests of the new community as it in turn can defend his; but the differences of nationality still remain notwithstanding.

Men may dedicate their lives to the cause of a foreign nation without losing their own nationality in so doing. Lafayette and Kosciusko, for instance, did not become Americans by their services to the American Colonies. The immigrant may become a naturalized citizen of his adopted country without becoming nationalized. The two processes are not necessarily synonymous as was pointed out in the discussion of citizenship. Civil wars and revolutions on the other hand do not destroy the fact of nationality; the political exile, the traitor, and the criminal may lose their status in the community, but they still retain their nationality. Although a community which is animated by the spirit of nationality desires to have a common government peculiarly or exclusively its own, it does not always follow that there should be harmony in the community with respect to the form of government which is desired. More often than not there is disagreement and some portion of the community is subject to the will of the rest in this regard. The state as an organization of community can be entered into or renounced; but the distinctive characteristics of nationality are developed only through a long process of common training and common living which molds the individual into the

likeness of the community in certain ways of doing, thinking, and feeling, and only by means of a similar process can
these be changed. The loyalties which integrate the national
community are engendered by these likenesses; the sentiment
which creates the national state is grounded in the awareness of them; they unite men, not at one point, but at a
thousand.

The ease with which the stranger is absorbed by the new
milieu depends upon the adaptability to one another of both
the stranger and the community. The United States was
for a long time cited as the classic example of a national
melting pot supposedly capable of speedily transforming all
comers into citizens after its own heart and pattern. That
doubts and misgivings should later have arisen concerning
the rapidity with which this could be successfully accom-
plished is not strange in view of the difficulties of the process
of nationalization even under optimum conditions. And the
circumstances were not equally favorable for all groups of
immigrants; the difficulties to be overcome were greater for
some nationalities than they were for others. The differences in physical appearance, language, religion, family relations, modes of living, standards of conduct and morality,
and innumerable other more subtle ways of doing and feeling were more pronounced in some cases than in others, and
hence the problems of becoming adjusted to the new environment were more complicated. Michels in his analysis of
this aspect of the sociology of the stranger has listed several
conditions which tend to quicken the denationalization of the
stranger and so to prepare the way for his absorption by the
new milieu. These are: 1. Similarity of language so that
the stranger does not have difficulty in becoming understood.
2. The necessity, in case the stranger's language is an unfamiliar one, for him to acquire the new language in order
not to be wholly isolated and prevented from obtaining work.

3. The lack of a true affection for the former fatherland as in the case of the Russian Jews. 4. A feeling of gratitude toward the new country as a place of refuge on the part of exiled wanderers. 5. The ownership of landed property in the new country. This type of property more than any other makes the stranger seem like a native. 6. Intermarriage with a native family. 7. The interruption of immigration. This gives an opportunity for the guest-land to absorb the strangers already present without being overtaxed by a fresh influx from without. The percentage quotas of the present restricted immigration policy of the United States are directed toward this end.[26]

There is, however, a certain attitude of receptivity on the part of both the group and the stranger which perhaps more than all else determines the facility of assimilation. This attitude had characterized the people of the United States and also the earlier immigrants during the period of expansion, but changing conditions, not only in the United States but in the countries from which the later immigrants have come, have reacted upon it. The native American no longer feels that his is the duty and the privilege of offering a welcome and a home to all the oppressed peoples of Europe, and the immigrant, in his turn, has ceased to idealize the new country to which he has come as a land of freedom and of equal opportunity for all. There has been a loss of idealism on the part of both in this regard and a consequent slowing down or disrupting of the assimilative processes. An unfortunate aspect of this situation appears in the increased delinquency among children of immigration parents whose own records have been law-abiding. These young people are, as it were, men without a country. They do not share the loyalties of their parents for the former homeland, they are

[26] Michels, Robert, " Materialien zu einer Sociologie des Fremden ", *Jahrbuch für Sociologie*, vol. i (1925), pp. 296-317.

no longer a part of it, but neither are they a part in sentiment of the American nation. Their potentialities for the larger social loyalties of the community and the nation have never been awakened. Family ties have also been weakened in the new environment, and the gang spirit has developed in lieu of other loyalties. This problem is discussed again in more detail in the following chapter in which concrete instances of situations involving the question of nationality are considered.

Subject populations which cherish a desire to be self-determined also present problems due to a lack of receptivity to assimilation, but the situation which results differs radically from that of the unassimilated immigrant community. The latter group has parted with its old garment of nationality before it was fully ready to don the new and in the absence of the customary unifying loyalties a period of social disintegration and disorganization has followed. A nation-conscious subject population, on the other hand, although failing to merge with the neighboring community, nevertheless forms a strongly integrated community within itself actuated by definite ideals. The immigrant situation may be regarded as an unfortunate phase of retardation in the development of a new national spirit. The problems of small peoples who seek self-determination and of peoples occupying territory which has been severed from the fatherland as a part of the spoils of war by a victor nation are, on the contrary, complicated by an undue national fervor which makes compromise and cooperation difficult. The Turks and their Greek and Armenian subjects have evinced a striking lack of receptivity to assimilation in the past. They have lived neighbors to one another in Istanbul for nearly five hundred years without becoming merged in nationality. Each group still retains its own distinctive national characteristics and loyalties. The French in Canada have also maintained a more or less separate community life of their own for more than a century and a half even in the absence of any marked national aspirations of their own or friction with their English-speaking neighbors. Already entrenched in the land at the time that Canada passed from French to British control, they have held with a passive tenaciousness to their own language and manner of life. There has been no immediate urge to change, either from without or from within; they have been sufficient unto themselves. The exiled Acadians who settled in Louisiana also represent a group which has remained singularly unassimilated throughout a long period although surrounded by neighbors of the same nationality originally as themselves. The difficulties in this case, however, are those of social class rather than of nationality. The Acadians have been regarded as socially inferior by their proud southern compatriots.

Despite the obstacles which not infrequently stand in the way of the ready assimilation of the stranger owing to the differences of nationality, the bonds of nationality are nevertheless not inelastic in relation to their strength. They can be extended, although time is required for the growth of the sentiments upon which they are founded. They are not external and superimposed, but they derive their strength from associations which have become endeared to all within the community, both rich and poor. It is in this sense that Professor Stratton says, " war does not spring primarily from hate, but from mutual attraction. The hatred is secondary; it is a protective device to defend what is loved ".[27] And that which is loved above·all is the social order; it is this which men conceive to be endangered by the outsider. The other person, the other nation, is always believed to be the aggressor whose presence or whose action in some way endangers the safety or the progress of the group. It is conceivable, for instance, that, notwithstanding the circum-

[27] Stratton, *op. cit.*, pp. 242-43.

stances connected with the bombardment of Shanghai, the Japanese were sincere when, in presenting their side of the case, they stated that the Chinese were the aggressor nation. From their point of view this may doubtless have seemed to be true and their own action necessary and justifiable for the preservation of their own national group. The intensity of the sentiments which unite men of the same nationality tends to make them oblivious to the rights of other nationalities when there is a conflict of interest. Professor Stratton stresses the bearing of loyalty upon conflict in the following excerpt.

At the foundation of war is the passionate attachment of men to one another, albeit an attachment of limited scope. Tribal prejudice, the contempt of one people for another, their corporate suspicion and animosity—these . . . could not exist if there were no self-appreciation within the two groups. The self-appreciation, the coöperative spirit, may be strengthened by animosity toward others, but it is not created by it. The loyalty to one's own group, rather, is the prime source of the antipathy toward its rivals.[28]

Nationality as a basis of social integration, though solving certain problems, has thereby created others. The intensification of the distinctive traits of nationality and the deepening of the ties of national loyalty which have been a natural consequence of the growing awareness of belonging together of the national group have resulted in accentuating the differences between the various nationalities. This would seem to be inevitable, but that these differences between nations should necessarily lead to irreconcilable disagreements and warfare does not seem so. Just as the individual has realized his highest potentialities through an organized group life, is it not possible that the nation, too, may achieve its finest expression of selfhood as a member of an ordered community of nations?

[28] *L. c.*

PART THREE

THE STRANGER AND THE COMMUNITY PATTERN

CHAPTER VI

ALIEN COMMUNITIES

I. IMMIGRANT COMMUNITIES

THIS classification is a comprehensive one which includes those groups or communities which are composed of individuals who have migrated from their former homes and have settled in another country with the intention of making their homes there more or less permanently and of identifying their interests with those of the adopted country. Such persons on their arrival in the new country tend to settle in the same neighborhood with other immigrants of their own nationality, and thus our Ghettos, Chinatowns, Little Italies and so on have come into existence. Each of these foreign sections or communities presents its own peculiar problems. Differences of race, language, religion, standards of living, customs, cultural traditions, and ideals of government and moral conduct may be present which separate the immigrant colony not only from the people of the country in which they have settled but also from other immigrant groups who are living in the same vicinity. And even within communities of the same nationality there are differences. The members of the laboring groups will not respond to situations in the new environment in the same manner as those belonging to the professional groups or to the diplomatic corps. Nor will the reactions of a small rural community of immigrants agree at all times with those of a larger urban settlement. Thus the attempt to generalize from such heterogeneous material as that which is presented by the numerous immigrant communities within the United States, to say nothing of those in other countries, is at once a difficult and a precarious undertaking.   Yet, for the purpose of this analysis, it would be impracticable to attempt to consider each kind of immigrant community separately; and hence these are taken together although it is realized that the generalizations which are made are not equally applicable to all immigrant groups.

Careful studies have been made of some, though not of all, of the various immigrant communities within the United States and an examination of these for like elements, should any exist amidst a multiplicity of differences, reveals the prevalence of a conflict situation in varying degrees of intensity.   There is a struggle between the desire on the one hand to retain old customs and mores, to keep the cultural traditions and the identity of the group, and the desire on the other hand, particularly among the younger people, to adopt new ways which are more in harmony with the changed environment.   This conflict between the old and the new, between parents and children, is not peculiar to the immigrant community alone.   It is met with elsewhere today and other generations have also been faced by the same problem. Even as early as 2700 B. C. the Sumerians were bemoaning the deterioration of the times, children no longer obeyed their parents, there was graft among public officials, and, worse still, every one was seeking publicity by trying to write a book.[1]

The putting away of old things for new is in itself a natural process, but in the immigrant group this has become accelerated and the difficulties of rapidly adjusting old ways to new conditions has disrupted and broken the long established ties of the relationship that had formerly regulated behavior in the mother country.   The increased crime and

[1] Taken from an ancient Sumerian cuneiform tablet now in the National Museum, Istanbul, Turkey.

delinquency which the Sumerians complained of are attend-
ant problems which have frequently been observed to arise
under such conditions. The desire for publicity occurs likewise, although other means than literary achievement are,
unfortunately, more often sought for its gratification.

The requirements of a new environment necessitate the
changing of some of the patterns of behavior in the immigrant group; and, since the social organization of a people
is an integrated whole, these changes will in their turn precipitate others until at times complete demoralization is
threatened. The effect which the breaking down of some
customs has upon other customs, and even upon the whole
cultural life of a people, has been witnessed in instances of
the contacts between primitive and civilized peoples where
disorganization of the entire social order of the simpler
group has followed upon the loss of certain customs and
mores. Nor is such disintegration a phenomenon found
wholly within the less highly organized groups. The individual who has " gone native " is not altogether fictitious
character. I have myself known a number of such persons
both in Alaska and in the Philippines. The loss of certain
patterns of behavior, more often those pertaining to standards of sexual morality, has been followed by a letting go
of other standards also with a resulting demoralization. The
importance for the morale of a group, or of an individual, in
maintaining a solid front is appreciated in warfare, and also
in other kinds of conflict situations.

For the immigrant communities within the United States
the contrast between cultures has been of a different order
than that which exists between primitive and civilized peoples.
It cannot be said that the American culture is more highly
developed than that of most at least of the foreign groups
who have come to us, but only that it is different in various
respects. Circumstances have, however, thrown the burden

of readjustment and modification upon the new arrivals more largely than upon the older American population, although this has been by no means a one-way process.

Among the foreign elements within the United States the problems of assimilation have not been equally great for all; there has been less conflict in some cases than in others. The tensions have been less acute for the peoples from western Europe whose behavior patterns more nearly resembled those of the American people, originally from the same stock themselves, than they have been for the immigrants from southern and eastern Europe and from the Orient. For the immigrants from western Europe the changes required for readjustment were often more apparent than real. The fundamental family, political, religious, and economic relationships did not need to change greatly since these were essentially like those of the American people to begin with. Moreover, these nationalities met with less opposition from without; they were not driven back upon themselves as the Jews, for instance, have been. The story of this people affords an example of an age-long conflict relationship, which, although it is rather too extreme a case to be considered typical, is one that is familiar and that brings the situation forcibly before us.

When the Hebrews migrated as a nation into the land of Canaan, following their sojourn in Egypt, it was necessary for them to subdue the people who were already occupying the land, and this conquest was not complete. Even though the Hebrews possessed the land they still " dwelt among the Canaanites, Hittites, and Amorites, and Perizzites and Hivites, and Jebusites." (*Judges* 3 : 5). Moreover, Palestine, a small, narrow strip of country in itself, was traversed by one of the great highways of the world. The trade of countries far beyond its immediate boundaries passed that way and in times of war their armies also followed that route.

The Hebrews were thus in constant contact with outsiders, not of a few nationalities but of many, and as a result of this situation another conflict arose, not with their alien neighbors this time, although such conflicts were frequent enough, but in their own lives. The forces which tend toward assimilation and amalgamation when different peoples are in contact with one another were at work. The Hebrews "took their daughters to be their wives and gave their daughters to their sons and served their gods," (*Judges* 3:6). In opposition to this fusion, however, was the Hebrew conception of themselves as a "peculiar people" (*Exodus* 19:5), the "chosen nation" (*Isaiah* 43:20). Their leaders impressed this upon them and exhorted them not to forget the Lord, their God, and not to marry with the uncircumcised who had no share with Israel in her peculiar privileges. Thus even from this early period in their history it has been the fate of the Hebrews to be surrounded by alien peoples to an unusual degree, and the struggle through centuries to preserve the integrity of their own race and of their religious and social life against outside influences has tended to accentuate certain features of these. In commenting on this situation, Dr. Wirth, in his study of the Ghetto, says:

The Jew is a much more clearly defined social type than physical type. What is typical of the Jews as a group is their characteristic "run of attention", or the direction of their habits and interests which have become fixed through centuries of communal life in segregated areas. . . . Judaism has been preserved throughout the long years of Israel's dispersion by two factors: its separative ritualism, which prevented close and intimate contact with non-Jews, and the iron laws of the Christian theocracies of Europe, which encouraged and enforced isolation. . . . All the devices that operated to keep the Jew apart, at the same time made him crave contacts that were taboo. He lived on the periphery of two worlds, and not fully in either. As a result he developed that keen sense of self-consciousness which is often expressed in his awkwardness and lack of poise when in the company of strangers. He is either shy and self-effacing, or he over-compensates in the direction of aggressiveness. In either case. he is seldom himself. He finds himself haunted by loneliness in the outer world, and when he returns to his familial hearth he is restless and anxious to escape.[2]

The effect upon the more sensitive individual of thus being divided between two worlds, the one that he has deserted and the one that will have none of him, has been sympathetically interpreted in certain of Ludwig Lewisohn's writings as in *The Island Within*.[3]

Although the Jews are usually thought of as being " clannish " and emergencies have at times tended to mobilize all Jewry for collective action, Dr. Wirth brings out another and more individual aspect of the situation. The first Jewish immigrants in the United States were Sephardic Jews from Spain and Portugal, the second group were German Jews, and the third group Polish and Russian Jews. As this third group began pouring in in large numbers the earlier Jewish immigrants, who stood on the brink of assimilation, were keenly conscious of the problem involved in the increase in numbers of Polish and Russian Jews who differed from themselves.

[2] Wirth, Louis, *The Ghetto* (Chicago, 1928), pp. 72-3.

[3] To the question that arises in the mind of the social scientist as to the validity for his purposes of a certain type of interpretative fiction, Mr. Lewisohn has himself perhaps given an answer in the following quotation from a letter to the author. " In any ordinary sense *The Island Within* is not based on facts. A thousand hints were taken consciously or subconsciously from observed reality, but these hints were transmuted into structure and pattern and into those new creative symbolic ' facts ' which are, or ought to be, so much truer than truth. . . . I am merely and inadequately illustrating the common transmutting of life into art."

They sensed that all the progress they had made in breaking down barriers, in preventing the development of a ghetto, and in gaining recognition for themselves as persons, rather than as Jews, with their Christian neighbors might now, with the new connotation that was attached to the word Jew, come to a sudden halt. . . . These Russians were all right—of that they were quite certain—but, like the southern Negro, they had to keep their place.[4]

Interestingly enough, this situation seems to have had a parallel in the case of the attitude of northern Negroes toward the influx of Negroes from the South at the time of the World War.

In many northern cities the native colored inhabitants had been accustomed to a large measure of freedom and equality in participating in the public and educational life of the town. With the coming of the migrants, these northern Negroes found themselves being differentiated from other inhabitants on account of their color and felt the barriers of dislike and prejudice strengthening against them. Inevitably many of them were inclined to hold the migrants responsible for these increasing social restrictions and tended to resent the influx of other blacks, many of whom were inferior in education and culture to the northern Negroes and most of whom were unaccustomed to northern standards of living and modes of conduct. There are various indications that numbers of northern Negroes did not eagerly welcome the migrants but, instead, sought to keep aloof from them. In many instances this resentment was probably only a temporary first reaction; so few facts are known concerning the extent and permanence of this feeling, no statements as to its duration can be made.[5]

The first Jews were generous in giving charity to the unfortunate of the later arrivals, but in doing so they assumed

[4] Wirth, *op. cit.*, p. 183.

[5] Kennedy, Louise Venable, *The Negro Peasant Turns Cityward* (New York, 1930), p. 222.

a patronizing attitude. They did not wish to have these
other Jews too close to them. Dr. Wirth also describes
another interesting relationship of the Jews in Chicago, that
with their Polish neighbors.

The two groups detest each other thoroughly, but they live
side by side on the West Side, and even more generally on the
Northwest Side. They have a profound feeling of disrespect
and contempt for each other, bred by their contiguity and by
historical friction in the pale; but they trade with each other on
Milwaukee Avenue and on Maxwell Street. . . . These two
immigrant groups, having lived side by side in Poland and
Galicia, are used to each other's business methods. They have
accommodated themselves to one another, and this accommodation persists in America. . . . The members of the younger
generation mingle in school and are members of the same
gangs.[6]

Even after the Jew has succeeded in leaving the ghetto,
the area of second settlement is also pre-eminently an area
of conflict—conflict within the family and the community.
"Families tend to disintegrate under the stress of contra-
diction between behavior patterns which results from the
importation of extraneous cultural influences into the home
by the children of the immigrants."[7]   The situation of the
Jewish immigrant group is thus one of tension both from
without and from within. There is the old antagonism
between Jew and Gentile, which is modified by a tendency to
become friendly and to be attracted, and there is also the
additional strain of the conflict within the family brought
about by the influence of the changed environment upon the
young people. These opposing forces create a tenseness and
a consciousness of self from which extremes of behavior are

[6] Wirth, *op. cit.*, p. 229.

[7] *Ibid.*, p. 253.

disposed to follow when contacts with strangers occur. The tendency on the one hand is to be attracted and on the other to hold aloof. " In frontier regions," Dr. Wirth notes, " the Jew plunges into the political and social life of the community with such zest and enthusiasm that he soon makes himself conspicuous as a Jew by his very attempt not to appear strange, and to be a real member of the community." [8]

Because of the peculiar circumstances of their history is is the Jews who are usually placed in the position of the stranger when the contact is between alien groups. The Christian groups are accustomed to assuming the initiative toward them and there is an inclination to feel resentful if the Jewish reaction to the somewhat dependent position in which they are placed is one of self-assertion and aggression and if they are over-zealous in demanding their rights. The situation is rarely an easy one for either group. To the Christian, the Jewish attitude seems that of a person who would eat his cake and yet have it too, that they wish to participate fully in everything without making any concessions themselves, while to the Jew it seems, and not at times without reason, that he is being discriminated against simply because he is a Jew and not because he would otherwise be objectionable as a person.

Although certain aspects of the conflict relationship of the Jewish immigrants arise from the fact that they are Jews, other features are a part of their general position as an immigrant group and are common to other such groups. The tendency, for instance, of boys and young men to form gangs is one that is frequently met with among immigrant groups as a consequence of various conflicts to which the young people are subjected. In his study of gang life Dr. Thrasher points out how the crowded, deteriorated areas in which the

[8] *Ibid.*, p. 256.

immigrant groups live afford a background for certain types of conflict.

Such a crowded environment is full of opportunities for conflict with some antagonistic person or group within or without the gang's own social milieu. The conflict arises on the one hand with groups of its own class in dispute over the valued prerogatives of gangland—territory, loot, play spaces, patronage in illicit business, privileges to exploit, and so on; it comes about on the other, through opposition on the part of the conventional social order to the gang's unsupervised activities. Thus the gang is faced with a real struggle for existence with other gangs and with the antagonistic forces of its wider social environment.

Play groups easily meet these hostile forces, which give their members a " we " feeling and start the process of ganging so characteristic of these unorganized areas.[9]

Back of this struggle, which tends to solidify the gang as such, lies another problem, that of the organization, or rather of the disorganization, of the immigrant home and community life which gives rise to it. Dr. Thrasher says of this:

The failure of the normally directing and controlling customs and institutions to function efficiently in the boy's experience is indicated by disintegration of family life, inefficiency of schools, formalism and externality of religion, corruption and indifference in local politics, low wages and monotony in occupational activities, unemployment, and lack of opportunity for wholesome recreation. All these factors enter into the picture of the moral and economic frontier, and coupled with deterioration in housing, sanitation and other conditions of life in the slum, give the impression of general disorganization and decay. . . . Thus the gang, itself a natural and spontaneous type

[9] Thrasher, F. M., *The Gang* (Chicago, 1927), pp. 26-27.

of organization arising through conflict, is a sympton of disorganization in the larger social framework.[10]

That the immigrant parents are unable to meet the demands of their children under such different and difficult circumstances is not strange, as Dr. Thrasher goes on to show.

Since about two-thirds of the parents of delinquent boys in Chicago are parents from rural areas and villages in Europe, it is not strange that they do not know how to manage their children in such a totally new and different environment. The language difficulty is only one part of the cultural discrepancy that grows up between parents and children. Family discipline cannot be maintained because of lack of tradition in the American community to support it, and the constant coming in and going out (immigrant succession) in many of the immigrant areas further increase the difficulty of developing any consistent tradition with reference to family control. In this sense the gang becomes a problem of community organization.[11]

Thomas and Znaniecki in their study of the Polish peasant also attribute the fundamental attitudes that are back of the social disorganization of this group in America to the development of new personal needs which cannot be met by the traditional systems of control. The growth of a new social system to meet these demands has not kept pace with the rapid decadence of the old which has been precipitated by the sudden transition to a different environment with its diverse and unaccustomed requirements. The sense of security and responsibility which comes from *belonging to something* has been lost in the breaking-up of the primary group organization before the forces making for individual efficiency have become sufficiently developed to carry on.[12]

[10] *Ibid.*, pp. 37-38.   [11] *Ibid.*, pp. 489-90.

[12] Thomas and Znaniecki, *The Polish Peasant in Europe and America* (Boston, 1918), vol. v, pp. 344-45.

Similar problems to these which have been cited exist in other immigrant groups in varying degrees of intensity. Conflict within the group tends to disrupt it, and the individual seeks other contacts irrespective of former ties, while conflict from without tends to unify the group. Newly arrived immigrants settle with those of their own nationality who are already here, or beside groups with whom they have had former contacts, even though these may have been antagonistic as in the case of the Polish and Jewish immigrants in Chicago. . Here, as among primitive peoples, that which is known, even though disliked, is less feared and suspected than something which is wholly unknown.

In those immigrant communities in which the former social order as a whole is being disintegrated more rapidly than an adequate reorganization can be made tensions arise and a condition of instability results. This affects the behavior that is manifested toward strangers, causing it to fluctuate now in this direction and now in that. Certain exigencies will tend to unite the foreign group as opposed to the American stranger, and at times even foreign groups who have for the most part disliked one another, as was the case of the Jews and the Poles, find a bond of common interest when both are alike strangers in a strange land. However, as the processes of assimilation and of amalgamation begin to make themselves felt, those members of the immigrant group who have achieved a degree of recognition within the American community, but whose place is as yet insecure, may be inhospitable to strangers of their own nationality, and even to former associates, if these are not so well assimilated as themselves. This attitude, which was displayed by the older Jewish immigrants toward certain later arrivals of their own race, is not an isolated instance nor one that is peculiarly Jewish. It is closely akin to the feeling of chagrin that is not infrequently manifested the world over

toward poorer and less sophisticated relatives whose relationship, if known, might entail ridicule or loss of prestige.   It
is a situation that has been a recurrent theme in literature
with the reader's sympathy, for the most part, directed
toward the unfortunate one who have been denied.   The
predicament of the Peters has been made a source of reproach
or of amusement; for, much as we may censure groups for
being clannish or exclusive, there is that within us which
echoes the sentiment of the old southern mountaineer, " Wal,
stickin' by air tha law."   Yet, in all fairness, it must be
admitted that the situation is a difficult and embarrassing one
for the older immigrant groups who see the place that they
have won for themselves in the community threatened by
an influx of newcomers of their own race.   The thoughtful
American who has been a tourist abroad can doubtless recall
instances when he has been deeply humiliated by the bad
manners and tactlessness of some of his own countrymen,
and can appreciate how serious a problem of this nature may
be for sensitive individuals among immigrant peoples who
have been able to make a place for themselves while others
of their family or group could not.   When situations occur
in which the interests of the individual are no longer best
served by the organization and interest of the group of
which he is a part, conflicts and tensions arise like those which
are so characteristic of immigrant groups in the United
States that are still in a process of assimilation.

The foreign groups that have been considered so far have
come to the United States with the intention of establishing
new homes there.   Although some individuals among them
do plan to return to their native country to live when they
can afford to do so, this is not the hope of all.   The immigrant group's position with respect to the community in
which they have settled is permanent rather than temporary,
except as they move from one section of the city to another,

or from one city or state to another. There are, however, a number of foreign groups among us of which this would not be true. The Chinese cherish the hope of eventually returning to China to be buried with their ancestors. Some Italian laborers hoard their savings that they might return to Italy to live. Our latest immigrant group, the Mexican, has no fixed abode. They are largely seasonal agricultural laborers moving with their families from point to point throughout the Southwest as their labor is needed for the various crops. Contacts of this transitory nature have as a concomitant a certain indifference on the part of both the migrant and the community. The sense of mutual responsibility and obligation that normally exists is weakened. The migratory worker on his part does not seek citizenship, and the community on its part is disposed to neglect the welfare of such persons or groups, as, for instance, it does the problem of child labor, difficult it is true to deal with, among the Mexican immigrants.[18]

The members of an immigrant group, whether their position in the larger community is to be a permanent or a transitory one, are separated by physical distance from their former environment. Innumerable associations and relationships of long standing have been suddenly broken by this removal, and the necessity for forming a variety of new relationships has been immediately thrust upon the immigrant by the exigencies of a different environment. These changes in the relationships of the members of a group also imply changes in its social structure. Normally such a modification would require a lapse of time and the observance of ritual ceremonies to assist in making the emotional transitions which accompanies the forming of new social bonds.

[18] Taylor, Paul S., *Mexican Labor in the United States*, vol. i (University of California Publications in Economics, vol. vi, Berkeley, 1930), *passim*.

These conditions are lacking in the case of the immigrant, and hence there follows a longer or shorter period of emotional strain and instability until adequate readjustments are made and assimilation finally effected. During this interval of stress the customary behavior patterns with respect to strangers of different types are distorted by the tensions within the social structure, and they do not follow their former recognized channels; but they turn now toward this extreme, and now toward that—now welcoming the stranger and now withdrawing from him.

2. FOREIGN COLONIES

The communities contained within this category differ from the immigrant communities which have just been considered in that their members and the descendants of these still continue to owe allegiance to the former mother country, while for the immigrant such obligations are largely broken when he leaves his native land, and in most instances, his children born in the new country grow up as citizens of it by right of birth. The children born in the United States of immigrant parents are American citizens irrespective of the nationality of their parents. On the other hand if the citizens of a country migrate to any of its foreign colonies or dependencies, they still remain under the aegis of the mother country and their children born in the new home do not lose their citizenship. The children born in Canada of English parents, for instance, are at once loyal British subjects as well as loyal young Canadians. The obligations imposed by these two different loyalties do not preclude one another. They are supplementary rather than antagonistic as is the case with the immigrant whose new obligations toward the state conflict with his former duties in this regard. There is thus a vital difference in the orientation of the foreign colony and of the immigrant community which brings about a correspondingly different realignment of the relationships within the two types of groups.

The problem of the readjustment of relationships in the immigrant community, with its ensuing conflicts and tensions, has been made the subject of a number of careful sociological studies and a rather wide literature dealing with this situation is available. In the study of the foreign colony, however, a somewhat different condition exists. The field here is also a heterogeneous one, as was true of immigrant communities, and there is practically no limit to the amount of literature of various kinds which bears upon different aspects of it. This material, however, is like a mountain of ore, which, although it contains precious metal, is of such a low grade that it does not yield this in a sufficient amount to repay the labor of extracting it under the present conditions. Many of the works on foreign topics—travel, history, economics, diplomatic relations and so on—would, if carefully analyzed, contribute much toward an understanding of the social relations of the people concerned; but this information is so widely scattered throughout a vast quantity of unrelated material that I have been under the necessity of waiving it for the most part. The conclusions which are being offered here are based largely on my own experience as a member of certain foreign colonies.

From the standpoint of the social relationships involved three main types of foreign colonies may be distinguished: first, colonies such as Australia which have been founded in regions that were only sparsely populated by a primitive people; second, colonies which have taken possession through conquest of an already well-populated territory belonging to a people of an advanced culture as in the case of the British in India or the Americans in the Philippines; and, third, colonies of foreigners who still seek to maintain their own racial and cultural integrity although living in an alien land

having an independent government. The foreign groups in
China, for instance, British, American, French, German,
Russian, Japanese and so on as the case may be still remain
loyal to their own countries even unto the third and fourth
generations. The land in which they have taken up their
abode does not become home to them nor yet to their children who are born there. Their interests at best are only
partially identified with those of the country in which they
are living. It may be objected that communities of this third
type should not be classified as foreign colonies since the
territory where they are established is independent. Their
inclusion seems justified, however, in that it is customary
to designate the alien residents in a country as a colony if
these are living together as a community. The foreign
groups in such cities as Shanghai, Istanbul and Jerusalem
are referred to, for example, as the American Colony, the
British Colony, the German Colony, and so on. A further
reason moreover for their consideration at this point exists
in the fact that these groups closely resemble in a number
of particulars the second type of foreign colonies which was
distinguished above. To illustrate, the American Colony in
Shanghai is oriented with respect to the Chinese in much the
same manner that the Americans in Manila are oriented to
the Filipinos although the Philippines are a dependency of
the United States and China is not. Certain problems of
the British in India, though by no means all, are repeated
again in China. Communities of the first type on the other
hand, which are true colonies as the term is more often
defined, differ from the two other types because of the fact
that the problems which are presented by contacts between
peoples of different races and cultures have been largely
solved by the unfortunate extermination of the native population. The position of such colonies is therefore unlike
that of the foreign colonies which are subjected to close con-

tacts with a native group differing from themselves in cultural traditions, nationality and race, and this difference is a significant one in understanding the social relationships of the communities.

The freedom from external pressure which is characteristic of the first type of colonies is also a feature of frontier settlements. In fact, when such colonies are first established they are frontier communities. When, for instance, the American Colonies were first founded, they represented the European frontier in much the same way that the settlements which later grew up beyond the Allegheny Mountains and in the Far West were, in their turn, the frontier outposts of the earlier settlements in the East. As the population of a frontier community increases, and as greater facilities for transportation and communication are introduced and the mode of living is improved, the problems change and either are gradually merged with those of the parent country of which the community is an offshoot or give rise to antagonisms which eventually result in the establishment of an independent state, or at least in the attempt to win independence. These same processes may also be observed in the growth of foreign colonies of the first type and these similarities make it possible to simplify the immediate problem of describing the social relationships of the different kinds of foreign colonies by combining the study of the first of these types with that of the frontier settlement which is to be taken up at another point.

Certain aspects of the problems associated with the second type of foreign colony, that situated in a dependency with national aspirations, have long been of general interest and have been widely discussed. The pros and cons of the questions of granting independence to the Philippine Islands and of acceding full autonomy to India have been matters of debate for the last several years, and much information, reliable and otherwise, has been brought forward. One phase of the situation has received little attention, however. This is the effect which has been produced upon the American group in the Philippines and upon the British in India, both of which are relatively small communities, by living in contact with large numbers of native peoples by whom they are regarded as foreigners. Because of the subordinate position in which the Philippines stand to the United States government and in which India stands to Great Britain it has become customary for those of us who live at home to think of the Filipinos and the Indians as the alien group, but it must be remembered that from the point of view of these peoples it is the Americans and the British who are the foreigners and not themselves. The over-lordship of the minority groups does not alter this fundamental fact in so far as the Filipinos and the Indians are concerned; they were born in the land and their fathers before them; it is home to them by right of birth and tradition. The justice of this point of view becomes the more readily apparent if the relative numbers of the different peoples are taken into consideration together with their respective places of birth. If we realize that there are but five to six thousand Americans in the Philippines in contrast to more than ten million Filipinos who were born there and that the British-born population of India is less than a hundred and twenty thousand persons [14] as opposed to over three hundred million Indians who are natives of the country, there can be but little question as to which groups are alien, irrespective of where the governing power lies. Similar situations also exist in the Dutch Col-

[14] The *Census of India, 1921* (Calcutta, 1923-1924), vol. i, part ii, table xi, gives the population of India who were born in the United Kingdom as 115,606 out of a total population of 318,942,480 in 1921. The *Report of the Indian Franchise Committee* (London, 1932) gives the British-born population in India for the 1931 census as 116,916 and the total population of India as 352,837,778.

onies in the East Indies, and in the colonial possessions of
the French in Indo-China, the Japanese in Chosen, and the
various European nations in northern Africa. The situation in central and southern Africa, where the native negro
peoples belong to simpler, less highly organized groups,
presents a different set of problems from that of those dependencies in which the subject peoples have national aspirations. In discussing the social relationships of colonies of
this latter type, our interest is centered primarily upon the
behavior of the ruling groups who are living in what is after
all foreign territory even though this is nominally at least
subject to their mother country. The emphasis is being
placed on these groups rather than on the native populations
with whom they come in contact since, for the purpose of
our analysis, these small foreign communities present problems in social adjustments which are of particular moment.

The Americans in the Philippines may be thought of as a
single community in spite of the fact that they are scattered
here and there throughout the Islands from Laoag in the
north to Zamboanga in the south, a distance of a thousand
or more miles, with poor facilities for communication and
transportation. Manila, with its mountain resort, Baguio,
is the focal point. More than one half of the American
population in the Islands lives there, and, sooner or later,
more or less frequently, all of the others come and go through
Manila. What is said and done by the American Colony in
Manila in regard to the behavior toward the Filipinos determines the attitudes of the other Americans living throughout the provinces, even in the most isolated stations where
mails are infrequent and months may pass without outside
contacts. Although some things may " go " in the provinces
that would not in Manila, or the other way around, these are
not many. In fact the smaller and the more isolated the
group is, the more conscious do its members often become

of their relations to, and dependence upon, the larger American community in the Islands. Their lonely position which is a consequence of the physical environment brings home to them all the more forcibly the tragedy of that greater isolation which devolves through social ostracism, and they would be reluctant indeed to break the ties that bind them to their own people and to forego the thrills of occasionally visiting Manila or Baguio or of unexpectedly meeting other Americans, even though strangers, who might by chance visit their out-of-the-way station.

The use of social ostracism as a weapon of social control is in no sense peculiar to the American Colony in the Philippines or to foreign colonies elsewhere. It merely operates with singular force in such situations. In one form or another ostracism has been universally resorted to throughout the ages by groups seeking to maintain their own solidarity. In most places today, however, the individual who meets with the disapproval of his own group can, as it were, lose himself in the crowd and ultimately find some other group with which he can become associated. This is not possible in the Philippines. With all its manifold diversities the American Colony, scattered all through the Islands though its members are, functions as a unit in all those matters which pertain to its relations with the native population. An American who had fallen from grace in this regard in one locality would be equally unfortunate wherever he might go in the Islands. Who he was and what had happened would be known. Such news travels. Soon after my arrival in the Islands, I remember asking one of the old-timers if the Filipinos were bad gossips. " No," he said with a sad shake of his head, " that is one thing they are good at." The same thing might have been said with equal truth of the American group. During the vacation months, April and May, Baguio becomes the clearing house for the gossip of the Islands in very much the same way that Kipling has shown Simla to do for that of India. Any gossip that has not already been disseminated in other ways is exchanged at Baguio and circulated from there when the season closes and people return to their stations. Gossip thus becomes a means by which the group imposes its standards and achieves unity of behavior throughout a wide area.[15]

The code which governs the nature of the social relations with the Filipinos is difficult to define from without but easily sensed from within. There is no stigma attached to eating with Filipinos as there is to eating with the Negro, nor to attending social functions with Filipinos of the higher classes socially. The two races may even dance together on these occasions without inciting criticism. In fact, the more formal the entertainment is the more nearly do the two races meet upon a plane of equality. It is in the intimate affairs of daily life that the social distance between the two groups becomes most carefully gaged. There is little informal entertaining or visiting back and forth, nor are Filipinos ever invited to the Army and Navy Club in Manila even for formal occasions. For an American to associate more freely and more intimately with the Filipinos than the group as a whole has decreed means criticism and disapproval, and, if persisted in, social ostracism. The line is drawn less stringently for men than it is for women, but it is drawn nevertheless. An American man who has married a Filipino woman is, in most cases, no longer recognized socially by his own group, at least by the women, and his children by the marriage are also regarded with disfavor. Notwith-

[15] Malinowski in *Crime and Custom in Savage Society* (New York, 1926), pp. 101 *et seq.* describes an interesting instance of an extreme form of ostracism, exile, among the Trobriand Islanders. The use of ostracism in the early history of civilization is familiar knowledge.

standing this attitude some mixed marriages do occur, but
for the most part the amalgamation which is taking place
between the two races goes on in an illegitimate way. The
American Guardian Association, which was organized a few
years ago for the protection of neglected *mestizo* children
whose American fathers had deserted them, discovered some
eighteen thousand of these unfortunate young persons in the
Islands.

The solidarity of a group which assumes superiority has
of necessity to be maintained at a cost to its own number if
for some reason it feels compelled to drop any of its members. It cannot continue to hold the position that has been
taken and at the same time recruit new members from those
groups which are regarded as inferior, nor can it tolerate
actions on the part of its members which detract from its
prestige in the eyes of these other groups. The American
Colony in the Philippines and other foreign colonies of this
type are thus faced by the double problem of keeping their
numbers as intact as possible and of preventing all digres-
sions from their code of behavior which might affect the
prestige of the group as a whole. Thence originates the ex-
ceptionally strong degree of social pressure which is wielded
by such groups in those matters which are of concern for the
preservation of their integrity. In most other respects the
attitudes of the foreign colony are inclined to be more
lenient than intolerant.

Unlike the immigrant community, the foreign colony is
not disturbed by a conflict between parents and children
growing out of the contact with an alien group; for, no
matter how democratic by nature little children may be, they
develop into little autocrats with surprising ease when
placed in an environment that is congenial to the assumption
of authority and superiority. They follow the lead given
by their parents in this regard and there is little or no tend-

ency to deviate from it in favor of adopting the customs of the supposedly inferior native group.

Conflicts of other kinds do exist, however, within the foreign colony. Bitter disagreements and jealousies arise and now and again it happens that the half dozen or so Americans in an isolated station who should take comfort in each other's company are not on speaking terms. Nevertheless, such discord, serious as it is, would not keep them from presenting a united front should an issue occur affecting the relations between Americans and Filipinos. Their common nationality is a bond that carries with it the obligation to stand by each other, if there should be need, irrespective of personal animosities. Even the social outcast who has " gone native " in the most extreme sense of the term and who has lost the respect not only of his own group but also of the Filipinos would be helped.

In the process of time the foreign colony becomes a rather highly selected community for one of its size. Those individuals who do not fit in, as a general rule, do not remain for long. They are made aware of the fact that there are " boats going back " and that if they are not satisfied with the existing order of things, why everyone would be happier if they left. The circumstances under which the new arrivals have come are frequently such that, if they find the life is unsuited to them, it is possible for them to return to the mother country within two or three years or even sooner in some cases. In this way the dissatisfied element in the colony is seldom a permanent one, a fact which is responsible for the comparative stability of the organization of the foreign community. The newcomer who objects to things as they are seldom finds it worth his while to attempt a reform. The line of least resistance is to acquiesce, make the best of matters for the time being, and leave as-soon as it becomes convenient to do so. Thus those who are out of sympathy with the attitudes of the colony do not as a rule create friction. Often, too, like the congregation which "came to scoff and remained to pray," those who were the most disgruntled at first become the most ardent supporters of the status quo in the end. The cloak of superiority is easily donned, albeit it is sometimes ill-worn.

The foreign colony despite its conservatism in certain particulars does not suffer from stagnation as some types of isolated communities do. A portion of its membership is constantly changing and new persons come to take the place of those going home and bring new ideas with them. The older inhabitants determine which of these ideas shall flourish, rejecting those which might interfere with their vested interests, but welcoming others. A stranger of the same nationality, or even race, automatically belongs to the colony by virtue of this fact. His presence can not be ignored since his behavior may become a matter of concern to all. He is therefore the object of attention and scrutiny. A great deal may depend upon the kind of person that he turns out to be. In the isolated provincial stations the happiness and peace of mind of the little community for the ensuing year is at stake. If he seems to be the right sort, he is assured of a cordial welcome, of assistance, and of well-meant advice. On the other hand even if he appears to be a misfit, he must still be given hospitality for so long as he is a stranger; but, recalling my own attitude in a case of this kind, I must confess that there have been times when it was none too graciously extended. However, no matter how unprepossessing the stranger might appear the extreme penalty of social ostracism could only come to him after he had been in the colony long enough to become acquainted with its customs and then had broken with its traditions and "gone native."

The problems of the English Colony in India as these

affect the stranger are similar to those of the Philippines but proportionally increased in magnitude with the greater numbers involved and the greater financial and political difficulties which have to be met. The basic problem is that of maintaining the unity and prestige of the English group, the dignity of the Empire. Even before I landed in Calcutta, this had been impressed upon me by the English people whom I had met on the steamer. Although I was an American tourist whose vagaries much must be forgiven, there were certain things which were required of me as an English-speaking woman. For one thing I must always dress for dinner in the evening. For another, I must have my own personal man servant; not only must I employ him while I was at the hotel in Calcutta but when I traveled across India I must take him with me also and then pay his fare back to Calcutta from Bombay. I saw my slender travel budget cut into by this unexpected, and it seemed to me wholly unnecessary expense, and I protested that I was accustomed to waiting upon myself and to traveling alone; but this was not the point. There was no question about my being able to manage these things for myself. It was simply that it would be beneath the dignity of a white woman to do so. In the end I succumbed. I was not free to do otherwise since I was made to feel that my behavior affected others than myself, a subtle form of group pressure that it is difficult to withstand.

Of India before the southwest monsoon breaks in June some one has said that it is " hot as hell and twice as nasty " and it certainly seemed so the night that I spent at Benares. The thermometer stood at 123 degrees and in the dining room the desultory motion of the old-fashioned punkas, which had not yet been replaced by electric fans, did but little to relieve the oppressiveness of the close, humid air. And there was no ice for the water. But, notwithstanding these things, the three Englishmen present were faultlessly, if uncomfortably, dressed in formal black evening attire, their stiff white collars bravely upholding the dignity of the British Empire at first, but wilting perceptibly under this burden as the hot moments dragged by. They were nice young men, but it was not difficult to detect that they did not come from those classes in England which can afford the luxury of dressing for dinner in the evening. Their doing so in Benares was a demand put upon them as members of a group which must command respect at all times, and costs. There were no English women present, they had all gone to the hills to escape the heat; but besides myself there was another little group of Americans, one of whom had dared to make himself comfortable in a soft shirt and khaki shorts. Nor did he seem in the least concerned about any possible loss to his own prestige or to that of the English-speaking peoples because of his unconventional dinner garments. Perhaps he did not need to be: he was the well-known son of a famous president of the United States.

The custom of dressing for dinner under all circumstances and of the observance of certain formalities serves, moreover, another purpose besides that of creating an atmosphere of social dignity and distance. It also proves effective in keeping up the morale of persons living under the disheartening conditions of some of the lonelier stations where to yield to the temptation to relax in a few things might easily lead to carelessness in others and eventually to complete demoralization. Thus, the strict adherence to certain forms of behavior becomes an obligation which the individual owes not only to his group but more intimately to himself as a person. To feel constrained in this way creates a degree of tension which may account in part for the tendency " to fly to pieces " at seemingly trivial provocations which is so characteristic of individuals belonging to foreign colonies of this type. The standards which they must live up to are in a sense artificial and imposed, and their behavior cannot be altogether natural under these circumstances. Relatively speaking, the average member of the foreign colony occupies a more prominent place in the life of the community than he would have filled in most communities in his home land had he remained there. In the narrow environment of the foreign colony, position and prerogatives tend to become matters of undue concern, giving rise at times to much envy and acrimony. Yet, with all its affectations, its bickering, its gossip, and its loneliness, life in the foreign colony possesses a certain fascination. Its monotony is relieved by its potentiality, the dynamic quality that is inherent in tense situations; although nothing has happened, something may. Excitement and a heightened interest are manifested in the relationships within the foreign colony and in the manner in which these are extended to the stranger.

The foreign colonies of the third type, consisting of persons residing abroad in territory which is not under the jurisdiction of their mother country, present a graduated series. In those instances where the civilization and culture of the foreign country closely resemble those of the native land from which these persons have come they tend to mingle with its citizens rather than to form small communities by themselves. The sense of belonging together as opposed to the natives of the country is a latent rather than an active factor in their lives except as this may be aroused by some circumstance which endangers the prestige or safety of the group, or of one of its members, in such a way that this might react to the detriment of the others. Crises in which the mother country is involved also tend to arouse a group spirit as do certain gala occasions. The pride and rejoicing which followed Colonel Lindbergh's arrival at Le Bourget established for the moment a bond of fellowship among the

Americans in Paris as members of a group having the same nationality.

In instances, however, in which the background of the alien residents in a country differs decidedly from that of the native people there is a strong tendency for the former to foregather in little communities of their own nationality and to live a more or less separate existence from that of the people by whom they are surrounded. This same propensity to settle together was noted in the immigrant situation, but with this difference: as immigrants become acquainted with the customs of the new country and are economically able to do so they usually seek to escape from the close confines of their own nationality groups and to merge with the community at large. The members of the foreign colony, on the other hand, do not do this. The social distance which separates them from their neighbors does not lessen perceptibly with the passing of time. Regarding themselves as superior, they direct their efforts toward strengthening the barriers rather than toward breaking them down. If these are to be eventually demolished, the initial pressure must come from without, as, indeed, it is doing in Turkey and in China, two countries in which characteristic colonies of this third type have flourished. The rights of extraterritoriality formerly granted to members of various foreign colonies in Turkey have been withdrawn under the present Turkish regime and three American women were recently tried in the Turkish courts and convicted of the offense of breaking the law regulating the teaching of religion in the schools. The sentence imposed was an inconsequential fine, but the school, which was under the auspices of an American mission, was closed. Both deliberately and unconsciously the strong nationalistic spirit that is manifest in Turkey today is exerting pressure against the unassimilated elements within its population. Although recognizing the right of persons to

differ in their customs and beliefs the Turks are sensitive
and insistent with regard to their own right to be treated
with dignity and equality and are eager to be accorded the
little courtesies of genuine friendship.

Owing to the changes that are taking place in the social
organization of the Turks at the present time, the status of
the foreign colonies is also a changing one since the position
which these communities occupy is definitely related to the
nature of the social media in which they occur. The situation is one which requires tactfulness, sympathy, and forbearance in order that the necessary readjustments may be
made and a more stable condition of mutual confidence and
good will reached. Suspicion must be alleviated. For this
reason the members of the foreign colonies in Turkey are
inclined to regard strangers of the same nationality as themselves with a certain degree of anxiety. There is the possibility that the newcomer may not appreciate the circumstances and that some unwise act of his may precipitate their
nationality group as a whole into difficulties.

The position of the foreign colonies in China, where the
differences are not only cultural but also racial, is more
sharply delineated than is the case in Turkey. The foreign
quarters are localized in particular sections of different cities
which have been conceded to the various nationality groups
through purchase or other agreement. Within its own con-
cession each of the foreign colonies is a law unto itself, exer-
cising the right of extraterritoriality and maintaining a rigid
aloofness toward the native people. This is true even for
those groups of foreigners whose purpose in China is phil-
anthropic rather than economic and who are primarily interested in the religious and educational welfare of the Chinese.
Whether or not these groups could do differently under the
existing circumstances is another matter. The problems
faced by the foreign colony are far from simple. However

much one may deplore the manner in which colonies of both the second and third types are oriented with respect to the native peoples by whom they are surrounded, it must be recognized that it would be difficult indeed for such communities to organize along other lines. Where radical differences exist between the cultural backgrounds of peoples it is easier to maintain ordered relations if a degree of social distance is observed whether the attitudes of superiority which give rise to this can be justified or not. A finer courtesy and a greater appreciation for the feelings and rights of others might reasonably well be inculcated, but an entire reorganization of the system of values which determines the forms of relationship that unite certain persons into groups as opposed to others would be necessary before the present situation in China could be greatly altered. Such changes are a slow growth which would have to be rooted in the mother country before they could bear fruit in the foreign colony.

The barriers which the foreign colony erects about itself hold its members together in spite of differences which under other circumstances would separate them into smaller groups along the lines of their more immediate interests. The bond of a common nationality become an active factor in the situation and one of first importance. A stranger of the same nationality is perforce a member of the foreign colony as was the case in the Philippines and in India. The colony is therefore interested in him and he is closely scrutinized. Position and prestige are matters of moment, and there is a good deal of "putting on face" as the Chinese express it, which contributes a certain tenseness.

CHAPTER VII

ISOLATED COMMUNITIES

I. PIONEER OR FRONTIER SETTLEMENTS

PIONEER or frontier settlements, which include those foreign colonies that have been established in thinly settled regions, belong to the early stages in the development of a new territory. A few generations, or at times even a single generation, may witness their transformation. Their status is therefore a changing one and the problems which are characteristic of the first period of growth disappear or take on new aspects as the population increases and as better facilities for transportation and communication incorporate these new settlements within the life of the older parent communities from which they have·sprung, or so accentuate conflicting interests between them that revolt follows and a new state is established.

In America the westward moving zone of pioneer settlements which has played so prominent a part in its history has come to be definitely associated with the region "lying at the hither edge of free land " [1] and known as " the frontier ". This meaning differs widely from the European concept. Although in both instances the frontier signifies a boundary or marginal area of separation, in America it is practically unsettled, undeveloped territory that lies beyond the frontier, whereas in Europe the frontier separates two neighboring countries both of which may be densely populated. Obvi-

[1] Turner, F. J., *The Frontier in American History* (New York, 1920), p. 3.

ously the problems associated with these two types of frontiers will be dissimilar. Those peculiar to the European frontier grow out of a condition in which people living in close proximity to one another are separated by the fact that they belong to different national units. The relationships that would naturally be formed by people living as neighbors are circumscribed by the fact that those on one side of the boundary have certain loyalties, traditions, and customs as opposed to those of the persons just across the line from them. The geographical boundary or frontier as politically determined is thus an outward manifestation of a separation between people on the basis of certain differences in their interests. It is not the source of these differences, but is instead a consequence of them, and it may be changed as such interests change. Nor, unfortunately, does it always need to coincide with them. Through the fortunes of war political boundaries are sometimes drawn in such a way as to separate people from their former mother country, to which they are deeply attached by ties of sentiment. Many vexed problems are created by this situation and various frontier zones have tended to be storm centers throughout long periods of history.

The so-called geographic or natural frontiers of European countries are thus, De Greef points out, " in reality social frontiers, ever varying according to the conditions of internal or external equilibrium of each society. They are not the *cause* of the group's adopting them as limits, but the *effect* of the structure of the group in its relation with the shifting social environment." [2] A frontier of this nature has a two-fold function as De Greef goes on to show. " It separates and at the same time it relates the society within its bounds. The first function is always more conspicuous and

[2] De Greef, Guillaume, *La Structure Générale des Sociétés* (Paris, 1908), Tome ii, p. 39.

was actually paramount at first; but it is the second that is really more significant." [3]

Dr. Douglas, in summarizing De Greef's characterization of European frontiers, says:

1. Frontiers are never primarily geographic. They are social and equilibrative—the point where the sum total of the internal forces of a society meet in balance with the sum total of the forces of the neighboring societies and nature.

2. The function of the frontier is always relational as well as separative, the point usually of the society's intensest life. Even in its most primitive form, the frontier absorbs as well as repels much of the life of the neighboring groups. It is the greatest single causal agency for internal differentiation.[4]

The problems of the European frontier are thus problems of the contact of different national groups, of nationalism as opposed to internationalism.[5] The pioneer settlement of the American frontier, on the other hand, is not faced by questions arising from international contacts. Its specific problems emanate from other sources and are different in kind. Primarily, they are a consequence of the sudden transition of individuals from the complex life of a civilized community into the simplicity of the primitive isolated conditions of the wilderness. The pioneer community is composed of persons who although they are imbued with the past are yet in many respects beginning life over again under new conditions. As individuals and as groups they have separated themselves from former affiliations and have become dependent upon their own resources. Confronted by the

[3] *Ibid.*, Tome iii, p. 273.

[4] Douglas, Dorothy Wolff, *Guillaume De Greef* (New York, 1925), p. 309.

[5] For an appraisal of the significance of De Greef's theories of frontiers see Prof. A. A. Tenney's article " Some Recent Advances in Sociology ", the *Political Science Quarterly*, 1910, pp. 502-8.

exigencies of a strange environment they are often forced to take the initiative in situations for which there are no guiding traditional precedents. Old patterns of behavior are necessarily transformed and new ones are evolved. This may mean greater possibilities for a higher form of individual freedom, for tolerance and for self-reliance, or it may mean lawlessness and tyranny. The challenge of the wilderness, its hardships and its rewards, its equality of opportunity, does not necessarily call forth uniformity of behavior. In the following excerpts from *The Winning of the West*, Theodore Roosevelt comments upon this fact.

The frontier, in spite of the outward uniformity of means and manners, is preeminently the place of sharp contrasts. The two extremes of society, the strongest, the best, the most adventurous, the weakest, most shiftless, and vicious, are those which seem naturally to drift to the border. . . .

All qualities, good and bad, are intensified and accentuated in the life of the wilderness. The man who in civilization is merely sullen and bad-tempered becomes a murderous, treacherous ruffian when transplanted to the wilds; while, on the other hand, his cheery, quiet neighbor develops into a hero, ready uncomplainingly to lay down his life for his friend. One who in an eastern city is merely a backbiter and slanderer, in the western woods lies in wait for his foe with a rifle; sharp practice in the east becomes highway robbery in the west; but at the same time negative good nature becomes active self-sacrifice, and a general belief in virtue is translated into prompt and determined war upon vice.[6]

Other writers have also noted this same tendency of pioneer life to intensify certain qualities of human nature. The categories are fewer and less finely graduated than those of older more densely populated districts, but they are at the same time more outstanding. Paxson writes:

[6] Roosevelt, Theodore, *The Winning of the West* (New York, 1905), vol. i, pp. 166-167.

Individuals as well as problems have emerged from the line of the frontier as it has advanced across a continent. In the conflict with the wilderness, birth, education, wealth, and social standing have counted for little in comparison with strength, vigor and aggressive courage. The life there has always been hard, killing off the weaklings or driving them back to the settlements, and leaving as a result a picked population not noteworthy for its culture or its refinements, but eminent in qualities of positive force for good or bad. The bad man has been quite as typical of the frontier as the hero, but both have possessed its dominant virtues of self-confidence, vigor, and initiative. Thus it has been that the men of the frontiers have exerted an influence upon national affairs far out of proportion to their strength in numbers.[7]

Schlesinger makes a similar comment.

The hardships and rewards of pioneer life served to accentuate these traits [energy, initiative, and ambition]. The settlers of the frontier states became self-reliant to the point of lawlessness. Their excessive pride was hardly to be distinguished from plain boasting; their unconventionality too often took the form of crudeness and coarseness. As some one has aptly said, they were "men with the bark on." Foreign visitors with their fastidious European background, like Charles Dickens and Mrs. Frances M. Trollope, saw only the unpleasant aspects of frontier existence—the rowdyism, debauchery, and lack of culture—and failed to perceive that these qualities were merely externals masking the essential soundness and strength of Western character.[8]

Charles and Mary Beard in comparing the colonizing movement in New England and California also call atten-

---

[7] Paxson, F. L., *The Last American Frontier* (New York, 1910), pp. 2-3.

[8] Schlesinger, A. M., *Political and Social History of the United States, 1829-1925* (New York, 1930), p. 4.

tion to the differences in the types of immigrants who are attracted to the frontier and to the changing character of the life of the pioneer community.

But how different the two migrations. It was the lure of a quick and easy fortune that swept most of the gold-rush immigrants into California — reckless adventurers fond of hard drinking, gambling and fighting, offering a curious contrast to the godly men who sought a humble livelihood by hard work under the leadership of Winthrop and Carver. Not many took families along. Indeed, relatively few women went out in the first days of roaring luck and some of those who did were, to say the least, not Puritans either. In the names of the mining towns were reflected the tastes of the occupants; in place of the Providences, Goshens, Salems, and Bethels of New England, there arose Slumgullions, Youbets, and Jackass-Gulches. When the miner burst into song, he chose " Highland Mary ", camp doggerel, or a drinking chant, rather than the Psalms of David. Even some " good citizens " were not ashamed to walk down main street of Poverty Flat with women who would have had to wear the Scarlet Letter in queer old Salem.

For years the exuberance and tempestuous life of the mining camps affected the character of the whole territory, not excepting the districts in the south devoted to cattle raising, grain fields, and vineyards. Even the distant and relatively peaceful city of Los Angeles could report in 1854 a murder a day on the average. " The Queen of the Cow Counties," wrote a vivacious editor of that town, " bangs all creation in her productions. Whether it be shocking murders, or big beets, jail demolishers, expert horse thieves, lynch justices, fat beeves, swimming horses, expounders of new religions, tall corn, mammoth potatoes, ponderous cabbages, defunct Indians, secret societies, bright skies, mammoth pumpkins, Shanghai chickens, grizzlies, coyotes, dogs, smart men, office seekers, coal holers, scrip, or fights. . . . She stands out in bold relief challenging competition.

If such was the state of that sedate settlement so far from gold regions, what must have been San Francisco, where a fever for speculation raged, as millions from mines and gulches poured in there for export? Quickly overcoming the slump that followed the first exodus to the mines, real estate dealers, hotel keepers, tapsters, and outfitters waxed fat at their trades. Riotous living racked the town and shooting frays made life precarious.

In the tumult, matters went from bad to worse until the more sober elements were driven to form extra-legal associations, known as Vigilance Committees, rough and ready agencies which dealt out summary justice to the most incorrigible and brazen disturbers of the public peace, hanging murderers, and banishing ballot-box stuffers. Under the press of business, mistakes were sometimes made but, on the whole, the work of the Committees was salutary — at least until the organized police force was strong enough and decent enough to function in a normal fashion.[9]

Turner likewise points out essential differences in pioneer communities due to the place element and the time element.

It is evident that the farming frontier of the Mississippi Valley presents different conditions from the mining frontier of the Rocky Mountains [10]. . . . French colonization was dominated by a trading frontier; English colonization by its farming frontier [11]. . . . In general, the Northern stream of migration was communal, and the Southern individual [12]. . . . Whereas the type of hero in the Southwest was militant, in the Northwest he was industrial.[13]

Yet, in spite of numerous differences in the character of the pioneers themselves and in the types of communities

---

[9] Beard, Charles A. and Mary R., *The Rise of American Civilization* (One Volume Edition, New York, 1930), pp. 612-14.

[10] Turner, *op. cit.*, p. 10.   [11] *Ibid.*, p. 13.

[12] *Ibid.*, p. 125.   [13] *Ibid.*, p. 259.

which they formed, certain common qualities tended to emerge in the life of the frontier. Schlesinger designates the three outstanding traits of the West in 1829 as " the individualism of the people, their belief in the capacity of the common man, and their strong nationalism." [14] Turner agrees in this.

But the most important effect of the frontier has been the promotion of democracy here and in Europe. As has been indicated the frontier is productive of individualism. Complex society is precipitated by the wilderness into a kind of primitive organization based on the family. The tendency is anti-social. It produces antipathy to control, and particularly to any direct control. The tax-gatherer is viewed as a representative of oppression.[15]

In brief then those characteristics common to pioneer communities which would seem to have a more or less direct bearing upon the behavior that is manifested toward strangers are a strong individualistic tendency combined with or opposed to a strong social one, a desire, in other words, to secure one's own rights and at the same time to grant equal rights to others. If properly adjusted to one another, these tendencies are not incompatible, but in the stress and change-fulness of frontier life they often failed to harmonize. The frontiersmen joined hospitality to strangers with a suspicion of them. They were suspicious that the stranger might in some way infringe upon their rights, or that his or her presence might in some way prove to be a disturbing factor in the new community. Roger Williams and Ann Hutchinson were banished from the " land of the last word and the final good " no less than were certain citizens from Poker Flat in the early days of California. But there also existed a certain

[14] Schlesinger, *op. cit.*, p. 4.
[15] Turner, *op. cit.*, p. 30.

obligation to treat the stranger hospitably since it was recognized that in the wilderness he was altogether dependent upon such good will. Moreover, if the stranger proved an agreeable person, his visit was a welcome break in the monotony of the social life of the frontier and he was more than welcome. Roosevelt quotes a letter written by Colonel Thomas Hart of Lexington in 1795 which illustrates this.

I can say with truth that the society of this place is equal, if not superior, to any that can be found in any inland town in the United States, for there is not a day that passes over our heads but I can have a half dozen strange gentlemen to dine with us, and they are from all parts of the union.[16]

The two contrasting attitudes of distrust and cordiality with which the stranger is regarded on the frontier are a familiar part of my own experience. My childhood was spent on a cattle ranch in Wyoming and I can recall with vividness the excitement and pleasure of having a stranger as a guest for the night or even longer, provided of course that we felt assured of his intentions and that he was good company. There were other times, however, when strangers stopped at the ranch to whom hospitality could not well be refused, for the nearest town was a day's journey away, but to whom it was grudgingly given since they were viewed with distrust as possible claim-jumpers, cattle thieves, or outlaws of one sort or another.

Later as a young woman when traveling in isolated sections of the Western States and of Alaska I again encountered the same attitudes, but this time expressed toward myself as the stranger. For the most part, hospitality and courtesy were extended without hesitation and without question, but now and again I have met suspicion. A young woman friend and I were once refused accommodations

[16] Roosevelt, *op. cit.*, vol. vi, p. 31.

by the proprietress of the hotel in Medicine Bow, Wyoming, the same Medicine Bow of Owen Wister's *The Virginian,* on the grounds that she kept a respectable house! However, the town of Medicine Bow had witnessed our discomfiture and, strangers though we were, champions of our cause were not lacking. We were offered the hospitality of a private home during our stay and my friend, a journalist, was given willing assistance in collecting the material that she wished for a western article. The simplicity of pioneer life and the sparsity of the population necessarily limits the number of categories into which the stranger, particularly if a woman, can be placed, and mistakes sometimes follow. The frontiersman is inclined to be direct and straight-forward himself and to look for these qualities in others. He is not particularly concerned with the stranger's antecedents or with his past; he is, however, interested in his present purpose and the person who attempts to conceal this is liable to find himself himself an object of suspicion. I once attempted the role of the mysterious stranger myself, but was glad in the end to abandon it and to assume once more the commonplace character of a country school teacher. I was going to a place in Alaska called Ouzinkie to relieve a teacher who wished to return to the States. This was in December, a time of the year when there was very little travel northward on the Alaskan boats, and it happened that I was the only woman passenger among a number of men. I was still very young and unsophisticated and it occurred to me that I should have more fun on the trip, which took about ten days, if I concealed the fact that I was a teacher. I had observed that other young professional women were less subject to criticism and had more freedom generally than teachers, who were expected not only to instruct their young charges but also to be their moral guardians. Therefore, I jokingly turned aside the questions that were asked about my reasons for making the trip at that uncomfortable season. Going to Alaska was too much of an adventure and I was having too good a time to notice the persistence with which certain men pursued this point or to be annoyed by the unaccountably hostile attitude that the stewardess, a prim, respectable widow, had assumed toward me. At Skagway another woman passenger came on board. She was young, attractive, and well dressed, and I welcomed her. A little later the captain, who had been particularly kind to me, saw us together and he called to me to join him without inviting the other woman. This seemed odd, but I went. Once out of hearing the captain explained to me who the woman was and why I must not be seen talking to her. This was Alaska, and I was young and alone. He wished to protect me from embarrassment. There were men on board who might misunderstand. I felt sick. Certain things took on a new meaning and I made haste to take refuge in my own profession, which, prosaic though it might be, was always a guarantee of safe conduct along the frontier.

Roosevelt with his customary insight has noted another trait which crops up from time to time among frontier people, particularly among the young people who have grown up there without the cultural advantages of the older settlements.

The regular army officer and the frontiersman are trained in fashions so diametrically opposite that, though the two men be brothers they must yet necessarily in all thoughts and instincts and ways of looking at life, be as alien as if they belonged to two different races of mankind. The borderer, rude, suspicious, and impatient of discipline looks with distrust and with a mixture of sneering envy and of hostility upon the officer; while the latter, with his rigid training and his fixed ideals, feels little sympathy for the other's good points, and is contemptuously aware of his numerous failings.[17]

[17] Roosevelt, *op. cit.*, vol. vi, p. 32.

It is the mixture of envy and hostility mentioned above which is significant. In spite of the frontiersman's self-sufficiency, his pride, and his certitude that every man is as good as every other man, which makes him scorn the little refinements of life, he is none the less envious of them. He may be contemptuous of the stranger whose manners seem fastidious and over nice, and yet, if he can afford to do so, he sends his own children away to school that they may acquire these same ways of doing things. As time passes the character of frontier life is modified in this way as well as by the influx of new settlers who come in, and by the increasing ease with which necessities and comforts can be obtained. Change comes to be associated with pioneer life. The atmosphere is one of hopefulness and expectancy. The frontiersman looks ahead and takes chances; he is building for the future and whether mistaken or not, the frontier has been, and is permanently a region of ideals.[18]

2. RETARDED DISTRICTS

" In sociology ", according to Professors Park and Burgess, " the essential characteristic of isolation is found in exclusion from communication." [19] Among the various factors contributing to such isolation by preventing normal social intercourse and the interchange of ideas, an inaccessible geographic location is perhaps the most familiar, although by no means the only one. Certain social differences, such as those of caste or class, or of racial or religious divergencies, may also act as barriers which exclude some elements of the population from enjoying full participation in the life of the community. Such groups develop many of the same characteristics that are to be found among peoples who have

[18] Turner, *op. cit.*, p. 214.

[19] Park and Burgess, *An Introduction to the Science of Sociology* (Chicago, 1921), p. 228.

been deprived by an unfavorable geographic environment of contacts with other groups and of the stimulation of competition and of sharing in progressive new movements. An isolated environment, whether due to social or to geographic causes, is rarely in itself a creative one; it tends rather to intensify already existing qualities. The fact that prophets and philosophers have gone into the wilderness for meditation does not mitigate against this; the ideas which they sought to contemplate in the uninterrupted solitude of the desert were born amid the busy life of the thronged market place. Quiet was needed for their fruition, but their conception could have taken place only in an environment in which interstimulation was possible.

Isolation tends to check or to retard the normal development of the individual or of the group. Lacking the leavening influence of new ideas from without, such isolated persons or groups tend to become individualistic and their own unique peculiarities are emphasized. Isolated communities of long standing are the strongholds of conservatism, clinging tenaciously to the old customs, beliefs, and mores to which they have become habituated through an extended association. They differ in this regard from pioneer settlements, which are also isolated from other communities, but which have only recently become so. The behavior patterns of the frontier settlement are flexible, whereas those of the older isolated communities have become rigid and static. This distinction is an important one in understanding the reactions of the two types of people. The deeply ingrained customs of the older communities resist change and yield reluctantly to pressure from without when presented, while on the frontier new developments are anticipated, and in many instances, welcomed. The old-time frontiersman who, to use a western expression, " pulled up stakes " and moved onward each time that the advancing tide of civilization caught up with him acted as an individual. His behavior was not as a rule typical of the pioneer community as a whole. Where changes affected the vested interests of the frontier settlement, these were resented naturally enough, but on the whole the attitude toward the outside world was an open one.

Long isolation tends to produce a homogeneous people while the frontier attracts a highly heterogeneous population. Even in those instances in which the first settlers of a region were all members of a well-organized group of kindred spirits, as were the Pilgrims of Plymouth and the Mormons of Salt Lake City, but a short time had elapsed before outsiders of different views were seeking to penetrate these communities. When, however, pioneer communities have somehow become lost from the main stream of advancing civilization in an inaccessible locality and forgotten as the southern mountaineers and some of the western miners and ranchers have been, the passing of a few generations may witness their transformation from a forward-looking people to a retarded one which holds to its former ways and is fearful of all outside intervention. The behavior patterns of the isolated community become stereotyped in the absence of new and stimulating contacts, whether the obstructing barriers are the result of the geographic location or of less tangible social differences.

The southern mountaineers are a well-known instance of an isolated people certain of whose outstanding peculiarities may quite clearly be traced to the influence of their exceedingly limited social environment. Their history and characteristics before settling in this lonely, inaccessible region are known, and there are also other groups who have come from the same original stock but who have lived in more stimulating places that may serve in a sense as control groups whose behavior patterns may be compared with those of the mountain folk. Within the narrow confines of the isolated neighborhood a few types of relationships suffice as they do among primitive peoples. Those of the family are of paramount importance and among the members of a kin group the ties are generally close. Even though disagreeing among themselves, blood kin are in honor bound to stand together and to avenge one another. Between families in the neighborhood who are not related quarrels are frequent and smoldering suspicions and hatreds break into open warfare at the slightest pretext. The least affront, real or fancied, renews an old feud. Toward strangers from beyond, " lowlanders ", " furriners ", suspicion and contempt are commingled with fear, the fear that resists that which it does not understand and that which threatens to destroy the existing order.

In a group of stories of the southern mountains Fiswoode Tarleton has vividly portrayed the nature of the three principal types of relationships of the isolated community which were just mentioned.[20] The incidents which he describes reveal a sympathetic insight into the life of the mountain folk which gives perhaps a truer picture of the reality than would a purely behavioristic, objective account of actual observed instances of these relationships.

The following passage gives an idea of the extremely restricted environment of many of the hill folks.

Maw Collet's never seen steam-cars and locomotives. Sometimes she imagines them as small cabins on wheels, sometimes as large, long wagons with seats and a smoking stove in front, her boy, Ed, feeding the stove with wood.

She knows that railroad trains bring Government men to Anathoth and that they drive or ride over to Porky and Misery to snoop on hill folks. It's only thirteen miles from Porky to

[20] *Bloody Ground, A Cycle of the Southern Hills* (New York, 1929).

Anathoth but it might as well be a hundred. It's outside the district, her clan's district. Bounded by Leeston seven miles away on the west. By Misery Mountain four miles east. Cone Mountain five miles south and Little Porky Ridge three miles to the north. Within these bounds Porky folks stay mostly. May be walls beyond. Strange people. Strange animals. Maw Collet's mind can't come to grips with anything beyond.[21]

Nevertheless, in spite of the limitations of her meager background, Maw Collett is not insensible to the appeal of new things if these gratify the yearning of her starved nature for pretty things. She, and neighbor women like her, are won over to the cause of a proposed automobile road along the top of Porky Ridge by an advertising booklet of colored pictures of automobiles with smartly dressed lowlanders in them. And this, even though the new road means invasion, as her kinsman, old man Bodie, tells her.

Means a highway across Porky cluttered with automobiles, "chug-wagons" full of strangers invading the district. Strangers stopping to ask questions at mountain cabins. Federal men rolling in regularly. Folks on mules or horses or afoot won't dare travel the road. Hill hounds lying in the middle of the road will be run over. Game will be frightened away to remote districts. Porky folks won't be able to call their souls their own if the road goes through. . . . "Wal, we-uns air a-goin' tuh stop'em. Time tuh do hit's now. . . . Wal, tha furriners cain't build a road lessen they lay hit out with stakes an' they cain't drive stakes lessen they look through 'at contraption o' thar's. Gee-almighty, thar's somthin' 'bout 'at air contraption 'at's funny. Tha furriners don' know whar that a'goin' lessen they peek through hit. Hit air funny, shore!"[22]

[21] *Ibid.*, p. 99. See Horace Kephart, *Our Southern Highlanders* (New York, 1913), pp. 21-24 for similar instances.

[22] Tarleton, *op. cit.*, pp. 111 *et seq.*

The suspicious and hostile attitude taken toward the presence of strangers by the mountaineers is in part at least accounted for by the fact that until the recent advent of the district nurse and other missionary workers the few strangers who found their way into the remote districts were, in all probability, revenue officers looking for stills. The mountaineers regarded the making of liquor as one of their legitimate rights and not without more justification than is sometimes realized. In the absence of roads and markets there has been no possibility in the past for these people to dispose of their corn crop. Liquor could, however, be transported much more easily than corn over the rough mountain trails on mule or horse back and a ready sale for it could be found. Thus to dispossess the mountain moonshiner of his still was to take from him the one source of his monetary income and to deprive him of a part of his scanty livelihood that he had no legitimate means of replacing. There are extenuating circumstances therefore in the case of these lawbreakers which do not exist for the majority of offenders against the Federal regulations with respect to the manufacture and sale of intoxicating liquors.

In the selections which follow Mr. Tarleton has pictured the attitude of the hill men toward the Federal officers.

Men in the hill country feel the fetters of new laws. Federal men on the hunt for liquor can't efface their marks in the hill country; can't disguise their hardness of eyes; can't help strutting; can't be mistaken for drummers or their like. When the three Federal men got out of their spring wagon a few minutes ago the storekeepers and the men wandering into Leeston from the hills closed their mouths tight and forced stupidity on their faces. While the Federal men tied their horses in the sun men all along the street were pulling their hats down farther over their eyes and sitting down on stoops or leaning against the buildings. They stopped where they were and prepared to watch. . . .

" Cain't go now. Cain't go 'til tha Government men pull out. An' hit looks like thar not a-goin'. Funny tuh me hill folks don' look sharper when thar a-makin likker. Allus a-gettin' caught. Porky Ridge men allowin' strangers tuh nab 'em. Huh, Lowlander dudes a-goin through the hills on their own hook, nabbin' yuh Porky men an' showin' up county officers, a-showin' up Sheriff Floyd. Yuh must been a-sleepin'."

Davey Wellcome and the other two prisoners hang their heads. They pull their hats down farther over their eyes. When Davey Wellcome speaks in a minute he doesn't lift his head.

" Hit war luck. Federal men stumbled on tuh us-uns. Federal men war a-tryin' tuh fin' thar way out o' tha gap. Didn't know at first we-uns war a-making likker. Still war not a-smokin'; we war a-fillin' jugs when one o' 'em called from Noah Rock, a-wantin' tuh know tha way out. One o' 'em suspicioned. Hit war luck." [23]

The hill men in no sense feel that they have done wrong in making illicit liquor. The sheepish manner of the prisoners comes from the fact that they, hill men, have permitted themselves to be caught by " lowlander dudes "; but, as Davey Wellcome explains, this " war luck " and not clumsiness on their part.

Among the mountaineers the older, more primitive custom of blood law has not been fully replaced by the modern conception of the administration of justice as an impersonal matter and the duty of the larger community as a whole. A man's kin were in duty bound to avenge the injuries done to him and to protect him from the vengeance of others even if he were the offender. It was a matter of family honor and one that was not debatable.

" Law," says Sol Jett. " Huh. Thar hain't but one law fitten tuh trust. An' yuh reckon Clem's kin air a-goin tuh set

[23] *Ibid.*, pp. 1 *et seq.*

quiet when the Daniels pack o' skunks come hyar. Reckon we-uns seed to hit 'at our own folks'll be a-ready. Blood law. 'At's hit. Law air a-settin' in the blood. Law hain't in co'te-houses.

The sheriff gives a sigh. His face remains passive.

" Yes, blood can be trusted, though the law doesn't sit in it. You don't mean law, anyway. You mean loyalty or something like that. You mean sticking by."

" Wal, stickin' by air the law!" [24]

The sheriff, who here upholds the law, is a young hill man himself, but one who has had the opportunity of going away to school and who combines the sterling qualities of the mountain people with the broader outlook that education and wider contacts have given him. The young people of the backwoods accept new truths readily enough; it is the older generation which is fearful. In the story from which the illustration given below is taken, the children see the reasons that the teacher is giving to show that the earth is round, but the older hill man does not.

Way down in Ted Valentine's soul something begins to seethe. Teacher Bankey is challenging the truth of scripture, breeding lies in the heads of mountain children, hatching sin in the schoolhouse. Seems to Ted that the hills have suddenly become worse that impious, that they are infested by the devil. The lie becomes an image. He sees the lie as a strange wild beast stalking in the ravines and coves, devouring the souls of children.[25]

The poverty of the social life of the isolated community combined with a lack of educational opportunities and new interests and of many of the usual comforts and conveniences of better settled regions tends to distort the individual's sense

[24] *Ibid.*, p. 272.
[25] *Ibid.*, pp. 232-33.

of values about some things. Those that pertain to his own personal rights and freedom appear of undue importance, and he is inclined to be self-centered, egoistic, and non-social. He lacks the imagination to grasp another's point of view where this differs from his own. With little else of interest to divert his attention, the trivial disagreements, petty grudges and jealousies which would be lost sight of in a fuller life are brooded over until they become a source of suspicion and quarrels. Among the southern mountaineers the fear and distrust manifested toward strangers are not due to timidity and cowardice in the usual sense, but to the limited range of their contacts and the unfortunate character of these in many instances. They are capable of acts of heroism and self-sacrifice, and they gladly share the little that is theirs to offer with those strangers of whose good will they have become assured. The absence of many of the customary ties of community life which are found in less isolated regions is brought out by Emma B. Miles in her book, *The Spirit of the Mountains,* from which the following excerpts are taken.

There is no such thing as a community of mountaineers. They are knit together, man to man, as friends, but not as a body of men. A community, be it settlement or metropolis, must revolve on some kind of axis, and must be held together by a host of intermediate ties coming between the family and the State, and these are not to be found in the mountains. A center might be supplied by their common interest in things not of the earth, if the church met together regularly, week after week, as in the towns; but a body that beholds itself, as it were, but once a month—and that always " if no providential hinderance "—cannot exert much influence as a bond.

Our men are almost incapable of concerted action unless they are needed by the Government. The traditions of the Revolution, persisting through generations, have sent them headlong into every war in which the United States becomes concerned. . . . But between blood-relationship and the Federal Government no relations of master and servant, rich and poor, learned and ignorant, employer and employee, are interposed to bind society as a whole. . . . In short, the only classification is founded on character, and the only groups are those arising from ties of kinship.[26]

The social structure of these mountain people in its simplicity is thus similar in some respects to that of the simpler peoples and a number of its characteristics are the same. The blood feud, for instance, is a primitive family or clan custom which has persisted; but so has hospitality within the family group. These are kinship obligations, and when no suspicion attaches to the stranger, hospitality is extended to him in much the same spirit that it is among native peoples. And, Kephart tells us, there are " manners " which one does well to observe as among all peoples. " For example, when you stop at a mountain cabin, if no dogs sound an alarm, do not walk up to the door and knock. You are expected to call out *Hello* until someone comes to inspect you. None but the most intimate neighbors neglect this usage." Vance Randolph has also noted this same custom in the Ozarks.[27]

The mountain man's cabin is his castle, and even though the door stands hospitably open, it is very bad form for a stranger to approach it unheralded. Usually the barking of pot-licker dogs sounds the alarm, otherwise the traveller is expected to stop a little distance away and " holler " until someone comes out to look him over. However unprepossessing, he is almost invariably invited to " light down an' set a spell ", for even the poorest and stingiest of backwoodsmen feels himself bound by the tradition of indiscriminate hospitality.

[26] Miles, Emma B., *The Spirit of the Mountains* (New York, 1905), pp. 71 *et seq.*

[27] Randolph, Vance, *The Ozarks* (New York, 1931), p. 23.

In the land where the path to one's door may be a warpath there is good reason for the custom of announcing one's arrival. Kephart also adds a further convention.

If you are armed, as a hunter, do not fail to remove the cartridges from the gun, in your host's presence, before you set foot on his porch. Then give him the weapon or stand it in a corner or hang it up in plain view. Even our sheriff, when he stopped with us, would lay his revolver on the mantel-shelf and leave it there until he went away. If you think a moment you can see the courtesy of such an act. It proves that the guest puts implicit trust in the honor of his host and in his ability to protect all within his house. There has never been a case in which such trust was violated.[28]

The mountaineers are eager for news and the coming of an unknown stranger will set the whole neighborhood gossiping. Every word and action of his will be discussed for weeks after he has gone. Kephart's description of the excitement which the coming of a stranger occasions is interesting.

Riding up a branch road, you come upon a white-bearded patriarch who halts you with a wave of the hand.
" Stranger—meanin' no harm—*whar* are you gwine? "
You tell him.
" What did you say your name was? "
You had not mentioned it; but you do so now.
" What mought you-uns foller for a living? "
It is wise to humor the old man, and tell him frankly what is your business " up this way-off branch."
Half a mile farther you espy a girl coming toward you. She stops like a startled fawn, wide-eyed with amazement. Then, at a bound, she dodges into a thicket, doubles on her course and runs back as fast as her nimble bare legs can carry her to report that " Somebody's comin'! "

[28] Kephart, *op. cit.*, pp. 194-95.

At the next house, stopping for a drink of water, you chat a few moments. High up the opposite hill is a half-hidden cabin from which keen eyes scrutinize your every move, and a woman cries to her boy: " Run, Kit, down to Mederses, and ax who *is* he!"

As you approach a cross-roads store every idler pricks up instant attention. Your presence is detected from every neighboring cabin and cornfield. Long John quits his plowing, Red John drops his axe. Sick John (" who's allers ailin', to hear *him* tell") pops out of bed, and Lyin' John (whose " mouth ain't no praar-book, if it *does* open and shet"), grabs his hat, with " I jes' got ter know who that feller is." Then all Johns descend their several paths, to congregate at the store and estimate the stranger as though he were so many board-feet of lumber in the tree or so many pounds of beef on the hoof.[29]

The mountaineer knows that he is an American, but his conception of America is vague. Outsiders are " furriners " no matter where they may come from in the United States. One native, when asked by a traveler what he would call a " Dutchman or a Dago ", studied a bit and then replied, " Them's the outlandish." [30] As Miss Miles has said, the two loyalties of the southern mountaineers are to his kin group and to the nation when the call to arms comes. He has not learned to pull with others nor to appreciate the advantages of cooperation; he is secretive, suspicious, and sensitive to criticism. His social life is a retarded one; he is still living in the eighteenth century, but he is facing toward a new era.

[29] *Ibid.*, pp. 101-02.
[30] *Ibid.*, p. 17.

CHAPTER VIII

Country Communities

I. THE RURAL NEIGHBORHOOD

THE difference between the rural neighborhood and the isolated groupings which we have been discussing is largely one of degree since these are all rural in their nature as contrasted with more densely populated areas. The pioneer community has been newly established, however, and its inhabitants are in the process of becoming adjusted to one another; whereas, in the older rural neighborhoods, relationships have become fixed and there is relatively little change. The typical rural neighborhood also differs from retarded regions such as are found in the Appalachian Mountains and in the Ozarks in the wider scope of its relationships, narrow though these often are. Professor Kulp II's definition of the neighborhood as " a series of relationships beyond the kinship group within which the control of personal wishes is most effective" [1] brings this point into relief. The southern highlanders were kinship groups with few, if any, neighborhood institutions and little or no community spirit. Kinship was the sole basis of unity, a condition which has become modified in rural neighborhoods which have been less isolated. Family ties have tended to become somewhat more specialized and more personal in their function and new ties of neighborliness have developed. These bonds are personal in their nature and unorganized. They grow up spontane-

[1] Kulp II, D. H., *Country Life in South China* (New York, 1925), p. 338.

ously over a period of time as a consequence of proximity and of mutual dependence in times of need; and they are consequently less specialized than those of groups which have been organized for a specific purpose. The functions of the relationship of " the good neighbor " are many and diversified. In the more lonely rural neighborhoods this relationship must satisfy all, or practically all, of the social needs of the individuals which are not fulfilled by the relationships of the family group. Its obligations are many and the manner in which these are met determines the character of the neighborhood to a large extent. The general attitude may be a cheery, obliging one or it may be suspicious and hostile, according to the way in which the different families which compose the neighborhood respond to each other and to outsiders. Country neighborhoods differ widely in this regard and there is thus a basis of truth for the two very divergent opinions often expressed concerning the nature of the social relationships of the country neighborhood. One observer's experience may have been in a kindly neighborhood, while another may have fallen in with churlishness and suspicion. Both types exist. Rose Cohen, in writing of her childhood in a lonely Russian neighborhood, gives a glimpse of the kindlier type.

These were pleasant days during winter. But there were others, days that were cold and dark and dreary, when we children had to stay a greater part of the time on top of the oven, and no one came, not even a beggar. But when a beggar did come our joy was boundless.

I remember that grandfather would hasten to meet the poor man, as we called him, at the door with a hearty handshake and a welcoming smile, saying, " Peace be with you, brother. Take off your knapsack and stay over night."

Mother would put on a fresh apron and begin to prepare some extra things for supper. And grandmother, who was blind, and always sat in bed knitting a stocking would stop for a moment at the sound of the stranger's voice to smooth the comforter on her bed. Her pale face, so indifferent a moment before, would light up as if with new life, while we children, fearing, if seen idle, to be rebuked and sent in to a distant corner from where we could neither see nor hear the stranger, would suddenly find a dozen things to do.

On such a night after supper there was something of a holiday spirit in our home. We would light the lamp instead of a candle and place it on the milk jug in the center of the table. Then we all sat around it, grandmother with her knitting, mother with her sewing, all of us listening eagerly to the stories the stranger told. But more surprised even than any of us children about the wonderful things going on in the world was grandfather. He would sit listening with his lips partly open and his eyes large with wonder. Every now and then he would call out, " Ach, brother, I never would have dreamt such things were possible."

At bedtime grandfather would give up his favorite bed, the bench near the oven, to the stranger. Mother would give him the largest and softest of her pillows. And grandmother would give him a clean pair of socks to put on in the morning.

The next day after he was gone we felt as after a pleasant holiday when we had to put on our old clothes and turn in to do every day things.[2]

This description of the artless pleasure derived by this simple household from the unexpected visit of a mendicant stranger is suggestive of the numerous folklore stories in which the poor beggar who is given hospitality proves to be the Christ Child or an angel in disguise whose blessings reward the family that has entertained him. The situation is very unlike that which is revealed in the following quotation from Hamlin Garland's *Main-Travelled Roads,* in which the

[2] Cohen, Rose, *Out of the Shadow* (New York, 1918), pp. 10 *et seq.*

man who has remained on the farm speaks bitterly to his well-dressed, successful brother from the city.

Singular we fellers here are discontented and mulish, ain't it? Singular we don't believe your letters when you write, sayin', " I just about make a live of it "? Singular we think the country's goin' to hell, we fellers, in a two-dollar suit, wadin' around in the mud or sweatin' around in the hay-field, while you fellers lay around in New York and smoke and wear good clothes and toady to millionaires? [3]

The unfortunate condition that is responsible in part at least for the farmer's attitude as here expressed is the fact that, to quote Dr. Wilson, " country life is dominated by labor. No other aspect of modern life is so industrialized as country life. It appears that no one, broadly speaking, has remained in the country except those who stay there for a livelihood. . . . There is no leisure, and no leadership." [4] The social life of the countryman is organized with reference to his manner of gaining a living to a far greater extent than is that of the city-dweller. His social relationships are more inexorably bound up with his economic interests than are those of workers in most other types of industry. As farming and ranching are carried on in America the homesteads are separated from one another, sometimes, as in the far western states, by a distance of several miles. The unity of the farm family group is thus emphasized by its isolation. The farmer's family is a closely knit cooperative unit, and voluntary cooperation on a small scale is an integral part of rural life. The family is the central institution of the rural world, and familism the basic form among all the relationships that in their totality compose rural social organization,

[3] Hamlin Garland, " Up the Coolly " from *Main-Travelled Roads*, p. 93.
[4] Wilson, W. H., " Social Life in the Country ", *Annals of the American Academy of Political and Social Science*, vol., xl, pp. 119 *et seq.*

according to Sorokin and others.[5] These writers also observe that the bonds which unite the rural family are
greater in both number and power than those which unite
the urban family. The relationships of the agricultural
family are more stable and more integrated than those of
the urban family. They are also more organic and spontaneous than contractual in nature.[6] The rural family relationships which have been so strikingly portrayed in
Hamsun's *The Growth of the Soil* and Mrs. Buck's *The Good
Earth* are of this elemental, natural type; they are rooted in
the soil and wither in an urban environment. The numerous parellels in these two narratives are of interest. Diverse
as the cultural patterns of the Norwegians and the Chinese
are in most respects, the rural relationships of these two
peoples revealed in their stark simplicity are shown to have
much in common. The farm family is a cooperative, largely
self-sufficing unity whose social attitudes have been conditioned by the physical environment, as Dr. Williams also
makes clear in his observations of rural life in America.

To return to the two general approaches to life, the physical
and the social, we note that people who are predominantly in
contact with nature are apt to lack attitudes that fit them for
smoothly getting on with people. They are not particularly
fond of being with any people except their few intimates.
They do not like solitude itself, but they like the freedom of
solitude. For, being with people requires a finer and more
thoughtful adjustment then the freedom of solitude. So
people who are predominantly in contact with nature are apt to
acquire the habit of ignoring associates a good deal and of
insisting on freedom to work as they please so far as others
are concerned. . . . Because the nature configuration was pro-

[5] Sorokin, P. *et al.*, *A Systematic Source Book in Rural Sociology*
(Minneapolis, 1930), vol. ii, pp. 3-4.
[6] *Ibid.*, p. 46.

nounced in the farmer, in his social approach to people he regarded them with a kind of awkwardness, a self-distrust, a feeling of not being at home, of losing time from work when merely meeting people socially. He was at home only with his few neighborhood intimates, possibly only his family circle. The farmer did not have to say anything when in the company of intimates. They could be ignored. He did not want to be alone. He wanted to know his family was there. He wanted his wife always to be at home. "Woman's place was in the home." But he was moved mostly by attitudes to nature. He wanted to be let alone, and to be free to work as he pleased. This attitude of liberty which is distinct from freedom passed into our national life.[7]

Outside of the associations of the family group and of temporary gatherings to meet the need of combined effort in certain labor as at threshing time, and in the cattle country for the round-up, the social life of the country is dependent upon the church and the school, and, most important of all in Dr. Wilson's opinion, upon the casual meetings which occur informally at places of trade, such as stores and barber shops, or places of public necessity, as railway stations and post offices. Of the effect of such meetings, Dr. Wilson says:

These casual meetings in the country community are, it is admitted, a wholly insufficient socializing experience. I desire to note them because of that fact, and as a means of showing further that they impress themselves upon rural society in intensifying the purely economic nature of it. The fact that the country community people meet nowhere except in the store or post office, the railroad station, the blacksmith shop, the grain elevator, and on the sidewalk saturates the social mind with economic commonplaces. People are under the influence

[7] Williams, James Mickel, *The Expansion of Rural Life* (New York, 1926), pp. 8 *et seq.*

of the occasional small talk of buying and selling, of prices and of the bare necessities of life. There is in these casual meetings little of politics or religion and nothing of art, literature, or social reform. The substance of conversation and discussion in such meetings is conditioned by the environment. Traditionally, the farmer talks politics at the country store and discusses religion in the post office; actually, he talks in the store butter and raisins and horses and harnesses and the commonplace experiences which would naturally suggest themselves in a country store. There is, indeed, an occasional tendency, dependent largely upon personalities, to launch into the two fields of politics and religion, but it is doubtful whether the political or religious discussion under such auspices is of value to the state or the church. The environment of the discussion would probably prevent it.[8]

Dr. Wilson's conclusions in this regard are corroborated in a general way by the fact that men of talent who have been born in rural districts, as many have been, have not attributed their inspiration to achieve to these informal discussions of the store or post office. Their awakening has come rather from books which they were fortunate enough to possess or to be able to borrow, or from the inspiration of some teacher or preacher of vision in the neighborhood. In many New England neighborhoods, however, politics do take a somewhat more prominent place in the conversation than Dr. Wilson has indicated; but this fact represents the survival of a strong native interest in the face of the handicaps of an unsuited environment. Politics together with religion and education form a part of the New England tradition. The New England town meeting is a democratic governing institution which still functions and its influence is felt through the community although the voting may often be determined more largely by bias, or may be more leth-

[8] Wilson, *op. cit.*

argic, than is consistent with a true spirit of discussion.
Religion as a topic of intellectual interest is more generally
left for women's meetings, while only certain aspects of
education, principally those pertaining to the school finances,
are matters of moment.   In this respect both the church and
the school fulfil less significant roles as socializing influences
in the rural New England community than was formerly the
case.   In the earlier history of New England the church and
the school, especially the academy, were centers of intellectual
life for both old and young in the community.   The teacher
and the preacher occupied positions of leadership which gave
stimulus and direction to the thinking of the neighborhood.
Today such guidance is lacking in the more isolated neighborhoods.   The country church and the school, in conformity
with modern trends, have each become more specialized in
the manner in which they serve the community and no new
organizations have appeared to take over the wider socializing functions, or to supply the leadership which these institutions formerly provided.

The density of the population of a country district is fixed
within a certain upper limit by the productivity of the soil,
and when this maximum is reached, migration or a lowering
of either the birth rate or the standards of living becomes
imperative.   In the United States this situation has generally
been met by migration westward or to the cities, thus deplet-
ing the eastern country neighborhoods of an undue proportion of their young and more energetic citizens.   A source
of potential leadership is withdrawn in this way from the
rural sections and goes to augment that of the city.   At the
same time contacts are established with the city and the
farmer becomes aware of his position in contrast to that of
the city-dweller.   He realizes that he is at a certain disad-
vantage as compared with city men.   He is not well-dressed,
as they are, and he lacks their ease and assurance of manner

and their fluency of speech. Yet, withal, he feels that he is the better man. He has a secret contempt for the city man's inability to do farm labor, which is the criterion by which the farmer tends to measure a man's worth. He regards the city man as one who neither toils nor spins and he feels that any suggested change which emanates from the city must therefore be at the expense of the country. He questions the value of proposed innovations in a self-defensive attitude, and he is chary of proposals which are cooperative in their nature where such cooperation means a possible loss of his own right to act independently. Individualism and conservatism are rural characteristics. Dr. Williams has noted an amusing instance of rural conservatism in the treatment of the stranger.

Several farmers were sitting in a country store when a young man, a stranger, came in. " Looks a little like rain," he ventured affably. No response. Finally one farmer queried, " What may your name be? "

" James Hammond. My grandfather used to live just a mile up the road."

" Oh, Bill Hammond. Ye-es, it does look a little like rain." [9]

At another point Dr. Williams comments further on the attitude toward strangers.

Farmers who had a decided preference for the unfamiliar migrated west or to the cities and left the home-loving type on the farm. They loved the familiar faces, the old homestead, the old church. To be sure the farmer was curious about a stranger who drove along the road and wondered who he was and where he was going. He was hospitable, too, if a stranger asked for shelter. At the same time he had a suspicion of strangers, a certain reaction against them just because they were

[9] Williams, *op. cit.*, p. 32.

strangers, unless a stranger could prove relationship with familiar people.[10]

The method of establishing a bond of relationship with the stranger by means of identifying his kinship or friendship with some one in the community is a familiar one among both primitive and civilized peoples. Among the Australian natives the only method by which the stranger could be admitted to the group was by showing his kinship to some one in it. Other means are possible in the rural neighborhood, but the kinship method is the one which is usually resorted to first. If this fails and no association with familiar people can be shown, then some other common ground is sought. The frank personal questions asked by country people, and so often resented by the stranger, are generally prompted by a sincere desire to find a basis for establishing relationships with the stranger. The most direct way of doing this is to discover if the stranger is related to persons who are already known. If he is, a basis exists for regulating the manner of behaving towards him; but if he is not, the distrust lingers. Not all of the questions which are asked the stranger, however, are prompted by a desire " to place him ", as it were; many are impelled by mere vacuous curiosity and others by a love of gossip. I have become keenly conscious myself of the differences in these types of questions and the attitudes which they imply through my own long residence in country neighborhoods and through numerous experiences as a stranger in such communities.

I began teaching in district schools in Vermont when I was just seventeen. Except for three years at normal school all of my life had been spent on a Wyoming cattle ranch and I was a stranger to my new environment. I could not understand why people should be curious about my personal affairs

10 Williams, *Our Rural Heritage* (New York, 1925), p. 3.

or why they should gossip about me and I shrank from the close scrutiny to which I was subjected. Naturally retiring, I tended to become more so and then I wondered why I was thought snobbish. At that time the school year in Vermont was divided into three terms of ten or twelve weeks each and the teacher was engaged by the term rather than by the year. Changes were frequent, and every term for the first two years I sought a new position in a different locality and somehow I got it. It was a kind of succession of flights from ills, and yet, trying as some of these situations were, they were not without their compensations. Among the most loyal friends that I have today are some of my pupils from those little district schools or the families that I lived with for those brief intervals. The relationships formed at that time have deepened with the passing years and we now laugh together over many things that were painful to me then. The following little incident illustrates the kind of country curiosity which was once so annoying to me, but which in retrospect seems amusing.

I had just gone into a new district to teach and was fortunate in having a congenial boarding place with an interesting old lady who lived alone and who stood by me loyally. The farmer's family who lived opposite included two or three young people who were inordinately interested in all that pertained to the new teacher. It was one of the mores of that district, of which this particular family constituted themselves the guardians, that the teacher should do her personal laundry on Saturday mornings. Unaware of this, I arranged to have mine done for me and I went walking instead. The second Saturday that this happened it was too much and the curious and cleanly came to investigate. " When," they demanded to know, " does the teacher do her washing? " They had watched, they said, all that Saturday and all the Saturday before to see me hang out my clothes

and I hadn't even so much as put out one pocket handker-
chief.   My landlady was a woman of spirit.   " I can assure
you," she retorted, " that the teacher does not go dirty."
And with this reply they were obliged to be content until,
in scanning the Monday morning clothes lines of the neighborhood as was their wont, they espied my things and the
mystery was solved.

The automobile, the radio, and the abundance of cheap
reading material, both good and bad, have extended the
farmer's horizons and many of the country attitudes are
changing.   Rural isolation is being penetrated by urban
influences and the scope of rural interests has been greatly
widened in recent years.   The nature of the farmer's occupation still contrives, however, to dominate the character of
his social relationships, emphasizing the personal, face-to-
face relationships of the family and unorganized primary
group.[11]

2. THE SMALL TOWN

Although the United States Census Bureau for its purposes
distinguishes but two main population groupings with respect
to numbers, rural and urban, ample evidence exists to justify
making a third grouping and considering the relationships
of the small town apart from either those of the city or those
of the open country.   Significant differences in the composition of the village population as compared with that of its
hinterland and also with that of cities of the same region
have been revealed by the statistical data compiled under the
direction of the Institute of Social and Religious Research
in the series *American Village Studies*.   Mr. Cressman
found differences in nativity grouping, sex, age, marital con-

---

[11] A clear analysis of the interrelations existing between the organization of the family group and the conditions imposed by rural life may
be found in Prof. R. M. MacIver's *Society: Its Structure and Changes*,
pp. 363 *et seq.*

dition, literacy and occupational status between villages and the open country from which he drew the conclusion that rural districts as opposed to urban included two separate elements, varying but distinct.[12]   Dr. Fry compared villagers and city-dwellers in these same respects and concluded that here likewise the differences were of moment and justified regarding the villagers as a separate grouping.[13]   Writers who have been interested in country life from other points of view than the statistical have also noted the individuality of the village or small town as compared with either the country or the city.   Hartman describes the village as " neither grass nor hay ".

Its problems are radically different from those of the open country, but it has not settled itself into the well regulated ways of a proper urban development.   The grass in the meadow may not become hay in the stack without undergoing a certain curing process to adapt it to the needs of its new environment.   The village stage is the curing stage in urban development.   The village problems are serious or light in proportion to their advancement toward substantial and ideal urban conditions.

Those of us who are interested in the village problems have no claims for the superiority of urban over rural conditions but they are different, and when urban conditions commence, they must be met by changed methods because of changed relationships. . . . The complications begin in the village where the proximity of people gives their actions and customs a more than personal significance, because they affect other people. It is here that the community is born, if it gets born on time, and that regulation of the actions of the individual by all becomes a necessity.

The great need in the village is for a community consciousness.   The village here suffers a severe handicap.   It has

[12] Fry, Luther C., *American Villagers* (New York, 1926), Appendix C by L. S. Cressman, p. 179.

[13] *Ibid.*, pp. 23-25.

problems of a serious nature and it has not the impersonal nature of law enforcement which is common in larger places. In the village a man knows all his neighbors. In the city he knows almost none of them. To do the work of the village properly there must be a fundamental understanding of the problem and a determination to work unitedly towards its solution. This calls in the village for a community sense which is different from that in the country and greater by far than that even necessary in the city.[14]

In the selection just quoted attention is focused at the crucial point in the problems pertaining to village social relationships, the adjustment between the direct personal relationships of the neighborhood group and the more indirect contractual relationships characteristic of more densely populated areas. It should be noted, however, that although the problems of the small town resemble in some respects those of both the city and the rural neighborhood, they are identical with neither. The small town does not develop into a city except under particular circumstances. It is not in this sense a stage in an evolutionary process, even though, generally speaking, village populations have enjoyed a favorable rate of increase in recent years. The village is " neither grass nor hay " and yet it does not become hay in the process of time. The village is itself; it has its own individuality, although its problems, like the reverse sides of a coin, are stamped with different designs. One face bears the impress of the country, the other that of the city. And like a coin that is tossed, now " heads " come uppermost and now " tails ". In one situation the village reaction may be a personal one and in another it may be impersonal; in one town the outlook as a whole may be predominantly rural in con-

[14] Hartman, E. T., " Village Problems and Characteristics ", *Annals of the American Academy of Political and Social Science*, vol. xl, pp. 234 *et seq.*

trast to the more sophisticated point of view of another community. Villages differ among themselves, indeed, as Thomas Hardy has observed in *Tess of the D'Urbervilles,* a book which radiates the atmosphere of the English country side, " Every village has its idiosyncracy, its constitution, its own code of morality ". Not all small towns are Main Streets by any means, although the drab type which Sinclair Lewis has pictured in the novel of this name does exist, unfortunately.

The social organization of the village is one in which family and neighborhood relationships largely prevail, but the greater number of persons involved and their closer proximity to one another have created new problems and new relationships unlike those of the more sparsely settled farming districts. Readjustments become necessary and the success or failure in making these determines the character of the small town. Some towns have achieved a happier adjustment than others between the simple intimate relationships of home and neighborhood and the more impersonal specialized relations of a group life of greater complexity. The main characteristics of small-town life, however, are those which Blumenthal has noted in his study, *Small-Town Stuff:* " close acquaintanceship of everyone with everyone else, the dominance of personal relationships, the subjection of the individual to continuous observation and control by the community." [15]

The intimacy of village life, like the intimacy of the family, tends to mold its members into certain likenesses, and into patterns of behavior which conform with one another and which form an integrated whole. Although the villager belongs to a number of associations outside of his own immediate family, his circle of contacts is still a rela-

[15] Blumenthal, Albert, *Small-Town Stuff* (Chicago, 1932), p. xii.

tively limited one in that it is " the same old crowd " that he meets at every turn. If, for instance, he is out of harmony with the group at church, this fact will affect his relationships with other groups since his fellow church members are also his neighbors and his business associates. He cannot be at variance in one particular without strain resulting at other points. He is thus under a greater compulsion to think and act as others do than either the farmer or the city man. The very isolation of the farmer gives him a certain independence of action; he has to take the initiative and to make up his own mind about many of those things which come within the sphere of his activities. The city man on the other hand achieves his independence by virtue of a freedom of choice, and his failure to meet the approval of one group does not necessarily affect his relations with other groups since these are not, for the most part, comprised of the same people. Consequently, the villager is less individualistic than the farmer and less socialized than the city-dweller; his manner of reacting to others is more nearly prescribed for him. H. P. Douglass in his study of the little town has discerned this.

With all the town's large allowance for the personal so long as its vagaries keep within the established social traditions, there is little patience for it when it wanders in untried ways. In the city, it is a normal attitude to regard life as a venture in which stakes should be offered and risked. The reality and solemnity of personal responsibility for novel decisions is well recognized. The little town will have none of this. The serious issues of life are not to be questioned. The individual may be eccentric and perverse, but he must not make novel choices nor depart essentially from the ways of the fathers. Society is essentially unadventurous and non-initiating. Personality in its profoundest aspects is not respected.[16]

[16] Douglass, H. P., The Little Town (New York, 1921), pp. 92-93.

The pace of each is set by the pace of the whole and this tends to be conservative. Several factors contribute to produce this attitude. Among these are the undue proportion of old people in the village population and the relatively large number of persons who are property owners. The greater homogeneity of the village population as compared with the city is also a stabilizing influence. Patterns of behavior have become more deeply entrenched than would have been the case if new realignments had been necessitated from time to time in order to accommodate unlike elements. When alien groups do present themselves they are left largely undigested by the village social order.

The occasional family of another nationality or race is indeed taken in without great embarrassment to most of the privileges of the community; but let any considerable number of such people present themselves and they are quickly formed into an almost impenetrable clan on the town's outskirts. In spite of their small numbers, the process of their assimilation is relatively slower than in the city. The world war has shown that some of the most un-American communities in America are small towns in the Middle-West. There is not the keen sense of life-and-death struggle to assimilate or to be submerged by the alien mass, which the city knows so well. Hence the town's assimilating processes are feeble and unsteady. Under the stimulus of the frontier, where all comers start life in essential equality, the alien of nearer lineage, like the Scandinavian in the Northwest, assimilates in a generation. Even under these favoring circumstances the Slav may remain alien indefinitely. Old towns especially prove utterly inadequate to the task of making over into their own likeness any new group entrenched in a mass-life of alien sort. As a class, also, the little town strangely fails to achieve the higher more spiritual unity of the city.[17]

[17] *Ibid.*, pp. 84-85.

The greater difficulty which the small town experiences as compared with the city in establishing satisfactory relationships with alien groups is due in part to the nature of its own social structure and in part to the fact that the village environment offers the foreigners less incentive for changing their former customs than does the more competitive urban environment. Broadly speaking, the foreign group and the villagers are each self-sufficient in a greater measure than is true of the endlessly diverse yet closely interlocking groups which comprise the social composition of a great city. Within the village group itself each individual is bound to every other by more than one set of relationships. Not only do they live near each other as neighbors, with all that this implies in village life, but they belong to the same social organizations and to the same business groups. The members of the alien group are also bound together in a similar way. To gain an entrée into either one of these systems involves establishing, not one set of relationships, but several. The stranger is thus judged by the criteria of several types of relationships rather than by that of one type alone. The examination covers a general field instead of a specific, though some forms of minutiae are not overlooked. It is not easy for the foreigner to meet so varied a list of requirements at one time and unless he is alone and dependent upon the villagers for the satisfaction of his social needs, he is not inclined to make the effort to do so; but he turns more than ever to his own group, thus strengthening its solidarity and delaying assimilation.

The relationships which bind the individuals of the city into groups within a larger whole are largely specialized; a person may belong to many different groups and not meet the same people in any two of them. He is thus united to the members of each group by but one set of relationships while in village groups the members are bound together by several

sets of ties.   This is an important difference for the social
structure of the two types of groups.   The strength of the
bonds which unite a group that has been brought together
for one purpose only and which is composed of persons who
are not bound together in other ways is dependent upon the
strength of one specific set of values.   Such relationships are
relatively clear-cut and definite; whereas, in groups composed
of persons who are united to one another by the obligations
and duties of relationships of more than one kind there is
an overlapping and confusion of values.   In the small town
the personal relationships of the family and neighbor tend to
dominate over the other forms and thence comes the pronounced personal attitude of the villager in all of his relationships.   This factor is difficult to eliminate from human
affairs and it is not easy to form an unbiased judgment when
it is present.   The village frequently tolerates a nuisance
which the city would not for the simple reason that the
people hesitate to bring legal action against a neighbor.
The number of social organizations of various kinds is sur-
prisingly large for the average village community.   Brunner
found an average of 21.1 non-church and non-school organizations and an average of 16.1 church organizations for
the villages communities which he studied.[18]   This means
that many of the groups are small and there is a duplication
of effort and also that the membership will be much the same
in some at least of the groups.   Villages as a whole are over-
organized into small groups, but are lacking in community
organization.

The existence of a multiplicity of relationships of various
kinds among the persons who comprise a group tends to
inhibit change and to encourage conservatism.   The obligations of one form of relationship cannot change without also

[18] Brunner, Edmund DeS., *Village Communities* (New York, 1927),
pp. 90-92.

affecting other interrelated relationships and unless these are modified in conformity with the initial change, strain and even distintegration will result.   A greater amount of energy is required, however, for overcoming the inertia of a number of established relationships and introducing new features into these than is needed for changing a single system of relationships.   In rural life, for instance, the marriage relationship also involves certain economic and service obligations which have been largely separated from it in urban life. Consequently, divorce is a more difficult act for country people than it is for city-dwellers since breaking the marriage bond disrupts other ties to a far greater extent than it does in the city.   The interests of the small town are interrelated and most of the members of the community are concerned with several of them so that group pressure is exerted at a number of points and a greater degree of conformity is secured.   The conservatism of the small town is inherent in its social structure, which is that of both a primary group of individuals and a complex of voluntary associations.[19]

The presence of a stranger is a matter of interest to villagers since, if he remains, they must come into contact with him in many ways.   The newcomer therefore finds himself subjected to a close scrutiny.   The usual procedure, like that of the open country, is to attempt to identify the stranger with familiar persons, or with a known class of people, as tourists or summer boarders.   If the stranger fits into a recognized category, and this is one which is approved, the small town is friendly, but otherwise the process of assimilation is slow.

The " outsider " or stranger is also likely to find himself conspicuous and yet isolated from the bosom of Mineville in

---

[19] Cf. Sanderson, Dwight, The Rural Community (Boston, 1932), pp. 663-66.

some ways. He must be in residence for many months, or years, before "the old guard" considers him to be a Mineviller. By nothing excepting long participation in the activities of the town do the people grow to accept him as one of them. He is apt to find stubborn discrimination against him in numerous respects—particularly in regard to getting some jobs. . . . Conversely, "hometowners" complain that you have to be a stranger to get any privileges in this town.[20]

Village reaction tends to be whole-heartedly for or against the stranger rather than discriminating. To accept in part and to reject in part is difficult, as we have shown, because of the overlapping nature of the relationships involved. Conformity is enforced in small matters as well as large through gossip. In Mineville the people soon discover by a "ferreting-out process" whether or not the newcomer "has anything to be stuck up about"[21] and this is true for small towns generally. The small town has time in which to be interested in small matters. Hardy brings this point out when he says: "The Emminister congregation looked at her [Tess] as only the congregation of small country townsfolk walking home at its leisure can look at a woman whom it perceives to be a stranger".[22] Trivial things often come to assume an undue importance because of the attention which they receive when other more vital interests are lacking. The stranger is often talked over and gossiped about simply to gratify the desire for novelty and excitement. Villagers have more leisure than farming people and fewer diversions than city people; and, hence, the small town is a fertile field for gossip. Obedience to the traditional folkways and mores of the town is secured through a fear of what will be said if one diverges

[20] Blumenthal, *op. cit.*, p. 121.

[21] *Ibid.*, p. 105.

[22] Hardy, Thomas, *Tess of the D'Urbervilles* (New York and London, 1891), p. 342.

from them.   The stranger is relatively less influenced by this
and the townsfolk may resent such independence, as was the
case in Mineville.

Of all offenders the stranger is most readily arrested because
there is a community antagonism against " outsiders who think
they can do as they ' damned ' please in this town ".   But even
he is usually given an opportunity " to get out of town " since
there is unpleasant notoriety for the police officer in making
an arrest, to walk to the jail involves climbing a steep hill, and
the sheriff's wife is obliged to cook the meals for the prisoner—
a task which she prefers to avoid, for the most part.[23]

The personal considerations which enter into the question
of making an arrest in Mineville are an interesting illustration of the small-town attitude in such matters.   The relationships are personal rather than contractual in their nature
and seemingly irrelevant things affect them to a greater
extent than is true for the more objective impersonal relationships of urban life.   It is only fair, however, to say in
justice to the small town that such added considerations are
often sympathetic and kindly.   The New England town
which has been my home for a number of years received my
own family in a neighborly way when we moved there as
strangers from the West.   It is true that we do not belong to
the community in quite the same sense that families do who
have always lived there; but there has been no want of warm-
hearted sympathy in times of sorrow, and whatever little
measure of success we have achieved has been generously
recognized.   The relationship of " the good neighbor " of
the small town is a valued one that we should seek to preserve in an era of changing social relationships.

[23] Blumenthal, op. cit., p. 196.

CHAPTER IX

The City

THE problem of discovering the nature of the social bonds which distinguish the modern city from other types of social groupings is not a simple one. The complexity of the life of the city resists an easy formula. One cannot point to this or that particular type of unifying relationship as forming the basis of the social structure of the city since many types contribute to this end no one of which may be excluded. The city is at once more personal and more impersonal in its relationships than the country, more lenient and more critical in its judgments of others, more tolerant and more intolerant in its attitudes toward outsiders. It is not in any one distinctive form of relationship, therefore, that the source of the unity of city life must be sought, but, rather, in the manner in which manifold highly differentiated relationships have become adjusted to one another. Such an adjustment does not, however, imply a fusion of relationships but the opposite. It has been the peculiar function of the city to accentuate the specific character of the various types of relationships found within it rather than to merge these into a general uniformity. The city separates and segregates, but it has a thousand criteria for so doing. It compounds and recompounds, now from this angle and again from that, and consequently, the pattern of social integration becomes an intricate one. A perspective is difficult to attain, and, as emphasis has been placed upon one feature rather than another of city life, different, and even opposing, interpretations have been given to the social significance of urban relationships. From one point of view the city becomes a kind of gigantic Juggernaut, crushing even as it civilizes mankind as in Spengler's theory, while from another it becomes a symbol of release from the tyranny of the soil. For it is only as the earth has yielded a surplus above the needs of the tillers that the city can exist; hence, the growth of cities has been concomitant with man's conquest of the soil. In this sense the city represents a form and degree of human emancipation; it belongs to epochs when men have been free to direct a portion of their energies to other pursuits than the immediate wresting of livelihood from the earth. That such other pursuits may often be more arduous and less rewarding than the rural occupations is true. The question is not one of the relative advantages of this or that way of gaining a livelihood, nor yet of leisure for some classes at the expense of others. It is rather a question of the increased opportunities which cities afford for the exercise of more highly specialized abilities and inclinations. Such opportunities, even though hemmed in by restrictions of many kinds, imply a certain freedom of individual choice, and, hence, the growth of cities has also witnessed the development of a new form of individualism, that of personal uniqueness.

The individualism of the farmer has been commented upon at another point. It embodies a certain rugged independence and self-sufficiency that is suspicious of socialized cooperation other than that which is found within the family group or small neighborhood circle. The individualism of the city-dweller, on the other hand, is the product of a selective social environment; it is born of contacts with men rather than with inanimate objects, and it depends for its fruition upon the recognition of others. These two forms of individualism, i. e., individual independence and personal uniqueness, are different in their sources and in their content and they give rise in turn to different reactions when the problem of establishing new relationships is presented. The frequency and the variety of the contacts to which men are subjected in an urban environment make it necessary for them to respond readily and yet with discrimination. Each different situation requires a specialized response, and, since much of the success of the city-dweller is dependent upon his ability to " get on " with others, he must acquire facility in working with others and in meeting new people and new situations. In answer to this need various types of impersonal, secondary relationships have been evolved. Such relationships, Simmel has noted, are based more largely on intellect and less on feelings and emotions than are country relationships.[1] While all emotional relationships are based on individuality, the intellectual relationships reckon with men merely as figures, or with indifferent elements that are of interest only because of their performance, which may be objectively evaluated. This situation gives rise to an attitude of sophistication, all objects appearing uniform and unimportant. It also affords the individual a kind of measure of personal freedom since his affairs are of no interest to those with whom he comes in contact unless a specific reason exists for their being so.

The personal freedom which the individual secures through the development of social relations of an intellectual, impersonal type in most of his dealings with others is offset to a certain extent by an enhanced desire for personal recognition and response from particular persons or interest groups with whom he is more immediately concerned. He reacts against being wholly submerged in the crowd. The attraction which the freedom of city life affords is not that of a complete

[1] Simmel, Georg, " Die Grossestädte und das Geistesleben " in *Die Grossestadt* (Dresden, 1903), pp. 187-206. For a further discussion of Simmel's article see Sorokin *et al.*, *A Systematic Source Book in Rural Sociology* (Minneapolis, 1930), vol. i, pp. 242-248.

absence of the more personal relationships with their peculiar obligations, privileges and restrictions; but it is rather that of an increased opportunity to form such relationships more nearly in accord with the individual's own wishes. The social environment of the city offers the individual a wider choice from which to select his more intimate associates than is found among primitive peoples and in rural communities. The city-dweller is not of necessity bound to the same few people at all points of contact and his relations with one group are relatively unaffected by his status in another group. His freedom lies in this and in the restriction of intimate, personal relationships to only the more immediate members of his own family and to companions of his own choosing.

The significance of personal relationships in the formation of the urban social structure is frequently overlooked or minimized because of the greater prevalence of the intellectual or contractual types of relationships. Their role, however, though a less conspicuous one, is none the less essential. Men have congregated in cities for the sake of congenial companionship as well as for economic and cultural advantages or for the opportunity of following a particular trade or profession. The loneliness of city life which is a frequent theme in literature is more often the loneliness of the stranger heightened by the contrast of his position with that of the hurrying multitudes about him, all of whom seemingly belong somewhere and to some one while he alone does not. The poignancy of such loneliness is not to be denied; but it seems reasonable to assume that if this were the common lot of those who live in cities, urban life would not be as attractive as it is actually known to be. Few men wish to be wholly without some personal relationships which involve sentiment, mutual understanding and emotion, however much they may crave the freedom to live their own lives in their own way unhampered by the restrictions imposed by such relationship and however high the barriers of reserve which they may rear to shield themselves from the intrusion of the people about them. The absence of all bonds of intimacy results in a condition of social isolation which is unnatural, and, which, although it is not infrequently met with in cities, can by no means be regarded as general for the millions of people who live in an urban environment. In spite of all that has been said about the distintegration of the family under the influence of the city, the closer family relationships have persisted. They have retained their vitality even if shorn of many of the duties and obligations which characterize rural family life.

As the relationships of the urban family have become narrowed in their scope they have also become more specific and more exacting in their character. They are less a matter of course or of expediency and more a matter of individual choice. The generally higher divorce rate and the lower birth rate of cities are expressions of the changing nature of the family relationships, but not necessarily of their dissolution. A marriage which ends in a divorce may represent a failure to meet the demands of a specific relationship rather than the lack of a desire to participate in such a relationship. The higher and more individualized the demands of any particular relationship become the more difficult it is to fulfil these and the more often will there be failures to do so. From this point of view the percentage of urban marriages which are successful may be taken as evidence of the strength of this relationship to hold two people together in its own right and independent of the buttressing of other inter-connecting relationships and of the mores of the group with respect to divorce. Among rural peoples the marriage relationship involves a greater number of accessory bonds than it does in urban groups and these additional ties tend to increase the stability of the major bonds of the relationship.

This is also true for the other family relationships, such as those between parents and children. In the city various extra-familial interest groups take over certain of the functions which are normally associated with these relationships in the country, and the parental-filial relationship is more restricted in its content and more definite in its nature. The presence of children in the home is more largely a matter of choice than of chance. The values intrinsic in the relationship sustain it independent of secondary considerations. Urban influences have not as yet destroyed the fundamental primary family relationships. Although these have become somewhat more limited in their scope, they still form strong cohesive bonds between those persons who come under their aegis; and a discussion of the types of relationships which characterize the city must take note of them.

As the family group has relinquished one after another of its less specific functions under the influence of urban conditions these have been taken over by other agencies or special interest groups. These groups form one of the most distinguishing features of the social organization of the city. Their number is legion and they are both organized and unorganized, public and private. In the larger metropolitan centers, organizations exist for serving every conceivable wish and whim of mankind whether these are physical or social in their nature. The interests of an individual must be most unusual, indeed, if some group with kindred likes cannot be found. The problem of the stranger, and often of the city resident as well, is one of gaining admission to such groups. The city group tends to be selective and to be critical and intolerant of those who do not measure up to its specific standards. The trend of city life is competitive and a struggle for recognition ensues. Economic success is frequently the criterion for such recognition, but it is by no means the only one. The efforts of a certain class of newly-rich people to gain an entrée into the more exclusive social circles have been widely caricatured. Wealth alone has not sufficed, nor will it secure the form of recognition for which writers, artists, musicians, actors, scientists, and many others are seeking. The commendation of a select few of the initiated who are interested in the same pursuits, and even the general acclaim of a less critical public, are values without price. That such recognition usually brings with it a highly desired and much needed monetary reward cannot be gainsaid; but this satisfaction is different in its nature from the former and to attain it has not been the primary urge. Men still contend mightily for the Olympic olive-branch and for a wreath of laurel. These values are social in their origin; to possess them gives the individual a certain status in his group or community. The simple " Well done " of the master, the approval of one's associates, the applause of the public, all signify relationships that are more personal and more charged with sentiment and emotion than are the contractual, bargaining relationships; and like the family relationships they too have a significant place in the social structure of the city.

As the extra-familial interest groups of cities have become more and more specialized in their functions, it has become necessary for the city-dweller who possesses a fairly wide range of interests to belong to a number of different groups in order to satisfy these. Even in the city of " Middletown " with its relatively small population the Lynds found that a successful lawyer, for instance, would probably belong to " the Bar Association, Chamber of Commerce, Rotary, the Republican party, one of two or three leading churches, a high order in the Masons, the Country Club, and be a director of the Y. M. C. A." His wife would be a member of the more fashionable women's clubs, the group directing the charities, and so on. A successful banker belongs to the same group, save that the Bankers' Association replaces the Bar Association." [2] Loyalties are linked since the same persons belong to a number at least of the same associations and in this way a degree of unity is engendered among the business class as a whole. In the larger urban centers the distinctions between the various groups are sharper and the membership of different organizations tends on the whole to be more mutually exclusive although it may not be entirely so. There is a tendency for groups of friends to join the same clubs and organizations; moreover, class discrimination enters in cutting across the other determinants for group membership and limiting eligibility to a comparatively small number of persons in the more exclusive circles. The same persons belong to all the groups which are organized within such circles since no outsider is welcome and the small number within the class itself makes this identity more or less inevitable. Loyalties are linked in this way, as in Middletown; a feeling of unity within the class is strengthened, and the gulf between it and other social classes is widened.

The obligations of the relationships between people of the same class and those which exist between people who belong to unlike classes differ in certain important respects. Those between members of the same class are based on like or shared interests and involve some element of personal sympathy, whereas those between unlike classes are based more largely on the interdependence arising in the social division of labor, and, hence, are contractual in their nature. The differences in the forms of unity or group solidarity which result from these two types of relationships have been summarized by Professors Sorokin and Zimmerman as follows:

First, there is solidarity based on the social similarity or the homogeneity of individuals or, as Professor Giddings styles it,

---

[2] Lynd, R. S. and Lynd, H. M., *Middletown* (New York, 1929), p. 492.

on " like-mindedness ". The second solidarity is based on the social heterogeneity of individuals, particularly on the social division of labor. The first form of solidarity is more intimate, less formal, more active, and comes, so to speak, from the hearts of men. The second is " colder " and represents not so much active solidarity and vivid sympathy as the dependence of one not self-sufficient individual or group upon another. It ties together various members of a society with a great division of labor in which no member or no particular group is self-sufficient and needs the exchanges and contacts with others in order to satisfy primary necessities. The solidarity based on heterogeneity and division of labor is more of a dependence than an active sympathy.[3]

Both the types of solidarity described in the foregoing paragraph are essential for the social integration of the city. The members of the family, the special interest groups, and the social classes are drawn together by ties of a personal nature and the units which are thus formed are again in their turn joined to one another to form the larger framework of the city, partly by relationships growing out of the division of labor, and partly by a certain community of feeling based on nationality and on the historical tradition of the city. To ignore the presence of either of these two fundamental types of social solidarity in an analysis of urban relationships is to over-simplify the problem. Both forms must be taken into account in order to understand the attitude, or more precisely the attitudes, of the city-dweller toward strangers. According to the circumstances of the contact, one type of solidarity rather than the other may be the predominant one and so determine the nature of the reaction.

In country neighborhoods where everyone is acquainted

[3] Sorokin, P. and Zimmerman, C. C., *Principles of Rural-Urban Sociology* (New York, 1929), pp. 516-18. See also Durkheim's *De la division du travail social* and F. Tonnies' *Gemeinschaft und Gesellschaft* for a fuller exposition of these two principal forms of social solidarity.

with everyone else the arrival of the stranger is noted at once and he becomes an object of interest. In the city, on the other hand, everyone outside of the city-dweller's own relatively small circle of friends and acquaintances is a stranger to him. He sees hundreds and even thousands of strangers in the course of the day and he is for the most part oblivious of them, as they in their turn are of him. The relationship between people who pass each other on the street or who crowd together into public conveyances is so highly formalized and impersonal that it is scarcely recognizable as a relationship, yet, since this behavior is in accord with an accepted social pattern and is social in its nature, the existence of a definite understanding of a reasoned, contractual type is evinced. It is a relationship of strangers to strangers on a like basis. There is no distinction as between the group and the stranger or between host and guest. In these casual contacts the residents of the city are as much strangers to one another as the newcomer is to them. The form of the relationship is a protective one. To take a personal interest in the affairs of others requires an outlay of time and energy and not infrequently of emotional feeling. If the city-dweller were to give more than passing heed to the throngs which press about him, he would be reduced to physical, if not also to financial, bankruptcy. A certain steeling of the emotions becomes necessary and consequently city people often appear " cold-hearted " and unsympathetic. Charity is organized and the city-dweller is inclined to feel resentful, and not without reason, of demands which are made upon him that do not come through authorized channels. The question as to whether or not he is less generous and less sympathetic in his attitudes toward his own immediate family and close friends than the countryman has not been investigated so far as I know; but from casual observation there seems little reason for believing him to be less

so. The indifference of the city-dweller to the multitudes
about him is an impersonal attitude born of the necessity for
conserving his own energies and for preserving a measure
of freedom and of privacy even though living in the midst
of crowds.

Business relationships form another large and exceedingly
important class of relationships of the impersonal, contractual
type which tend to lend their color to the whole of the urban
social order and to obscure the presence of other more intimate social bonds. The business of earning a livelihood in
the city involves dealing with others to a far greater extent
than it does in the rural occupations. The number of contacts which farmers, fishermen, lumbermen, trappers, and so
on make in connection with their work is limited, whereas
frequent contacts are the rule rather than the exception in
most urban industries. The ability to meet others easily and
to work well with one's associates is indispensable for both
employer and employee. If he succeeds, the city-dweller
must be cooperative and he must acquire facility in making
new contacts readily and in accommodating himself to new
situations and to the peculiarities of others. He meets those
strangers who come to his attention more easily than the
countryman, but the relationship which ensues tends to
remain impersonal in its nature. There is less constraint in
the process of becoming formally acquainted, but there is a
greater reticence in revealing the more intimate side of one's
nature. The plaint that one never really gets to know people
in the city is a familiar one. The reserve with which the
city-dweller normally shields certain aspects of his personality
from all but a chosen few is baffling to the person who does
not understand it and who is accustomed to sharing a greater
degree of intimacy with his associates. The more formal
intellectual and contractual relationships do not satisfy the
emotional needs of his nature. In his contacts with city

people he is conscious of missing the warmth of the personal relationships and he is troubled by the greater difficulty of establishing these.

The fact that intimate relationships are established less easily in an urban environment than are the more impersonal types does not, however, connote an absence of the first type. We have already observed the significance for the integration of urban life of the personal bonds which unite the city family and certain of the special interest groups. The need for congenial companionship, for appreciation, and for affection finds its satisfaction in those exclusive little circles whose privileged relationships are extended only to those who possess the magic passwords. The personal qualities of the individual are the prerequisites for these. There is little opportunity for establishing strong bonds of intimacy by the fact of living together in the same community as neighbors. In the country many people who would not have discovered much of interest in one another in a larger social environment often become attached to each other and find pleasure in each other's society through the growth of ties formed by sharing common neighborhood interests and by the exchange of the innumerable little services and kindnesses which characterize the neighboring of country life. The greater mobility of city life, on the other hand, and the general plan of its organization do not encourage the development of strong personal ties in this way. The contacts which afford opportunities for becoming acquainted with the kind of people whom the individual would like to know and among whom he may reasonably hope to find congenial friends must usually be made through other channels. The fact of living in the same block or in the same apartment house with others does not as a rule afford the basis for establishing intimate ties; but if these are already begun, it may facilitate their growth because of the greater ease with which people interested in each other can be together. People who have been attracted to one another in a first meeting may plan further meetings who would not have done so if, in the beginning, much time or effort had been required. The friendship which develops is founded, however, on personal rather than on neighborhood interests.

The problem of becoming acquainted with others in the city is to a greater or a less extent one of making contacts through special interest groups. The stranger who is actively interested in forming new relations presents whatever credentials he possesses which will give him an entrée into one or more of such groups. It may be a union card, or a certificate of membership in a fraternal lodge, in a church, or in some such organization as the Young Men's or Young Women's Christian Association. Or again it may be a letter of introduction to some person or group who may be of assistance to him in making the desired contacts. Some avenue for making acquaintances in the city other than that which is afforded by one's work or by the chance contacts of public amusement places is usually, though not always, available. Unfortunately, however, such avenues do not always lead to the type of contacts which an individual particularly desires; and even when they do so, he still may not be accepted as a member of the group to which he has been introduced. The selective aspect of city life is operative in those relationships which are more purely social in their nature as well as those which are of economic origin. The city group is critical and intolerant of those who do not measure up to the standards of its own peculiar social code, but it does not as a rule demand conformity in other matters which lie outside its defined field of interests. In this respect urban groups are less exacting than the small town community which seeks to regulate the whole life of the individual. The city-dweller is less inclined to assume the responsibility for being his brother's keeper. He carefully scrutinizes those personal qualities of the individual which are of special moment to him, but he is apt to be tolerant and uncritical of divergencies in other respects. To repeat, the city-dweller is at once more personal and more impersonal, more tolerant and more intolerant in his attitudes than the countryman. He is also more conventional and less conventional in his behavior as the case may be. He is no more ready to incur the ridicule or the unfavorable criticism of his own group than is the countryman. He adheres as closely to those customs which are valued in his own circle as his country brother does to the customs of his neighborhood. These values tend, however, to be specific and exclusive in city groups and outside their range the group does not exert pressure to secure conformity. Moreover, with respect to many things, the accepted order of the city tends to be a changing order. Fads flourish because it is the correct thing to be interested in the latest thing out. In other words it is conventional to be considered up to date. No courage is required to accept the new; indeed, it would be difficult to reject it.

The question of conservatism in both the city and the country is one of maintaining inviolate those values which are considered to be fundamental for the survival of those relationships which constitute the social order of the group itself. The group resists changes which it feels will destroy these values. The privileged classes of the city, for instance, cling as tenaciously to their rights as the farmer does to his. That they have relinquished prerogatives and accepted new theories which they at first regarded adversely more often than the rural classes does not necessarily imply a greater willingness to make such changes. The extent of the pressure from without to which they have been subjected must also be taken into consideration. The interests of the congeries of interdependent groups of which the city is com-

posed are antagonistic as well as complementary and the
mores of the city group are continually being assailed.   The
mores of rural people, on the other hand, are relatively protected from such external pressures by their greater isolation
and by the peculiar nature of the rural social structure which,
figuratively speaking, is rooted in the soil and does not lend
itself to a wide range of variations.   In this sense the life
of the peasant is " beyond history ", as Spengler has said.
The great social movements which have made history have
left rural life singularly untouched throughout the past.   In
the present era this situation is being modified by the closer
interrelation of city and country, and charges in the urban
social order of today tend to have their repercussion in rural
life to an unprecedented extent.   Distinctions between the
two social orders are less sharp than they have formerly been
and the country more nearly approaches the city in its values.

In making comparisons between city and country it is necessary to bear in mind that on the whole country life is simpler
and more uniform than that of the city and for this reason
it is easier to make generalizations with regard to it that are
representative than to do so for the city with its wide range
of variations.   Which, for instance, of the multitude of differentiated city groups can be regarded as typical of the
whole?   Shall we take the Gold Coast or the Slum?   Fifth
Avenue or the Bowery?   East London or West London?
Shall we consider the conservatism of the well-to-do, socially
entrenched classes or the radicalism of the Third Estate as
representative of the attitude of the city toward certain social
changes?   Or shall we ignore these more extreme views and
accept the reactions of other intermediate groups as typical
of urban life?   Obviously, the problem cannot be satisfactorily solved in this way; urban groups are so highly differentiated that there must inevitably be significant exceptions to
most attempts to generalize concerning the attitudes of city
people as a whole.   The social structure of the city is com-

plex and it is well not to be over-zealous in subsuming the
reactions of all city people under the same categories. The
very essence of urban life is its variety; and in making comparisons it is safer, if more laborious, to be specific with reference to which groups or which aspects of city life are meant.
Generalizations with reference to the social behavior of the
city as a totality must be carefully drawn in order to avoid
giving an undue emphasis to certain phases at the expense of
others which are perhaps no less vital; for, although the city
is a distinct community which is capable of a unified response
to certain appropriate stimuli, this larger unity is for the most
part in abeyance. As a rule the behavior reactions which
have been noted in most studies of city people are those of
specific groups or neighborhoods within the city and are not
general throughout.

Mention has already been made of the differences which
exist in the attitudes and underlying relationships of certain
types of city groups and classes. It remains, however, to
consider the nature and function of distinctive areas or
neighborhoods in the social organization of the city. The
uniqueness of such areas has attracted the attention of a
number of writers and in such studies as Bercovici's *Around
the World in New York,* Zorbaugh's *The Gold Coast and the
Slum,* Wirth's *The Ghetto,* Shaw's *Delinquency Areas,* Anderson's *The Hobo,* and Hecht's *1001 Afternoons in Chicago*
the distinctive aspects of various city neighborhoods have
been effectively portrayed. These sections are " areas of
habit " accordingly to Anderson and Linderman—" the physical groundwork or frame into which urban society has
woven itself, which bears witness to the order of urban existence, and in which it has its basis. . . . The most exclusive
street in the city, the most poverty-ridden, or the most de-
praved, each has a character of its own." [4]   The question as

[4] Anderson, N. and Lindermann, E. C., *Urban Sociology* (New York,
1928), pp. 83-84.

to whether the distinguishing traits of a particular area have been molded by the neighborhood itself or whether they are there as a consequence of the processes of urban segregation is a debatable one.   Plainly, the distinctive foreign areas of such a city as New York have come into being through a process of selection.   Immigrants have settled in the same neighborhood with others of their own race or nationality—drawn together by the loyalties which have united them in the past.   The sentiments and interests which they share in common are derived for the most part from other sources than those which are furnished by the area in which they have settled.   The new ties which the immigrant forms do not usually include a feeling of loyalty toward the particular neighborhood in which he first settles.   More often than not he seeks to escape from it and to make a place for himself in the larger community.   Proximity alone does not make neighbors in urban life.[5]   It does, however, as we have noted before, facilitate the functioning of unifying bonds which are already present; and it may under certain circumstances afford a basis for unification.   City neighborhoods sometimes unite against the intrusion of elements which they regard as undesirable or to further some project of common interest.   Such activities are usually temporary, however, and the relationships which they create dissolve when the emergency has passed.   Permanent unifying loyalties of the type which characterize country communities are largely absent from even the most distinctive city neighborhood.   Its unity depends upon the specialized interests which have brought certain people together and upon tradition rather than upon sharing a number of more general things in common.   The distinctive city area is the result of selective processes; but once formed it is capable of perpetuating its own legend.   A body of sentiment and tradition grows up

[5] *Ibid.*, p. 212.

about the region, customs become established, and the neighborhood exerts a subtile influence on those who dwell there. Although a constant moving in and out goes on the personality of the neighborhood persists.[6]   The unique culture area of the city not only attracts the like-minded but also weaves its own peculiar spell over others who come within its bounds.   Hobohemia, for example, is such an area and " whoever ventures near to partake of its life either finds himself contributing his bit or he feels uncomfortable ".[7] Bercovici mentions an interesting if somewhat unusual instance of neighborhood influence in the case of a Greek immigrant in New York City who learned Yiddish as the language of his adopted country.   The larger life of the great city as a whole lay undreamed of beyond the narrow horizons that enclosed the area in which he lived.

Physical distances and social distances do not always coincide in the city and people may live side by side who cannot, even with the best of good will, become neighbors because of the divergence of their interests and heritages.   The Near North Side in Chicago presents such a situation.   Twenty-eight specified foreign nationalities, the Negro, and category " all other countries " in addition to the native-born population are all crowded within a few hundred blocks.[8]   The Gold Coast and the Slum rub elbows, as it were.   Among the unique areas of this region is " The World of Furnished Rooms ".

. . . . A mobile, anonymous, individual world, a world of thwarted wishes, of unsatisfied longings, of constant restlessness; a world in which people in the effort to live are building up a body of ideas that free them from a conventional tradition that has become fixed, hard, and oppressive; a world in which

[6] *Ibid.,* pp. 83-84.

[7] *L. c.*

[8] Zorbaugh, H. W., *Gold Coast and Slum* (Chicago, 1929), p. 45.

individuation, so typical of the life of the city, is carried to the extreme of personal and social disorganization. People behave in strange and incalculable ways; quick and intimate relationships spring up in the most casual way, and dissolve as quickly and as casually. Behavior is impulsive rather than social. It is a world of atomized individuals, of spiritual nomads.[9]

The world of furnished rooms has an interesting corollary in the tendency for urban recreation to gravitate from the home and neighborhood to the outside world and to assume forms in which the effect of participation goes little beyond the stimulation of individual emotion and has little or no function for social integration. The taxi-dance hall, for instance, provides recreation of this type on a commercialized basis. The patrons, Dr. Cressey has discovered,[10] tend to be those who experience elsewhere certain social barriers and restrictions of a serious nature resulting in a sense of inferiority. The taxi-dancers are young women who have come in many instances from broken, disorganized homes which have failed to provide them with normal, wholesome social relationships.[11]

The anonymity which may be attained by a person who is not living with relatives or friends gives him a degree of freedom which is unknown in the country. Even if the villager were wholly without family ties, his activities would still be of intimate concern to his neighbors, he would still be a part of a group to whose folkways and mores he must give heed. The occupant of the furnished room has no obligations of this particular type; he is free to form only such relationships as he wishes, or is able to form. This may mean, however, that he is a very lonely person since

[9] *Ibid.*, p. 86.
[10] Cressey, Paul G., *The Taxi-Dance Hall* (Chicago, 1932), pp. 142-43.
[11] *Ibid.*, p. 81.

congenial contacts are not always easily made.[12]   The freedom from constraining family and neighborhood ties which
the individual so often covets does not necessarily bring
happiness.   Unless these bonds are replaced by other relationships which are more satisfying, loneliness and dissatis-
faction are apt to follow.

The processes which have created the unique culture area
within the city form a part of a general process which is
again manifest in the fact that cities themselves also differ
from one another in atmosphere.   The purposes for which
they have been founded and which contribute to their growth
vary and these differences are reflected in the life of cities.
Every great city has developed a characteristic atmosphere
and spirit of its own.   A body of tradition[13] has grown up
about it which lends a distinctive interest to the city and
which forms a bond of union among its inhabitants.   Cities
which have been too recently founded to experience the mel-
lowing influence and charm of historical tradition not infrequently compensate for its absence by placing an emphasis,
usually much exaggerated, upon their unsurpassed opportunities for future development.   Boosting is a characteristic of
frontier towns, a device for arousing a spirit of united effort
in new communities.   The city population is a selective one
in comparison with the country population as a whole.

[12] There is a larger percentage of unmarried persons in the city than
in the country, a condition which may be due, in part at least, to the
absence in the city of certain opportunities for young people to become
acquainted in a social way which the country offers. It must be kept
in mind, however, that the city also tends to attract the unmated. For
statistics concerning this problem see E. R. Groves and W. F. Ogburn,
American Marriage and Family Relationships (New York, 1928).

[13] Professor Park in defining the city (R. E. Park *et al., The City,*
Chicago, 1925, p. 1) calls attention to the significance of tradition in
making the city the thing that it is. "The city," he says, "is rather a
state of mind, a body of customs and traditions, and of organized attitudes and sentiments that inhere in these customs and are transmitted
with this tradition."

Selection is present when the peasant turns cityward and it appears again if he is so situated that he is free to choose one city rather than another as his goal. Cities differ in the kinds of economic and cultural opportunities which they offer, and, hence, they attract different kinds of people. The commercial city is unlike the manufacturing city in certain respects; its dominant economic interests are different and this fact has a marked effect on the type of immigration which is attracted as well as on other features of the life of the city. The larger metropolitan centers provide both the commercial and the manufacturing interests, but these tend to be segregated to a certain extent at least in distinctive areas within the city. For other cities, or for certain sections of the metropolitan area, the prevailing interest is a cultural one; the atmosphere is vibrant with learning or music or art. The potency of such environments in influencing the careers of men of genius has been brought out by M. Odin's study, *Genèse des Grands Hommes,* in which a positive correlation is shown between the relative frequency of men of genius, at least of the kinds of ability in which M. Odin is interested, and the educational opportunities which the environment affords. Durkheim has also distinguished between material and dynamic density in populations; and Ward, American protagonist of opportunity, is led to conclude from these studies and his own experience that the dynamic influence which is productive of genius is not due to density at all nor yet to the friction of mind upon mind. " It is rather," he says, "the contact of mind with things, with the kind of things that tend to sharpen it, such as some cities afford and others do not." [14]

The fact that cities differ from each other in their attitudes as well as displaying differences within themselves complicates the problem of discovering the common and general

[14] Ward, Lester F., *Applied Sociology* (Boston, 1906), p. 193.

in city life yet further.   Indeed, in a brief survey such as
the present one, it would seem as though only the phenomenon of specialization were general, and, hence, that no
statement could be made which would apply to the behavior
of city people as a whole.   And in a large measure this is
true.   The responses of city-dwellers tend to be more par-
ticularized and less uniform than those of country people.
The total social environment of the larger community, as
Anderson and Linderman have pointed out, " is highly seg-
mented in fractions, circles, or groups, some of which touch
the individual intimately, others remotely " [15]   The relationships within these different segments of the city vary in
character, some are intimate and personal, others are impersonal and remote, and behavior toward the stranger varies
accordingly.   The nature of the relationships which unite the
group and which must be extended to the stranger if he becomes a part of it has a direct bearing, as we have noted
with other types of groups, upon the manner in which the
stranger is received.   The frequency of contacts of mobility
and the relatively greater number of the secondary or indirect
form of group relationships combine to give prominence to
the impersonal attitudes and relationships in urban social
life.[16]   The place of the personal relationships, on the other
hand, is relatively more restricted in scope, but not less essential.   Both types of relationships are indispensable parts of
the social structure of cities.   The integration of city life in
its totality rests upon the adjustment of the obligations of
these forms of relationships to each other; and from this it
follows that the newcomer does not become a full partaker
in the life of the city until he has been included in the intimate
relationships of at least one, if not more, of its groups.
Until then he remains a stranger.

[15] *Op. cit.*, p. 282.

[16] Carpenter, Niles, *The Sociology of City Life* (New York, 1931),
p. 205.

PART FOUR

THE STRANGER AND THE SPECIFIC SITUATION

CHAPTER X

The Circumstances of Meeting

I. THE DEGREE OF MOBILITY

In the preceding chapters something of the manner in which the social structure of the group determines in what ways the stranger is received has been noted. The fundamental principle of unification of the racial or national groups to whom the interacting persons belong was seen to determine certain of the broader characteristics of the initial relationships. Other somewhat less general attributes were observed to depend more directly upon the nature of the local pattern of social organization of the particular type of community which the stranger had entered than upon the bonds of national or racial allegiance. There are, however, other factors than those immediately involved in the social organization of the group which may also have an important bearing on the relationship of the stranger. To illustrate, although the nature of the social structure of any particular group lends relative permanence and stability to the general form of the relationship of the stranger within that group, the exact contour which is assumed by any specific instance of this relationship is also dependent upon the conjuncture of circumstances which are present when the contact occurs. Each relationship is therefore the resultant of a number of factors which belong in part to the social organization of the group and in part to special conditions of the meeting which are never precisely the same for any two contacts. This latter category comprises an endless variety of factors which defy classification, but from among which it is possible to select for consideration certain ones whose presence more noticeably affects the nature of the ensuing relationships. The degree of mobility of the stranger is such a factor, for instance, and others will appear in the course of the discussion.[1]

The stranger is a wanderer in the sense that he is one who has just entered the group who did not formerly belong to it. He possesses a certain mobility because of this condition and the question of the probable length of his contact with the group is introduced. The relationship may be a transitory one, and recognized as such, or it may be one for which a greater permanency is anticipated. In either case it will be a matter of moment in determining the behavior of both the group and the stranger toward one another. Simmel's well-known analysis of the sociological " form " of the stranger was based on the transitory aspect of the relationship. Simmel defined the stranger as a potential wanderer, who, although he had gone no further, had not quite got over the freedom of coming and going.[2] His relationship with the group would therefore be regarded as a more or less temporary one and would be associated with a greater or a less degree of mobility accordingly. The concept of the

[1] The term mobility as it is here used implies an actual or potential freedom to come and go as opposed to fixation within a group or a locality. The contact has been brought about by the stranger's entrance into the group, and, hence, by movement on his part from one position to another in the social universe. The question of the direction of this movement, that is, whether it is horizontal or vertical as these types of movement have been distinguished by Professor Sorokin (*Social Mobility*, New York and London, 1927, pp. 2-10 and p. 133) involves a different problem from that of the degree of. mobility, or probable duration of the contact, which is being considered at this point. The significance of the direction of mobility on the relationship will be discussed in the final chapter.

[2] Simmel, *Soziologie*, pp. 685-91. See Park and Burgess, *Introduction to the Science of Sociology*, pp. 322-27 for a translation.

stranger as one who has just entered the group, but who did not belong to it from the first, is broader than Simmel's and as a consequence of this the influence of the factor of mobility has a greater variability.

The special sociological characteristics of the relationship of the stranger which Simmel presents are mobility, objectivity, confidence, freedom from convention, and abstract relations. Of these characteristics, mobility would seem to belong to a somewhat different and more general order than the rest, inasmuch as the degree of mobility which is present determines to a considerable extent the existence of all the other attributes. They are derived from it. If, for instance, it is assumed that the relationship will be a permanent one, these will be greatly altered or will be absent altogether. Hence, the attributes of objectivity, confidence, and so on, appear as special features of a situation which has been produced largely by the condition of mobility. Simmel does not make this distinction, but this in no way impairs the validity of his analysis. He was describing a sociological form in which a given degree of mobility was present. Our task is to discover how the relationship which Simmel has so ably delineated would be affected by changes in the degree of mobility.

The stranger, according to Simmel, possesses mobility because he is not a landowner, a term which Simmel uses not only in the customary physical sense but also in a metaphysical one to mean an individual leading "a permanent and substantial existence which is fixed, if not in space, then at least in an ideal position within the social order." [3] The stranger is therefore restricted to trade or to pure finance, Simmel concludes. This concept is, however, a limited one. Not all of the strangers who enter a community in modern times

[3] *L. c.*

are traders or financiers.   There are tourists, for instance.
Moreover, a newcomer who has purchased a home in a community has become a landowner and yet he is a stranger
when he first takes possession of his new property.   Either
of these situations will react upon the nature of the ensuing
relations, but in different ways, since the degree of mobility
is much higher in the one case than it is in the other.

The objectivity of the stranger is, as Simmel points out,
an expression of his mobility.   The stranger is " not rooted
in the peculiar attitudes and biased tendencies of the group,
he stands apart from all these with the peculiar attitude of
the ' objective ' which does not indicate simply a separation
and disinterestness but is a peculiar composition of nearness
and remoteness, concern and indifference." [4]   At the one
extreme there is the tourist who is ruthlessly indifferent to
the feelings of the native people among whom he is sight-see-
ing because he does not expect to see them again and their
good will does not matter.   Nor is this lack of regard wholly
confined to the tourist; native merchants, hotel keepers, cab
drivers, guides, and others frequently make a practice of
over-charging the tourist for the same reason.   The tourist
is for them a passing stranger who can be taken advantage
of without endangering future trade.   On the other hand,
there are rarer individuals who make every effort to leave a
good impression behind them since they feel that they may
not have the opportunity to pass that way again to correct an
unfavorable one.   A high degree of mobility may thus be
related to two quite opposite types of behavior depending
upon the attitudes of the people involved.   A third type of
behavior is more truly impersonal than either of the two
types just described in that the stranger does not consider
himself in relation to the situation.   He is neither indifferent
to the impression that he makes nor zealous that this should

[4] L. c.

be a good one. He views the situation impartially as an outsider, free from its prejudices and its obligations and with no axe to grind.   Because of his neutral position the stranger is often sought to settle disputes.   As an instance of this, Simmel calls attention to the practice of Italian cities of bringing in their judges from without.   In the familiar act from *The Merchant of Venice,* Portia is given the opportunity to be the judge because she is, supposedly, " a learned doctor from Padua " and, moreover, a stranger whose decision will be unbiased.

Another phenomenon resulting from the mobility of the stranger's position is manifested in a peculiar freedom from restraint which sometimes leads people to confide intimate personal affairs to strangers which they would not reveal to any of their own immediate associates. The stranger receives these confidences because his sympathy and his judgment are assumed to be unbiased and genuine; and, further, the temporary nature of the contact is thought to preclude any possibility of his repeating the secrets told him to those who might be concerned and thus causing embarrassment. One can perhaps recall instances in which he has confided things to strangers only to be greatly perturbed to discover afterwards that the stranger was in some way connected with the persons about whom the disclosures were made.   A certain tension is relieved by the mere telling of one's secret problems to a sympathetic listener, who is himself in no way involved, even though his advice is not being sought, or thought to be of assistance.

A somewhat different situation is that in which the stranger who has entered a group is taken aside by various members, more or less in turn, and told, " in strictest confidence, of course," about the idiosyncrasies and the shortcomings of the others.   The motives for doing this are varied.   In some cases there is a sincere desire to protect

the stranger from unpleasantness; but, again, the reason is
an entirely selfish desire to enhance one's own personal interests in some way at the expense of another. The stranger
who is discreet may come to occupy a position of peculiar advantage since he may enjoy the confidences of all the factions.
He may use this to gain his own ends by playing one side off
against the other, or he may endeavor to bring about harmony
between the warring factions as a neutral arbitrator. On the
other hand, unless the stranger is judicious, he may find
himself at outs with everyone concerned or forced to take the
part of one side against the other whether or not he really
wishes to do so. The position of the stranger in a house
that is divided against itself is not an easy one; tact is needed
if he does not himself wish to become embroiled.

The freedom from conventions is a further attribute of
the position of the stranger which Simmel has noted and
which, as he indicates, contains " all sorts of dangerous possibilities ", since the stranger is not confined in his action by
" custom, piety, or precedents." [5] Where the relationship is
to be a transitory one, the stranger need not be bound by
the conventions of those with whom he is in contact in many
cases, and he is, moreover, free from the conventions of his
own people for the time being since he is separated from
them. To certain persons this freedom gives a sense of
exhilaration and of adventure that is manifested in various
ways, and that may readily go to extremes. A measure of
the excitement of traveling is derived from this source as
well as from an interest in new surroundings. The traveler,
particularly if he is alone, is free from the criticisms of those
who know him and he therefore dares to do things which he
realizes would not be approved in Gopher Prairie, Middletown and Mineville. If his own inhibitions are not too

[5] *L. c.*

deeply ingrained, he can " let go " and oftentimes he does.
He ignores the social customs of the people among whom he
happens to be because he feels that they do not apply to
him and no one is present who is acquainted with him to
censor his behavior or to report it to his friends.   A different
situation is created, however, when the stranger enters a
new group with the intention of becoming a part of it.   He
cannot then afford to disregard its conventions; rather, he is
solicitous about conforming with them since his reception
by the group may depend upon this.   He does not wish to
appear odd in their eyes.   The adherence to conventions is
thus seen to be dependent not only upon the previous conditioning to which a person has been subjected, but also upon
the seriousness of the consequences involved in breaking
these.   The stranger is not rooted in the customs of the new
community and in this respect he may be free from its conventions; but if he wishes to remain among the people with
whom he is in contact, he may still find it necessary for him
to observe their conventions.   It follows from this that the
freedom from convention as an aspect of the relationship of
the stranger is relative to the degree of mobility which the
stranger enjoys.   The manner in which the group regards
the stranger's behavior is also influenced by this.   If the
stranger is merely a passer-by, his oddities may seem amusing and be tolerated; but, if he has come to stay, they may
prove to be annoying and may arouse resentment.

The fifth characteristic of the position of the stranger
which Simmel distinguishes is expressed in the more abstract
nature of the relations which are involved.   This characteristic is a more comprehensive and fundamental one than those
which have just been discussed in connection with the influence of the degree of mobility.   It is less directly an expression of the probable duration of the contact and more directly

an attribute of the position of the stranger as such. Simmel points out that the stranger only has certain more general qualities in common with the members of an intimate group who are allied by the very differences which distinguish them from those who do not share this intimacy. The more specific and intimate the bonds are that unite the group the more definitely the stranger who does not share these is regarded as an outsider. The stranger is near to or like the group, only in those qualities which because of their general nature are shared by a great many, perhaps by all mankind, and, hence, have but an attenuated value as unifying bonds. On the other hand, those interests which are shared by only the intimate members of the group, and in this sense are their nearest ties, are the ones in which the stranger is the farthest removed from the group. Thus results that unique constellation of the near and the far, of the intimate and the remote, which, accordingly to Simmel, characterizes the relationship of the stranger. This concept, is, however, an abstraction of a very general nature. If we wish to understand the manner in which it applies to any concrete instance of the relationship, it is necessary to discover the particular respects in which the stranger is near to or far from the group and what the conditions are which have brought about this alignment. This requires, as we have previously noted, a consideration of the social organization of the group and also of the specific circumstances of the meeting, since there may be special factors present which will affect the customary reactions toward the newcomer. The position of the stranger is responsive, for instance, to changes in the degree of mobility. It may also be affected by the intervention of extraneous factors of varied kinds which become of moment because of their relation to other elements which are present in a given situation.

2. THE INTERVENTION OF FACTORS OF MOMENT

Those circumstances which have been termed factors of moment are largely dependent for their significance upon the particular combination of conditions under which they occur. They are thus lacking in the relative stability and regularity of the factors which pertain to the social organization of the group. The dependence of such factors upon the nature of the circumstances under which the contact takes place makes it difficult to generalize concerning the influence which any factor of this character may have since every contact represents a more or less unique situation and a factor which has one effect in one setting may have quite the opposite in another. A serious catastrophe may, for example, prove a unifying factor in one situation or it may widen already existing social distances in another. The Japanese earthquake in 1923 tended to bring the Japanese and Americans closer together. Racial differences were forgotten for the time in the common purpose of relieving suffering. On the other hand, the antagonisms between the Japanese and the Koreans were heightened by the calamity and the Japanese in a kind of hysteria of fear attacked numbers of unoffending Koreans.[6] The usual behavior sequences between the racial groups involved—the Japanese and Americans, and the Japanese and Koreans—were deflected from their accustomed channels by the same factor; but, in the one case, this deflection tended toward convergence or unity of feeling and in the other toward divergence or an increased animosity. It is necessary therefore when noting the changes which are brought about by the intervention of an accidental factor to bear in mind that these are the consequences of the conjuncture of circumstances present in the total situation and are

[6] This information was given to me by friends living in Japan at the time whose attitude toward the Japanese is sympathetic and friendly.

by no means wholly due to the presence of the interjected factor alone. Such a factor may, as we have just seen, have a certain influence in one situation and quite the opposite in another. Like a chemical catalyzer the presence of an extraneous factor may often serve to accelerate reactions that are already taking place and thus to accentuate or intensify developing friendships or dislikes. At other times, however, the interjection of such a factor may tend to retard the normal processes of establishing new relationships or to deflect their direction, changing an inclination toward friendliness to one of distrust or vice versa.

In my own experience there are many instances of contacts with strangers in which the intervention of some unexpected event or of some unusual circumstance of the meeting has markedly affected the nature of the ensuing relationships. I once hiked alone and unarmed across the mountains of Northern Luzon from Baguio to Tagudin on the China Sea, a distance of nearly two hundred miles. A few passages adapted from my travel journal give an idea of contacts which I had with the native people of this remote region, the Igorots, whom I met from time to time along the lonely trail and for whom I came to have a warm glow of fellow feeling.

My admiration for the Igorot *cargadors* (carriers) whom I met on the trail grew apace; men, women, and even little children carried loads many times heavier than my pack with apparent indifference. And I was having difficulty with my pack; the Albatross, I called it. It would not stay in place and the straps hurt my shoulders. Toiling upward with it, I decided that if, like the Igorots, I had to pack all the appurtenances of civilization that I had on my back for days over mountain foot paths, I would forego the most of them, clothing included. . . .

If these once-upon-a-time head hunters felt any surprise at meeting a white woman on foot and alone in that isolated country, they gave no expression of this. The only English that most of them knew was "Good Morning", and they invariably greeted me with it no matter what the hour was, and I made the same response. One of the first white teachers among the Igorots was a Mrs. Kelly who taught her pupils to say, "Good morning, Mrs. Kelly". Ever afterward they said, politely, "Good morning, Mrs. Kelly", to whomsoever they met, man or woman. . . .

Down in the Bugias Valley all was sunshine and verdant loveliness, but up among the clouds where I was, a spiteful rain drenched and a cutting wind chilled. I had been walking six kilometers an hour, but now my muscles stiffened and ached and I stopped to rest when any shelter was available. A heavily laden Igorot cargador whom I met indicated that he, too, was cold when he saw that I was shivering and we commiserated with one another and became good friends as we huddled together under a protecting ledge waiting for the storm to pass. . . .

There had been heavy rains in the mountains and the Abra River ford, like that of the famous Kabul River, was "up and roaring". I was uncertain just how deep the water might be and its swiftness terrified me, for I am not a strong swimmer. I remembered, moreover, that an American man had been drowned at that same ford a few months before and I felt that it would be foolhardy for me to attempt to cross. I scouted up and down the stream looking for a more promising place, but there was none and it was rapidly getting dark. In the midst of my perplexity I suddenly realized that I was not alone. Three Igorot men whom I had seen behind me on the trail had come up and were making a camp under an acacia tree by the ford. I hurried over to them and explained by signs that I wanted to cross the river. One of them, a tall, dignified young man who was starting the fire, rose and signified that he was willing to take the plunge with me. I was soon ready and the "Big Chief" and I took hold of hands and waded in. It was quite dramatic and thrilling, and I was no longer afraid although the water was shoulder-deep and so swift that I kept my footing

with difficulty. My escort knew how to make the crossing.
We tacked up stream to a sandbar and then down stream to
another one and up again to the farther bank. I could never
have made it alone. I gave him a peso (fifty cents) and he
grinned his thanks and went back across the river. I looked
for him when I was ready to start on. He was standing on
the opposite bank with the gray and white striped mantle that
the Igorots sometimes wear when they come down from their
hills to civilization thrown about his shoulders with all the
dignity of a Roman senator. We waved each other a friendly
good-by.[7]

The unusual circumstances of these meetings, the fury of
the storm on the lonely mountain trail, the hazardous crossing
of the torrential stream, were exceptional factors the presence of which created an entirely different relationship from
the one which would normally have existed. The whole
gamut of differences which existed between myself and the
Igorots were swept away for the moment and the plane upon
which we met had become narrowed to a simple elemental
one of physical discomfort combined with an emotion of
awe inspired by the angry forces of nature which each of
us realized that the other also experienced and which formed
a bond of union. These relationships, fleeting though they
were, carried with them a content unlike that of other contacts, also friendly, which I had with Igorots during a vacation spent at Baguio. The emotional factor was absent from
these latter relationships and they were marked by a certain
social distance due to racial and cultural differences which, in
the contacts along the trail, had been obliterated by the exigencies of the circumstances.

Another instance of the effect of the intervention of an
incidental factor upon a casual relationship between strangers
is taken from my Turkish travel notes.

[7] Adapted from my unpublished Philippine notes.

A friend and I were making a tour of the Seven Churches of Asia and returning to Smyrna from Denizli, the modern city near the sites of the ancient Laodicea, Colosse and Hierapolis, we were crowded into a third-class coach filled with newly recruited soldiers.[8] It was during the Kourban Bairam holidays and a festive spirit prevailed. We were the only women in the car and we felt conspicuous and a little uneasy for fear the men might become rough and make it unpleasant for us. Happily, this was not the case. We soon noticed that some of the quieter men were busy practicing the letters of the new Turkish alphabet which had been adopted a few months before and which is based on the Latin characters rather than on the Arabic as the old Turkish alphabet had been. The new alphabet is similar in most respects to our own. We praised their efforts with smiles and the few Turkish words that we knew and we helped them to form some of the letters. They were delighted and within a few minutes many of the others had produced scraps of paper and stubs of pencils and were hard at work, eager for assistance and boyishly pleased with our approbation.

An awkward situation was here changed into a pleasant, friendly one by the presence of an incidental factor, the interest in the new Turkish alphabet. The feeling of tension that had existed disappeared, and in the temporary relationship of teacher and pupil which was formed we felt at ease with the young Turkish soldiers and they with us. The reader can no doubt think of times in his or her own experience when some happy circumstance has intervened and relieved an otherwise strained and uncomfortable situation between strangers. An amusing saying or act of a child, or

[8] We were traveling third class ourselves, ostensibly because one absorbs more local color that way, actually because college professors, women professors at least, are, like the apostles of old, an impecunious people.

even the antics of an animal, may open the way for friendly conversation. The readiness with which travelers become acquainted is frequently due to the fact that they meet under circumstances which are out of the ordinary and which each realizes are of moment to the other. This is particularly true if the situation is one in which the interest is associated with like sentiments and evokes a like emotional reaction. Among my own more intimate friendships there are two which had their beginnings under such circumstances, one at the Great Wall in China, the other on Mt. Lykabettos in Athens. In both instances the initial contacts were of such short duration that had they occurred under ordinary conditions hardly more than speaking acquaintanceships would have developed. In these meetings, however, a sympathetic bond was created at once through the medium of our surroundings. Something of the sentiment long attached to these historic places became associated with the other person, thus giving a background endued with a rich emotional content to relationships which in themselves were but newly formed.

Circumstances which are of sufficient import to arouse strong emotional reactions tend, at least for the moment, to unify, on the one hand, those whose response is the same although their other interests may be widely variant, and to separate, on the other hand, those who feel differently in this one particular matter even when they have much else in common. The spectators at a baseball game, for instance, often forget their natural reserve in the excitement of a good play, or in resentment at a decision of the umpire, and talk and argue freely with strangers. People who have never seen each other before nor will in all probability ever do so again are comrades, or antagonists, for the time; the emotions aroused by the game are so over-mastering that other likenesses and differences are submerged until these have subsided.

Trinculo's much quoted observation, " Misery acquaints a man with strange bedfellows ", expresses succinctly the familiar fact that a common difficulty which is of sufficient magnitude may out-weigh differences which would ordinarily be of significance in keeping people aloof. The welding power of a common enemy has long been recognized, and leaders seeking to achieve a degree of unanimity among divergent groups have frequently played upon this factor. During the World War the Allied Powers laid aside their own disagreements to present a united front to the enemy countries. After the Armistice, however, the conflicting aims and ambitions of the different nations again became apparent. At the time of the American Revolution, the Colonies were led to forgo their own petty rivalries in order that their efforts might be united in the struggle against the mother country visioned as an enemy of the interests of each and all alike. Benjamin Franklin's famous remark to John Hancock when the American Declaration of Independence was signed, " We must all hang together or assuredly we shall all hang separately ", is a cryptic statement of the situation. The presence of a common danger provides a strong motive for cooperation among unlike persons or groups and odd alignments of loyalties often occur at such times. George, an American Negro living in the Philippines, voiced the need for unified action rather aptly at a time when the relations between the Americans and the Filipinos had become somewhat strained. " Us Americans has got to stick together," George stoutly maintained—a sentiment which was shared by his white compatriots.

There are many descriptions in literature, some of them purely fictional and others based on facts, of oddly assorted groups of strangers who have joined forces because of some extremity. In Bret Harte's story, " The Outcasts of Poker Flat ", for example, a strange little company of the besmirched and the pure in heart are brought together and achieve a measure of unified feeling through the intervention of an adverse factor, the blizzard by which they are snow-bound in an isolated mountain cabin.

Not all of the circumstances or influences which bind together persons who would ordinarily be uncongenial are necessarily of an adverse character. Political life furnishes many instances of what President Butler of Columbia University has aptly described as " the cohesive power of public plunder ". The " tin box " may form a link connecting a corrupt office-holder not only with gangsters of the underworld whom he regards as socially beneath him, but also with men above him in wealth and social position who are unprincipled enough to stoop to seek their ends in an illegal manner. History also records instances in which kings have condescended to negotiate with thugs when some nefarious scheme was to be perpetrated.

The effect on the formation of new relationships of the interjection of some unusual factor may also be one of retardation. Oftentimes the presence of an adult among a group of children is a deterrent of this kind. Children who are strangers to one another and who feel self-conscious and ill at ease when there are grown-ups in the group will soon begin to get acquainted if left to themselves. Among older people the presence of some one in authority, or who is feared or disliked, may have the same retarding effect when new contacts are being made. Accidents which cause embarrassment or which make people appear ridiculous may also prevent them from responding in the way that they would naturally have done when meeting strangers. The series of cartoons entitled *Life's Most Embarrassing Moment* and the advertisement of a well-known cigarette which adjures people to be nonchalant and to conceal their confusion, as it were, behind a smoke screen, have an appeal because the discomfiting situations which they depict in an amusing way so frequently strike a responsive note in the reader's own experience. Many of these occur in the presence of strangers before whom one wishes to appear well and toward whom it is difficult to be composed after the incident. My memory of one particular occasion of this kind is still poignant. I had an appointment with a college trustee, an eminent professor and writer, concerning a position for which I was applying. A maid directed me to his study and I knocked on what I supposed to be the right door. A voice said, " Come in ", and I did so only to find to my intense chagrin that I had mistaken the door and had blundered into the dignified trustee's bedroom while he was having his toe nails manicured. That I was elected to the position is further evidence of the magnanimity of the great.

The particular circumstances which have immediately preceded a contact may also affect the nature of the initial relationships. A stranger who enters a family group in which a crisis exists, a quarrel perhaps, or some other difficulty, especially if this cannot readily be divulged, may be unwelcome because his presence complicates the situation. Again, there are times when his coming might create a welcome diversion and in this way help a harassing situation to right itself.

Other examples of special or unusual factors of various kinds which may affect the behavior of people toward one another when they are meeting for the first time as strangers will, in all probability, suggest themselves to the reader. The category of such factors is a large and an exceedingly flexible one, since the question of whether or not any accidental circumstance may be of moment is dependent upon the manner in which it is interrelated with the other factors present in the total situation. The same factor may be of moment in one situation and of little or no consequence in another. The whole combination of circumstances must therefore be understood in order to appreciate why a certain factor produces the reaction that it does in any specific situation. This involves taking into consideration, among other things, the characteristics of the interacting persons both as types and as individuals, a problem that has been reserved for the following chapter.

CHAPTER XI

The Evaluation of the Individual

I. THE ESTABLISHMENT OF POSITION

In face-to-face contacts the interacting persons will either have already established relationships with one another in former meetings or, in case the meeting is one between strangers, they will begin to form relationships through the process of interaction. If the relationship is a new one, the interaction will tend to follow accustomed pathways and the behavior toward the stranger will be based on the previous experience of the group with outsiders of various categories, to one of which the stranger is assigned, tentatively at least. To illustrate, among the Australian tribes the stranger is given one of two positions with reference to the group, he is either a tribal brother or he is not. In the first position, he has a definite place in the group and his behavior toward the members of the group and theirs toward him is already pre-scribed, while, in the second case, he is regarded as an enemy and a person to be killed if possible. It must, however, be determined to which of these two categories the stranger belongs and the first stages of the process of establishing his relation to the group are those of evaluation. A position, tentative in most instances, is accorded to the stranger almost as soon as his existence has been noted and this forms a point of departure for the beginning of the relationship. As the contact continues and further characteristics of the stranger appear, the position assigned to the stranger at first may be changed and the behavior toward him modified accordingly. In this connection Simmel has observed:

All relationships of people to each other rest, as a matter of course, upon the precondition that they know something about each other. . . That we shall know with whom we have to do is the first precondition of having anything to do with another. The merchant knows that his correspondent wants to buy at the lowest price and to sell at the highest price. The teacher knows that he may credit to the pupil a certain quality and quantity of information. Within each social stratum the individual knows approximately what measure of culture he has to presuppose in each other individual. In all relationships of a personally differentiated sort there develop, as we may affirm with obvious reservations, intensity and shading in the degree in which each unit reveals himself to the other through word and deed. How much error and sheer prejudice may lurk in all this knowledge is immaterial. Just as our apprehension of external nature, along with its elusions and its inaccuracies, still attains that degree of truth which is essential for the life and progress of our species, so each knows the other with whom he has to do, in a rough and ready way, to the degree necessary in order that the needed kinds of intercourse may proceed. . . . The customary reciprocal presentation, in the case of any somewhat protracted conversation, or in the case of contact upon the same social plane, although at first sight an empty form, is an excellent symbol of that reciprocal apprehension which is the presumption of every social relationship. The fact is variously concealed from consciousness, because, in the case of a very large number of relationships, only the quite typical tendencies and qualities need to be recognized. Their necessity is usually observed only when they happen to be wanted.[1]

Simmel adds further that it would be " profitable scientific labor to investigate the sort and degree of reciprocal apprehension which is needed for the various relationships between human beings." [2]

[1] Simmel, Georg, " The Sociology of Secrecy and of Secret Societies," translated by Albion W. Small in *The American Journal of Sociology*, Jan., 1906, vol. xi, pp. 441-498.

[2] *L. c.*

In the present study, in which the attempt has been made to discover something of the nature of the initial relationships between strangers, it has been noted that the kind of apprehension most frequently required is that which makes it possible to assign a position to the stranger. This may be a relatively simple problem or it may be an exceedingly complicated one. In primitive societies the number of categories into which the stranger may be placed is relatively limited; and, although it may be a matter of debate as to which of these is the right one, the question can hardly be said to require the fineness of discernment that is often necessary in a highly civilized society with its multitude of interwoven categories. In a highly organized and differentiated society the individual belongs to many categories at one and the same time and the additional problem of evaluating these arises. To illustrate, American Negroes are at once citizens of the United States and members of the black race, two categories which, from the standpoint of the white race, are associated with different types of relationships. Toward a fellow citizen the customary attitude is one of loyalty and toward a Negro it is more often one of antipathy, or of superiority. Which of these conflicting attitudes will predominate is a question of evaluation and the manner in which it is resolved will depend upon other factors present in the total situation. In the case of the reaction toward the Negro George during the Philippine agitation, nationality was of first importance and the feeling was that of loyalty, while in the incident in which Negroes were asked to withdraw from a church congregation, the issue was that of race.

The tendency to form categories and to evaluate the individual on the basis of the categories to which he is assigned, N. S. Shaler has termed the categoric motive.

We have seen that at the beginning of any acquaintance the fellow-being is inevitably dealt with in a categoric way. He is taken as a member of a group, which group is denoted to us by a few convenient signs: as our acquaintance with a particular person advances, this category tends to become qualified. Its bounds are pushed this way and that until they break down. It is to be noted in this process that the category fights for itself, or we for it, so that the result of the battle between the immediate truth and the prejudice is always doubtful.[3]

The method of establishing categories in dealing with new phenomena, whether they consist of human beings or of inanimate objects, is itself a necessary reasoning process. Its unfortunate aspect, where people are so classified, is the frequent limitation of the categories and the nature of the emotional qualities which come to be associated with some of these. In meeting strangers the most apparent categories for establishing relations are those that pertain to the larger population groupings which are distinguished by certain biological traits or by certain characteristic cultural patterns. The question as to whether or not the stranger is a member of one's own population group is a fundamental one. If he is, certain cultural similarities may be assumed and the subsequent behavior toward him regulated accordingly. If he is not, then the question of deciding to which of various other population groups he does belong must be met. This may be a careful and discriminating procedure which places the individual not only within a major population grouping but also within a definite sub-group. Or, again, it may be a rude decision which merely classifies the stranger as "some kind of a foreigner" without troubling to ascertain which kind.

If the stranger belongs to a different race, he will, in all probability, encounter already existing attitudes with respect to his race which may have been formed by previous contacts

[3] Shaler, N. S., *The Neighbor* (Boston and New York, 1904), p. 221.

with other individuals belonging to it, or by tradition and hearsay alone. If his racial or national group is regarded as inferior, because different, he may be designated as " a nigger ", " a Chink ", " a Jap ", " a wop ", " a greaser ", " a sheeney ", " a dago ", " a Siwash ", and so on and be placed forthwith in an unfavorable position which makes it difficult for him to establish pleasant relations with the group. On the other hand, if the stranger's racial group is one which enjoys prestige in the eyes of the other group, the position which is assigned to him will be one which will facilitate forming friendly relations. It is not so much the fact that the individual is judged to be a type that is to be deplored as the fact that the concept of the type is so often an erroneous one. If the concept of the type were a correct one, there would be no harm in assigning the stranger a preliminary position in this way and utilizing this as a basis for the development of relationships of a more specific nature as other attributes were discovered. Not infrequently, however, the concept of the type is a superficial one colored by prejudice. The type may be judged by the individual no less than the individual in his turn is judged by the type. This has been brought out in numbers of the personal documents secured by the Race Relations Survey on the Pacific Coast.[4] In describing their attitudes toward certain alien races many persons have indicated the very limited foundations on which these were based.[5] Certain of my own attitudes are also good illustrations of the role of a few vivid personal experiences in determining the manner in which another group is

[4] See Bogardus, E. S., *The New Social Research* (Los Angeles, 1926) and *Immigration and Race Attitudes* (New York, 1928).

[5] An interesting correlation is shown between the degree of information possessed by persons concerning oriental peoples and questions and their attitude toward these in Godwin B. Watson's unpublished monograph, *Orient and Occident*, prepared in connection with the Institute of Pacific Relations at Honolulu, July, 1927.

evaluated, and of the way in which this affects new relationships with members of this group.

In my first contacts with Greek students a few unhappy cases of cheating in examinations occurred, and, without my realizing what was happening, my attitude toward the Greeks as a people became biased by this. This bias was increased no doubt by the fact that the relations between the Greeks and the Turks were somewhat strained at the time and my sympathies were drawn toward the Turks. A conflict existed, however, between the new attitude that I was forming toward the Greeks and my deep admiration for the ancient Greek culture. It was difficult to reconcile the two, but I found a way out. I looked up all the evidence that I could find to substantiate the claim that the modern Greeks are not the lineal descendants of the Greeks of the Classical Period and hence have no rightful pride in that glorious tradition. This was purely a biased process on my part since I made no effort to weigh this evidence critically or to seek out the counter arguments. Fortunately, before I had become too set in this way of thinking to change, I had the opportunity to widen my contacts with Greeks in a number of pleasant ways and the absurdity of what I had been doing dawned upon me. Moreover, the Turks and the Greeks were making an effort to arrive at a better understanding and their leaders were wisely calling attention then to the benefits of cooperation and were pointing out the good qualities rather than the shortcomings of the other racial group. There had been bitter recriminations between the Turks and the Greeks over the question of the burning of Smyrna, each nation blaming the other for this unhappy tragedy, but as better relations were established the problem was solved in another way, at least by the man in the street. A Turkish chauffeur in Smyrna assured me that the Armenians had done it, and it is of interest in this connection that I accepted this statement willingly and uncritically since I was irritated with Armenians myself just then because of a propensity of some of my Armenian students to whine about their grades.

My relations toward the Chinese and the Japanese were also affected by minor incidents which to a certain extent still condition my initial reactions to individuals of these races whom I meet as strangers. The attitude toward the Chinese is a friendly one, not alone because of my high regard for the cultural tradition of the Chinese, but also because of a certain sentiment attached to a going-away gift of white lilacs from a Chinese ricksha boy whom I had engaged for the few days that I was in Pieping. For me, lilacs are a symbol of spring time in New England and seeing them again in the parks of far-away Pieping had given me a little thrill of pleasure. That my ricksha boy should have noticed this and should bring me a lovely bunch as I was leaving for Mukden was a wholly unexpected little act of thoughtfulness which touched me deeply and which always comes to mind when I meet a Chinese.

Toward the Japanese, on the other hand, my first reaction is a less kindly one. Realizing that this is so and the reasons for it, I can, and do, rule this bias out; but a certain effort is required in order to do this and my greeting is a less spontaneously friendly one than it would be if this bias did not exist. My emotional reaction in this case has its origin in two unpleasant experiences connected with sleeping-car reservations on Japanese railroads. In both instances I was taking a train late at night and reservations paid for in advance were not forthcoming. This inconvenience to me may have been accidental; but the circumstances inclined me to believe than it was intentional since I was an American woman traveling without an escort, and the Japanese felt resentful at the time toward Americans because of the difficulties of their own nationals in California.

The personal experiences which have just been related illustrate how trivial the circumstances may be upon which the concept of a type is formed and how this concept again affects the reaction toward others of the same grouping. Childish and unreasoned as some of my own attitudes have been, I hardly think that they were more so than those of many people whose contacts with an alien people have been comparatively limited. I have known tourists whose opinions of entire nations were based on whether or not they had liked the food and the hotel service. The wife of a prominent American clergyman whom I met touring the Near East had, figuratively speaking, eaten her way through Palestine and had found it hard and dry. Her reactions were altogether in terms of food that she had found unpalatable.

Professor Sorokin has summarized the method of locating a person's position in what he has termed *social space,* as " (1) the indication of a man's relations to specific groups (2) the relation of these groups to each other within a population, and (3) the relation of this population to other populations included in the human universe." [6] These three general types, or levels, of relationships tend, however, to become telescoped together, and the procedure in identifying the stranger's position is not always an orderly and logical one. The most salient relationship from the standpoint of the group tends to be the one which is first established with the stranger, the essentials of the other relationships being taken note of later as they happen to be wanted. The issue to be determined in the initial process is whether or not the stranger possesses those characteristics which are of most value for the type of relationships which are dominant in that particular group, either for the moment or for a protracted period. Is the stranger a good sport or is he not? Is he a communist

[6] Sorokin, Pitirim, *Social Mobility* (New York and London, 1927), p. 3.

or an adherent of the status quo? a good neighbor or a disobliging one? a Jew or a Gentile? a Catholic or a Protestant?—and so on, as the case may be.

Among the Australian tribes the sacred messenger brings his credentials, a cleft stick, or similar token, with him and his position is assured once he has presented these. In civilized societies, letters of introduction or letters of recommendation serve this same purpose in assisting the stranger to establish his position in a new community. Such documents are an indication of the stranger's former position and hence may expedite the process of establishing relationships in another group. If the newcomer brings no credentials with him, the effort to trace, if possible, some relationship between him and some one who is already known to the group is a customary procedure, especially in rural communities; but one which is by no means confined to these. To discover that the stranger knows some one also known to ourselves gives, as it were, a key to his position and forms a bond of relationship with him.

The position accorded to the stranger may be one which brings him in some way within the circle of the social organization of the group and extends to him the obligations, duties, privileges, and so on, of a position within the social structure, or it may be one which places him outside the group in a relationship of dislike, indifference, or open hostility. Both types of positions are in relation to the group; the fact that the stranger is regarded as an enemy and excluded implies a relationship of a definite, specific kind no less than if he were accepted as a friend. It is the obligations and privileges of the two relationships which are different. If the stranger is accepted as a friend, the new relationship carries with it an obligation of loyalty; but if he is classed as an enemy, the obligation may be to kill him instead.

The nature of relationships which may be extended to the

stranger is largely determined, as we have seen, by the kinds
of social relationships which form the structure of the group
itself. The question, however, of whether or not the reaction
is a friendly one and an effort is made to include the stranger
or whether he is summarily rejected is influenced in many
instances by the special circumstances of the meeting. And
there is yet a third aspect of the problem to be considered,
one which is by no means always of least significance
although it has been reserved until the last for discussion.
Even in the first stages of contact the personal qualities of
the individuals concerned, as distinct from the types to which
they belong, are often recognized and constitute a decisive
factor in determining the stranger's place in the group.

2. THE APPRECIATION OF PERSONALITY

The problem of distinguishing those qualities of the total
personality of the individual which are common to his type
from those other qualities which are unique with the person
himself is an intricate psychological task and one which need
not detain us here. It is sufficient for our present purpose to
recognize the fact that, although the individual is to a certain
extent a replica of the group, or groups, to which he belongs,
he is, nevertheless, a person in his own right possessing an
individuality of his own which is never identical with that
of another no matter how close the resemblance may be.
These unique traits of personality, both biological and psychological, which differentiate each individual from every
other tend to reveal themselves more slowly than the more
general characteristics which are associated with the type
and, hence, they are frequently less operative than the latter
in determining the nature of the initial relationships. If the
persons meeting as strangers are distinctly different in their
general types, these major differences, since they are more
easily recognized, tend to obscure the more intimate attributes

of personality which only become apparent as the acquaintance continues. Indeed, if strong biases exist with regard to group differences, or if the other person is regarded as an inferior or a rival for some reason, his own specific traits may never be noted or justly appraised even though the contact becomes a permanent one. These, however, are the more extreme conditions; normally, the personality traits peculiar to the interacting individuals become significant factors early in the formation of the relationship, and, at times, from its very beginning.

The relationships in which the more specific elements of personality have been taken into consideration differ from those which are based on type and position alone in their greater degree of complexity and in an added richness and import. This does not mean that to recognize the individuality of a person is synonymous with liking him, for this does not necessarily follow. Quite the opposite may be just as true. We hear people remark that the longer they know such and such persons the less they like them, or that so and so does not " wear well ", perhaps as often as we hear that the relationship has become a pleasanter one with a more extended contact. The question is not one of merely liking or disliking; it goes far deeper than that, touching the very wellspring of egohood. Consciously or unconsciously each seeks recognition in his own right. This quest is an expression of the desire for recognition which has been listed by Thomas and Znaniecki in their study, *The Polish Peasant,* as one of the four fundamental wishes or desires of mankind. And, however differently this wish may manifest itself, whether in seeking glory at the cannon's mouth, or in publicity from perching in trees, or in the range and intonation of one's voice in calling home the hogs, there would seem to be little doubt that in some form or other it is a universal trait. The manner of recognition that is wished for may vary, but the desire itself remains constant.

If the contact between strangers is a purely casual one, each may be indifferent to the impression which the other has of him; but if the relationship is to be of a more permanent nature, the desire for personal recognition becomes a factor. More often it is the stranger, who, because of his position as an outsider, seeks recognition from those within the group; but, at other times, if the stranger has prestige, the members of a group may be anxious that he should recognize them, not only as a group but as individuals also. In either case, however, the essential quality of recognition is its mutuality. It is a consequence of a form of interaction in which each person becomes aware of the other's individuality and each realizes that the other has done so. Such mutuality of recognition does not require that the persons involved should accept each other as equals; the relationship of position still remains and this may, or may not, have been one of like status. That which has been changed is the content of this form which has been supplemented by a personal, and therefore more intensive, feeling. When, for instance, I commend the little student who has spent long hours working over the drawings in her biology note book that these may be as perfect as possible and she says, very shyly and sweetly, " And all for you, Miss Wood," our formal relationship as student and instructor has not been removed, but to it there has been added an additional bond of recognition and affection which exists in conjunction with it.

Although the initial step in the formation of new relationships is that of establishing the stranger's position and the recognition of the more intimate aspects of personality must wait upon this, there are many occasions when the stranger's position has already been ascertained when he enters the group, and, unless this is of such a nature that more personal relations are automatically precluded, personality rather than position will then be the dominant consideration. To illustrate, let us say that the stranger who appears in a country village is know to be the new minister. The relationship of position already exists and the problem of the first contact is therefore one of the adjustment of personalities to each other from this point of view. People admire or dislike certain qualities in those who fill various relationships to themselves and the new minister is more than likely to be critically scrutinized. One member of his congregation may prefer that he should be "a good fellow," another may esteem reserve and aloofness in a minister.

Personal reactions are complex, rarely simple, and in many cases it is difficult for a person to explain why he feels as he does toward some one whom he has just met. I cannot always explain why I have been attracted by certain people and repelled by others. Nor are such first impressions always permanent. I have grown to care for persons whom I did not like at first. It is seldom that the opposite reaction has occurred. The personal relationships are, however, distinctly ones of interaction; my impression of the other person is strongly influenced by what I believe to be his impression of me. A friendly impulse which does not meet with a like response may be changed to one of bitterness. The opinions of others also impinge on the relationship. One does not wish to lose face by liking or disliking the wrong people. Strangers moving into a new community are anxious to meet "just the right people" and frequently their first reactions are based more largely on the opinions of others as to whom they should know than they are on their own feelings in this matter. Social prestige is here the controlling influence. Eventually, however, one's own nature tends to reassert itself and in the relationship which is ultimately formed the genuine feeling with which each person regards the other becomes significant. This, though, is a process which requires time; for, even if no untoward retarding factors intervene, the recognition of personality is more often a gradual unfolding than it is an immediate awakening. There are, to be sure, instances of love at first sight, but this precipitous appreciation of each other's personality is not the customary one. The initial contact seldom affords sufficient time for each to take, as it were, an accurate measure of the other person and to establish a relationship based on these findings. What may be achieved, however, by the reactions of the first meeting is a certain tentative conditioning which predisposes one to react in the same way at a future time. If the first impression is a favorable one, the acquaintance is renewed with pleasure; whereas, if the contact has left an unfavorable impression, further contacts will not be welcomed so readily. The impressions formed in the first meeting are therefore of importance because of this conditioning tendency. A person who believes, perhaps mistakenly, that he has been misjudged during the first contact is rarely quite natural in his behavior at the next meeting and a rift accidentally begun may continue to widen as time goes on because of an initial misunderstanding for which no actual necessity existed.

Although there are Uriah Heeps who take pride in their humbleness this attitude of depreciation is not the usual one. Most people desire to be thought well of from the point of view of certain standards, whatever these may be, and they are inclined to resent being judged solely on the basis of the position which they occupy with reference to the group, particularly if this position happens to be one which is regarded as socially inferior, either economically or racially. There are two somewhat different reasons for this resentment, depending on the individual. In the one case a servant, for instance, may accept as a matter of course and as right the fact that his economic and social standing are different from, and inferior to, those of his master and yet feel hurt or indignant because no attention has been shown to him personally as a servant. In the other case, a person occupying an inferior position may feel that he is as good a man as those who are above him socially and he may resent the fact that other criteria than personal merit have operated to determine both his position and theirs. In the first of these cases the resentment tends to be directed toward a particular person, while, in the second, it tends more and more to emphasize class distinctions and class bitterness unless the desired recognition is granted in some measure at least. If it is possible to obtain personal recognition and thus to move upward in the social scale, class tensions are alleviated and the problem becomes more largely an individual one between particular people rather than a conflict between social classes.

In contacts between strangers, other than those that are temporary and casual where recognition is immaterial, a certain feeling of tension exists until each has become cognizant of the personality of the other. Such cognizance may mean open warfare, but at least it establishes a definite relation which clears the atmosphere. And until this definiteness has been achieved the stranger remains a person who is in the group but not of it. To feel that he belongs to the group and is no longer an outsider, the stranger must not only have an acknowledged position within the group, with the relationships which this implies, but these relationships must have been further augmented by the nearer, more personal bonds which arise in the mutual appreciation of personality apart from position. I have been in groups in which I never felt at home although the contact lasted over a considerable period and my position was a satisfactory one entitling me to respect and courtesy. The warmth of the nearer relationships that have their source in mutual recognition, response, and an interest in one another and a common purpose was lacking. I remained a stranger throughout.

Simmel emphasizes this point of nearness and farness in his discussion of the more abstract nature of the relationship of the stranger. //

This is seen in the fact that one has certain more general qualities only in common with the stranger, whereas the relation with those organically allied is based on the similarity of just those specific differences by which the members of an intimate group are distinguished from those who do not share that intimacy. All personal relations whatsoever are determined according to this scheme, however varied the form which they assume. What is decisive is not the fact that certain common characteristics exist side by side with individual differences which may or may not affect them but that the influence of this common possession itself upon the personal relation of the individuals involved is determined by certain conditions: Does it exist in and for these only? Does it represent qualities that are general in the group, to be sure, but peculiar to it? Or is it merely felt by the members of the group as something peculiar to individuals themselves whereas, in fact, it is a common possession of a group, or a type, or mankind? In the last case an attenuation of the effect of common possession enters in, proportional to the size of the group. Common characteristics function, it is true, as a basis for union among the elements, but they do not specifically refer these elements to each other. A similarity so widely shared might serve as a common basis of each with every possible other. This too is evidently one way in which a relation may at the same moment comprehend both nearness and remoteness. To the extent to which the similarities become general, the warmth of the connection which they effect will have an element of coolness, a feeling in it of the adventitiousness of this very connection.

This constellation (in which similarities are shared by large numbers) acquires, it seems to me, an extraordinary and fundamental preponderance—as against the personal and individual elements we have been discussing—in defining our relation to the stranger. The stranger is near to us in so far as we feel between him and ourselves similarities of nationality or social position, of profession or of general human nature. He is far from us in so far as these similarities reach over him and us, and only ally us both because in fact they ally a great many.[7]

The formal aspects of the position which is accorded to the stranger are general in nature and are capable of a wide application while the affective aspects are dependent upon the personal traits of the particular individuals concerned and upon the circumstances of the contact. This distinction becomes more clear if we consider certain other familiar relationships, as, for example, those within a family group. Here custom prescribes the forms of the relationships between the different members, but the strength of the emotional aspects of these relationships varies exceedingly in different family groups. The ties of affection between husband and wife may be deep and lasting in one family and non-existent in another. Or again, the relationships between teacher and pupil have a certain form that is dependent upon respective positions; but in any specific instance of this relationship the question of whether or not the individuals concerned respect and feel affection for one another personally makes a vast difference. It is necessary to consider both aspects of a relationship in order to understand it; to dissociate the behavior pattern from the emotional values involved would give a partial idea only of the actual nature.

Professor Znaniecki in an article, " Study of the Antagonism to Strangers ",[8] stresses the importance of like or unlike systems of values in determining the relation of the stranger. When the contact takes place on the basis of a different system of values strangeness is experienced even between persons who know each other well in other situations, and if the system of values is not shared antagonism results.

[7] Simmel, *Sociologie*, pp. 688-91. See Park and Burgess, *An Introduction to the Science of Sociology*, pp. 325-26 for a translation.

[8] *Przeglad Socjologiczny* (Posen, 1931), vol. i, pp. 158-209.

The recognition of personality involves the recognition of the presence or absence in the other person of qualities or interests which constitute such systems of values. Such attributes, as was noted before, are as variable as human nature itself. There are, however, certain personal qualities which are generally regarded as values by most peoples and which evoke respect for those possessing them even if their position is that of an acknowledged enemy. Outstanding courage and a high degree of special skill are instances of qualities which tend to win such admiration. Even among the Seri Indians of Lower California, who have been notorious for their unsocial attitude toward all outsiders, McGee mentions three exceptions which were made in favor of persons whose courage or skill, medical in this case, had commanded respect, or at least tolerance.

Collectively the cases seem to define a germ, rather than a mature custom of adoption. In the first case a benefactor (by means regarded as magical), was formally inducted into the reigning family; in the second case the conquering hero (through what were again regarded as magical means) was formally recognized and venerated, even worshipped, as an all-powerful shaman; while in the third case a representative of the doughtiest alien tribe was enslaved, probably with motives akin to those expressed in the carrying of chargeless guns, the making of imitation machetes, and other fetishistic devices.[9]

This same recognition of personal worth, irrespective of all else, has been expressed by Kipling in the following much quoted lines:

> There is neither East nor West, nor border, nor breed, nor birth
> When two strong men stand face to face though they come from the ends of the earth.

[9] McGee, W. J., "The Seri Indians", *Seventeenth Annual Report of the Bureau of American Ethnology*, pt. i (Washington, 1898), p. 279.

Thus, even in instances where strong prejudice or actual enmity exists toward the stranger's type, it is yet possible for the personality of the individual to overcome these and to win a position of respect and good will in the group even though the more intimate forms of sympathy [10] are lacking. The problem of congeniality is ultimately one of personality. The attitude toward the stranger's type may be the friendliest possible and we may still find him a most uncongenial person in spite of this. The question of the manner in which individuals react upon one another is an extremely intricate one which has by no means been fully solved by our analysis of the more obvious factors which influence the nature of the relationships which are established with the stranger. The values which determine the finer adjustments of individuals to one another and which give rise to the relationships of intimate fellowship are more individualized, more personal, more varied, and therefore less easily discovered. Personality is compounded of many attributes and the question of their evaluation in forming close relationships of affection is so largely an individual matter that further research in this field is needed before generalizations are possible. The problem is an attractive one.

[10] Scheler, Max, *Wesen und Formen der Sympathie* (Bonn, 1923), has distinguished several forms of sympathy: compathy or emotional solidarity, mimpathy or emotional imitation, sympathy (genuine) or emotional participation, transpathy or emotional contagion, empathy or emotional intuition, and emipathy or emotional identification.

CONCLUSION

OUR study of the relationship of the stranger from the standpoint of the group has taken us far afield and into so many highways and byways that it seems well in closing to pause a moment to consider where it has brought us and what have been its rewards. What questions have been answered, in part at least, and what others are still awaiting further study? What aspects of the problem of forming new social relationships have been explored, and what others still remain to be investigated? Obviously, but a limited part of the field has been covered in the present small volume and there is much that is still to be done. The loneliness of the stranger's position and the psychological effect produced upon him by the manner in which he is received have not been considered. This problem is closely related to the whole subject of social isolation, whether of individuals, or of groups, classes and communities. The effects of being outside the normal circle of social relationships may be far-reaching and the problem is one which may well receive further attention.[1] For those aspects of the relationship of the stranger which have been surveyed in this study certain conclusions seem to be justified.

First, the types of fundamental unifying relationships which form the basis of the system of social integration of the community as a whole involve some measure of sentiment and emotion, and in order for the stranger to become fully assimilated it is necessary for him to come to share these

[1] On the problem of social isolation I myself hope to throw some light by a study now in preparation.

sentiments also. This process, in most cases, is one for which a period of time and certain ritual ceremonies are required, as in assuming the obligations of kinship through adoption or of citizenship through naturalization.

Second, in the more complex societies, local patterns of social integration develop within the larger configuration, and the nature of these more specialized relationships has an important bearing on the manner in which the stranger is received. The small town and the city, for instance, react differently to the arrival of the stranger.

Third, every contact of group and stranger is a unique phenomenon and the nature of the relationships which are formed will be influenced by the particular combination of factors which are present in the circumstances of the meeting. The presence of any unusual factor, or combination of factors, may bring about an entirely different alignment of relationships from that which would normally have occurred.

Fourth, the initial process in establishing a relationship with the stranger is that of assigning him a position with relation to the group. The nature of this tentative position will depend upon the character of the group and the manner in which it is organized. In complex, highly organized groups the number of categories in which the stranger may be placed is large and the personal characteristics of the individual are more carefully evaluated than is the case in some of the simpler societies which have but two categories to which the stranger may be assigned—that of the tribal brother and that of the enemy. Personality thus counts for more and the distinctions are finer in the more highly civilized groups.

Although each of the four conclusions which have been enumerated is distinctive in certain of its aspects, it is possible to discern a relationship among them and thus to be able to generalize to a certain extent concerning the nature of the reaction of the group to the stranger. *The broad determinant throughout is the character of the values about which the group is organized and the degree to which the stranger is adjudged an asset or a liability for the realization of such values, whether they pertain to kinship or to nationality, to expediency or to congeniality.*

BIBLIOGRAPHY

The following bibliography comprises, for the most part, only those works which have been quoted in the text and is in no sense exhaustive. The subject of the relationship of the stranger has so many ramifications that the works of numerous other writers who have dealt with various phases of the subject, and to many of whom the author is also indebted, have perforce been omitted.

Abbott, F. F., *A History and Description of Roman Political Institutions* (Boston, 1901).

Abel, Theodore, *Systematic Sociology in Germany* (New York, 1929).

——, "The Significance of the Concept of Consciousness of Kind," *Social Forces*, vol. ix, no. 1, October, 1930.

Anderson, N. and Linderman, E. C., *Urban Sociology* (New York, 1928).

Aristotle, *Politics*.

Beard, C. A. and Beard, Mary, *The Rise of American Civilization* (one vol. ed., New York, 1930).

Becker, Howard, "Some Forms of Sympathy: A Phenomenological Analysis", *The Journal of Abnormal and Social Psychology*, vol. xxvi (1931-1932).

Bercovici, Konrad, *Around the World in New York* (New York, 1924).

Bernard, L. L., "Social Attitudes", *Encyclopaedia of the Social Sciences*, vol. ii (New York, 1930).

——, "A Theory of Rural Attitudes", *American Journal of Sociology*, vol. xxii (1916-1917).

Bilby, J. W., *Among Unknown Eskimo* (London, 1923).

Bloomfield, M., "Hymns of the Atharva-Veda", *Sacred Books of the East* (ed. by F. Max Muller, Oxford, 1897), vol. xlii.

Blumenthal, Albert, *Small-Town Stuff* (Chicago, 1932).

Boas, Franz, "The Central Eskimo", *Sixth Annual Report of the Bureau of Ethnology, 1884-1885* (Washington, 1888).

——, "The Eskimo of Baffin Land and Hudson Bay", *Bulletin of the American Museum of Natural History* (New York, 1907), vol. xv.

——, *The Mind of Primitive Man* (New York, 1911).

——, *The Social Organization and Secret Societies of the Kwakiutl Indians* (Washington, 1897).

Bogardus, E. S., *Fundamentals of Social Psychology* (New York, 1924).

——, *Immigration and Race Attitudes* (New York, 1928).

——, *Introduction to Sociology* (4th ed., Los Angeles, 1926).

285

——, *The New Social Research* (Los Angeles, 1926).

Bourgeois, Léon, *Solidarité* (Paris, 1912).

Breasted, J. H., *Ancient Records of Egypt* (Chicago, 1906), vols. i and ii.

Briffault, Robert, *The Mothers* (New York, 1927).

Brinkmann, Carl, "Alien", *Encyclopaedia of the Social Sciences* (New York, 1930), vol. i; "Citizenship", vol. iii.

Brown, A. R. (see also Radcliffe-Brown, A. R.), *The Andaman Islanders* (Cambridge, 1922).

Browne, Lewis, *This Believing World* (New York, 1930).

Brunner, Edmund DeS., *Village Communities* (New York, 1927).

Bryant, W. C., *The Odyssey of Homer* (Boston, 1899).

Buck, Pearl S., *The Good Earth* (New York, 1931).

Burckhardt, J. L., *Notes on the Bedouins and Wahábys* (London, 1830).

Carpenter, Niles, *The Sociology of City Life* (New York, 1931).

Child, C. J., *Beowulf* (Boston, 1904).

Codrington, R. H., *The Melanesians* (Oxford, 1891).

Cohen, Rose, *Out of the Shadow* (New York, 1918).

Cook, A. S. and Tinker, C. B., *Select Translations from Old English Poetry* (Boston, 1902).

Cooley, C. H., *Human Nature and the Social Order* (New York, 1922).

——, *Social Organization* (New York, 1911).

Coyle, Grace L., *Social Process in Organized Groups* (New York, 1930).

Crawley, Ernest, *The Mystic Rose* (2nd ed., London, 1927).

Cressey, Paul G., *The Taxi-Dance Hall* (Chicago, 1932).

Czaplicka, M. A., *Aboriginal Siberia* (Oxford, 1914).

De Greef, Guillaume, *La Structure Générale des Sociétés* (Paris, 1908).

Denison, J. H., *Emotion as the Basis of Civilization* (New York, 1928).

Dickey, H. S., "Up the Orinoco into the Age of Stone", *New York Times Magazine*, November 2, 1930.

Dorsey, J. Owen, "Omaha Sociology", *Third Annual Report of the Bureau of Ethnology, 1881-1882* (Washington, 1884).

Douglas, D. W., *Guillaume De Greef* (New York, 1925).

Douglass, H. P., *The Little Town* (New York, 1921).

Durkheim, Emile, *De la Division du Travail Social* (5th ed., Paris, 1926).

——, *Elementary Forms of the Religious Life* (tr. Swain, London, 1926).

Ellwood, C. A., *Sociology in its Psychological Aspects* (New York, 1921).

Fletcher, A. C. and La Flesche, F., "The Omaha Tribe", *Twenty-seventh Annual Report of the Bureau of Ethnology, 1905-1906* (Washington, 1911).

Frazer, J. G., *The Golden Bough* (3rd ed., London, 1915), vols. iii and vii.

Frazer, R. W., *A Literary History of India* (New York, 1898).

Fry, C. L., *American Villagers* (New York, 1926).

Galpin, C. J., *Rural Life* (New York, 1918).

——, *Rural Social Problems* (New York, 1924).

Garland, Hamlin, *Main-Travelled Roads* (New York and London, 1899).

Garstang, John, *The Hittite Empire* (London, 1929).

Gibbon, Edward, *The History of the Decline and Fall of the Roman Empire* (London, 1897. First ed. 1776), vol. i.

Giddings, F. H., *Elements of Sociology* (New York, 1898).

——, *Inductive Sociology* (New York, 1901).

——, *Principles of Sociology* (New York, 1896).

——, *Readings in Descriptive and Historical Sociology* (New York, 1906).

——, *Studies in the Theory of Human Society* (New York, 1922).

Goldenweiser, A. A., *Early Civilization* (New York, 1922).

Grierson, P. J. H., *The Silent Trade* (Edinburgh, 1903).

Groves, E. R. and Ogburn, W. F., *American Marriage and Family Relationships* (New York, 1928).

Gumplowicz, L., *Sociologie u. Politik* (Leipsic, 1892).

Hadow, W. H., *Citizenship* (Oxford, 1923).

Hamsun, Knut, *The Growth of the Soil* (tr. Worster, New York, 1930).

Hardy, Thomas, *Tess of the D'Urbervilles* (New York and London, 1891).

Harper, R. F., *The Code of Hammurabi, King of Babylon* (Chicago, 1904).

Hartman, E. T., "Village Problems and Characteristics", *Annals of the American Academy of Political and Social Science*, vol. xl, March, 1912.

Hayes, C. J. H. and Moon, P. T., *Ancient and Medieval History* (New York, 1929).

Hecht, Ben, *Thousand and One Afternoons in Chicago* (Chicago, 1922).

Hobhouse, L. T., *Morals in Evolution* (New York, 1906), vol. i.

Hobhouse, L. T. *et al.*, *The Material Culture and Social Institutions of the Simple Peoples* (London, 1915).

Hobley, C. W., *Bantu Beliefs and Magic* (London, 1922).

Hogbin, H. Ian, "Transition Rites at Ontong Java", *Journal of the Polynesian Society*, vol. xxxix, June and September, 1930.

Hopkins, E. Washburn, *Origin and Evolution of Religion* (New Haven, 1923).

Kaegi, A., *The Rigveda* (tr. R. Arrowsmith, Boston, 1886).

Kennedy, Louise V., *The Negro Peasant Turns Cityward* (New York, 1930).

Kephart, Horace, *Our Southern Highlanders* (New York, 1913).

Kroeber, A. L., *Anthropology* (New York, 1923).

Krueger, E. T. and Reckless, W. C., *Social Psychology* (New York, 1931).

Kulp II, D. H., *Country Life in South China* (New York, 1925).

Lasker, Bruno, *Race Attitudes in Children* (New York, 1929).

Legge, James, "The Texts of Confucianism", *Sacred Books of the East* (Oxford, 1879), vol. iii.

Lévy-Bruhl, Lucian, *Primitive Mentality* (tr. Clare, New York, 1923).
——, *The Soul of the Primitive* (New York, 1928).
Lewisohn, Ludwig, *The Island Within* (New York, 1928).
Lipson, E., *An Introduction to the Economic History of England* (4th ed., London, 1926).
Lowie, R. L., *Primitive Society* (New York, 1925).
Lynd, R. S. and Lynd, H. M., *Middletown* (New York, 1929).
MacIver, R. M., *Community* (New York, 1928).
——, "The Foundations of Nationality", *Sociological Review*, July, 1915.
——, *The Modern State* (2nd ed., Oxford, 1928).
——, *Society: Its Structure and Changes* (New York, 1931).
Maine, Sir Henry Sumner, *Early History of Institutions* (London, 1875).
Malinowski, B., *Argonauts of the Western Pacific* (London, 1922).
——, *Crime and Custom in Savage Society* (New York, 1926).
McGee, W. J., "The Seri Indians", *Seventeenth Annual Report of the Bureau of American Ethnology, 1895-1896* (Washington, 1898), pt. i.
McKenzie, R. D., *The Neighborhood* (Chicago, 1923).
Michels, R., "Materialien zu einer Sociologie des Fremden", *Jahrbuch für Sociologie*, vol. i, 1925.
Miles, Emma B., *The Spirit of the Mountains* (New York, 1905).
Morgan, L. H., *Ancient Society* (New York, 1878).
Muir, Ramsay, *Nationalism and Internationalism* (London, 1916).
Muntz, E. E., *Race Contact* (New York, 1927).
North, C. C., *Social Differentiation* (Chapel Hill, 1926).
Odin, A., *Genèse des Grands Hommes* (Paris, 1895).
Old, W. G., *The Shu King or the Chinese Historical Classic* (New York, 1904).
Park, R. E., "Assimilation, Social", *Encyclopaedia of the Social Sciences* (New York, 1930), vol. ii.
—— *et al.*, *The City* (Chicago, 1925).
—— and Burgess, E. W., *Introduction to the Science of Society* (Chicago, 1924).
Paxon, F. L., *The Last American Frontier* (New York, 1910).
Plato, *The Republic*.
Radcliffe-Brown, A. R. (see also Brown, A. R.), *The Andaman Islanders* (Cambridge, 1922).
——, "The Social Organization of the Australian Tribes", *The "Oceania" Monographs* (Melbourne, 1931), no. 1.
Randolph, Vance, *The Ozarks* (New York, 1931).
Rivers, W. H. R., "Kin, Kinship", *Encyclopaedia of Religion and Ethics* (ed. by James Hastings, New York, 1915), vol. vii.
——, *Kinship and Social Organization* (London, 1914).
——, *Social Organization* (New York, 1924).
——, *The History of Melanesian Society* (Cambridge, 1914).

Rölvaag, O. E., *Giants in the Earth* (New York, 1927).

Roosevelt, Theodore, *The Winning of the West* (New York, 1905).

Roscoe, J., *The Bagesu and Other Tribes of the Uganda Protectorate* (Cambridge, 1924).

Ross, E. A., *The Foundations of Sociology* (New York, 1905).

Sanderson, Dwight, *The Rural Community* (Boston, 1932).

Scheler, Max, *Wesen und Formen der Sympathie* (Bonn, 1923).

Schlesinger, A. M., *Political and Social History of the United States* (New York, 1930).

Shaler, N. S., *The Neighbor* (Boston and New York, 1904).

Shaw, C. R., *Delinquency Areas* (Chicago, 1929).

Simmel, Georg, " Die Grossestädte und das Geistesleben ", *Die Grossestadt* (Dresden, 1903).

——, " The Sociology of Secrecy and of Secret Societies " (tr. A. W. Small), *The American Journal of Sociology*, vol. xi, January, 1906.

——, *Soziologie* (Leipzig, 1908).

Small, A. W., " The Scope of Sociology ", *The American Journal of Sociology*, vol. v, 1899-1900.

Smith, W. Robertson, *Kinship and Marriage in Early Arabia* (London, 1903).

——, *The Religion of the Semites* (London, 1894).

Sorokin, Pitirim, *Social Mobility* (New York, 1927).

—— and Zimmerman, C. C., *Principles of Rural-Urban Sociology* (New York, 1929).

—— et al., *A Systematic Source Book in Rural Sociology* (Minneapolis, 1930).

Spencer, Baldwin, *Native Tribes of Northern Territory of Australia* (London, 1914).

—— and Gillen, F. J., *The Native Tribes of Central Australia* (London, 1899).

—— and Gillen, F. J., *The Northern Tribes of Central Australia* (London, 1904).

Spengler, Oswald, *The Decline of the West* (tr. Atkinson, London, 1926).

Steiner, J. F., *The American Community in Action* (New York, 1928).

Stratton, G. M., *Social Psychology of International Conduct* (New York, 1929).

Sumner, W. G., *Folkways* (Boston, 1906).

—— and Keller, A. G., *The Science of Society* (New Haven, 1927).

Tarleton, F., *Bloody Ground: A Cycle of the Southern Hills* (New York, 1929).

Taylor, Paul S., *Mexican Labor in the United States*, vol. i (University of California Publications in Economics, Berkeley, 1930).

Tenney, A. A., " Some Recent Advances in Sociology ", *Political Science Quarterly*, vol. xxv, September, 1910.

Thomas, W. I. and Znaniecki, F., *The Polish Peasant* (Boston, 1918).

Thrasher, F. M., *The Gang* (Chicago, 1927).

Trumbull, H. C., *The Blood Covenant* (Philadelphia, 1898).

——, *The Covenant of Salt* (New York, 1899).

——, *The Threshold Covenant* (2nd ed., New York, 1906).

Turner, F. J., *The Frontier in American History* (New York, 1920).

Van Gennep, A., *Les Rites de Passage* (Paris, 1909).

Ward, L. F., *Applied Sociology* (Boston, 1906).

Ware, Caroline F., " Immigration ", *Encyclopædia of the Social Sciences* (New York, 1932), vol. vii.

Watson, Goodwin B., *Orient and Occident* (Unpublished Monograph, 1927).

Westermarck, E., *The History of Human Marriage* (New York, 1922).

——, *The Origin and Development of Moral Ideas* (London, 1912).

Wiese, Leopold v., *Systematic Sociology* (adapted and amplified by Howard Becker, New York, 1932).

Williams, J. M., *The Expansion of Rural Life* (New York, 1926).

——, *Our Rural Heritage* (New York, 1925).

Wilson, W. H., *The Evolution of the Country Community* (New York, 1912).

——, " Social Life in the Country ", *Annals of the American Academy of Political and Social Science*, vol. xl, March, 1912.

Wirth, Louis, *The Ghetto* (Chicago, 1928).

Wissler, Clark, *An Introduction to Social Anthropology* (New York, 1929).

Zimmern, A. E., *The Greek Commonwealth* (Oxford, 1922).

Znaniecki, F., " Object Matter of Sociology ", *American Journal of Sociology*, vol. xxxii, January, 1927.

——, " Study of the Antagonism to Strangers ", *Przeglad Socjologiczny* (Posen, 1931), vol. i.

Zorbaugh, H. W., *The Gold Coast and the Slum* (Chicago, 1929).

INDEX

VITA

THE writer of this dissertation was born in Cheyenne, Wyoming, December 20, 1888. Her childhood was spent on the noted Dollar Ranch on Bear Creek, Wyoming. A strong interest in the phenomena of the natural sciences dates from this early period, much of which was spent out of doors. She did not attend school until her family moved to Vermont when she was fourteen. She had, however, studied at home with her mother and was able to enter classes with students of her own age. At seventeen she had graduated from normal school and had begun to teach. Her career since then has been one which has taken her far afield and which has afforded the background for this study. She has had the opportunity to observe the manner in which new relationships are formed in many widely varying groups of peoples.

EDUCATION

1906, Vermont State Normal School, Randolph Center, Diploma. 1910, University of Wyoming, Laramie, B. Ped. 1917, University of Washington, Seattle, B. S. (Zoology). 1924, Columbia University, New York City, A. M. (Zoology). 1928, American School of Oriental Research, summer session, Jerusalem, Palestine, (Archaeology). 1930, Columbia University, New York City, matriculated for the degree Doctor of Philosophy in the Faculty of Political Science. Major subject, sociology; minor, genetics.

Experience

1906-1908, Rural school work in Vermont farming communities. 1910-1916, Elementary school work in small towns in Wyoming, New Mexico, Washington and Alaska. Coal mining, fruit and wheat farming, and fishing communities are represented. 1917-1919, Secondary school work in lumbering and fruit farming communities in the State of Washington. 1919-1920, Laboratory technician, Hygienic Laboratory, Washington, D. C. Also field work at Wilmington, North Carolina in rural sanitation. 1920-1921, Waukegan, Illinois; Portsmouth, Ohio; Washington, Louisiana. 1921-1923, Teacher-training work in the Philippine Islands. Travel in China, Japan and India. 1924-1925, Secondary school work in the Canal Zone. 1925-1927, Secondary and Junior College work, The Scudder School, New York City. 1927-1929, Professor of Biology, The American College for Women, Istanbul, Turkey. Travel in Europe and the Near East.

She has published articles in *Plain Talk, The Journal of Applied Psychology, Social Science,* and *The American Journal of Sociology.* She is a member of Pi Gamma Mu and of Phi Delta Gamma.